The Braid of Literature

The Braid of Literature

Children's Worlds of Reading

SHELBY ANNE WOLF

and

SHIRLEY BRICE HEATH

Harvard University Press

Cambridge, Massachusetts
London, England
1992

Library of Congress Cataloging-in-Publication Data

Wolf, Shelby Anne.
    The braid of literature: children's worlds of reading / Shelby Anne Wolf and Shirley Brice Heath.
        p.   cm.
    Includes bibliographical references (p.) and index.
    ISBN 0–674–08040–8 (alk. paper)
    1. Children's literature—Study and teaching—Case studies. 2. Reading—Case studies. 3. Children—Books and Reading—Case studies. 4. Children—Language—Case studies. I. Heath, Shirley Brice. II. Title.
LB1139.L3W56   1992
372.6'4—dc20   92–5057
                  CIP

For Lindsey, the heroine and heart of the story,
and for Ashley, with a clear sweet voice of her own

S.A.W.

For Jimmy Britton, who led us to listen—*truly* to listen—
to learn from every Lindsey and Ashley

S.B.H.

ACKNOWLEDGMENTS

Once upon a time an eager and anxious mother approached Albert Einstein for advice. Her young son was a budding scientist, and she needed help in laying out an appropriate course for his studies. "What should I read to him?" the mother queried. Einstein nodded his cloud of white hair and replied, "Fairy tales." Startled, the mother came back with, "Fine. But then what?" Einstein peered at the woman over his spectacles and said, "More fairy tales." Exasperated, the mother persisted, "And after that?" Einstein leaned closer to the woman, "Still more fairy tales." (Adapted from Graetz, 1979)

We begin with this language story because we must first acknowledge the enormous debt we owe to the world of fairy tales, folk tales, and fantasy literature. Like Einstein, we believe that entry into the world of the imagination is the best education and, to extend the thought, that the most enlightening instructors are the authors and illustrators who open the door to that world. Without Grimm, Perrault, Andersen, Hyman, Sendak, Steig, the Dillons, and countless others, the family in this book would be forced to live another narrative altogether.

As with all narratives, this book brings together many stories—some professional and some personal. Our professional acknowledgments begin with a line of British scholars ranging from James Britton and Nancy Martin to Harold Rosen, Margaret Meek, and Michael Armstrong, who have taught us to accept children's curiosity and to learn to learn by watching and listening. The voices of these scholars are joined by those of two major figures in the study of children's language in the United States: Charles Ferguson and Courtney Cazden. Both have encouraged long-term observations of children's written and oral language and have pushed for a deeper understanding of how the complexities of children's worlds of learning extend across cultures and settings. Scholars in early education and children's literature who have provided inspiration for our work include Rudine Sims Bishop, Anne Haas Dyson, Janet Hickman, and Dorothy White. Two others, Marjorie Martus and Jennifer Wheat, earned our gratitude for reading and commenting on this text and for testing it through their ability to anchor our words in their own long experience with education. Maria Ascher, our editor, helped us tighten our prose and faithfully sped this work on its way.

In addition, we want to thank our sources of support. The School of Education at Stanford University, under the leadership of Marshall Smith, provided Shelby with a research assistantship in 1989–90. During 1988–89, while Shirley was a fellow at the Center for Advanced Study in the Behavioral Sciences with support from the Spencer Foundation, she completed much of her work on this volume.

To these professional credits we each must add our own personal acknowledgments.

In the case of Shirley, it was Mildred Alexander, her foster mother, who first revealed the wonder of children's books to her. Many years later, Shirley's daughter, Shannon, helped her reenter that world through her own exuberance in reading literature. Both Mildred and Shannon, the latter now a grownup, still read children's literature for the pure enthusiasm and excitement it offers and for its reminders that the childlike qualities of curiosity, faith, and imagination often make the impossible possible.

For Shelby, though her daughters are at the center of the story, other family members helped keep the text alive. Her husband, Kenny, is first and foremost among these. Over the years, Kenny helped collect and analyze data, read and commented on countless drafts, consoled in times of despair, and celebrated in times of delight. His love has carried her through. Shelby's sisters, Martha and Karen, and her mother and father also deserve loving recognition, not only for the interviews granted and the advice given but for the stories told throughout a lifetime. Beyond the bounds of her family, Shelby owes special gratitude to Marjorie Siegel, who initiated the work and who continually provided encouraging and critical commentary. Through her guidance as both colleague and friend, she introduced Shelby to a dynamic way of reading, thinking, and understanding. Most important, she encouraged Shelby to read fairy tales.

And so, with the help of these distinctive voices, our tale begins.

CONTENTS

Life wells up and alters and adds. Even things in a book-case change if they are alive; we find ourselves wanting to meet them again; we find them altered.

Virginia Woolf, "Modern Fiction," 1925

Children's Creativity, Connections, and Criticism

One spring afternoon, a few months after Lindsey's third birthday, a friend telephoned our house and Lindsey ran to answer it. She had on two dresses, one over the other, to create a "ball gown" and she carried a long-stemmed tulip, which served as a "magic wand."

"Lindsey?" my friend questioned.

"No, this is Cinderella," Lindsey replied. She stated that there was no "Shelby" here and that since she was busy getting ready for the ball, she had little time to talk. (March 1986, 3;4—or 3 years, 4 months)

A young child can enter the world of story as easily as Cinderella stepping into the pumpkin carriage. Yet the adult, attempting to capture the child's response to literature, is left peering into the carriage window and wondering how to get inside. How can adults negotiate the winding paths of children's play, talk, emotions, and movements to understand what and how they learn from literature? How can adults move their attention from the act of reading to the experience of reading?

Documented in this book are the daily lives of Lindsey (born November 8, 1982) and Ashley (born December 27, 1985) for the years 1982 to 1991. Their stories bring together insider and outsider learning in the case of two children as they extend literature from its occasions of reading and develop a sense of its connections with the rest of their existence.

The insider is Shelby, playing the roles of social scientist, lover of literature, and mother of two children. Only someone in daily contact with Lindsey and Ashley could fully document the relationship between the stories they heard read to them and the way in which they used the rules and roles perceived in these stories to test, negotiate, control, and reshape their everyday world.[1] As mother and as social scientist, Shelby recorded, through fieldnotes, audiotapes, and video recordings, the ways that literature worked in the language and thought of her daughters during their preschool and early school years. As mother and lover of literature, Shelby selected and read stories to Lindsey and Ashley; discussed the plots, authors, and characters with them; and, during her nine years of observing and recording, reflected often on ways to ensure that the role of social scientist did not reshape the roles of mother and reader.

The outsider is Shirley, anthropologist and linguist, critic and co-interpreter of Shelby's notes and tapes. As curious social scientist, desiring more detailed case study data on how children learn to use oral and written language, Shirley saw in Shelby's notebooks the rare opportunity for nearly a full-time and certainly a long-term study of how young children learn with and through the language of literature. As critic and cointerpreter of Shelby's data, Shirley helped compare the cases of Lindsey and Ashley with other, more short-term, sometimes specially pleaded studies of children in different families, cultures, and times.

What brought us together to write this book was our mutual interest in the language of literature and the enduring patterns in which it enters the thoughts and expressions of young children. Authors and critics alike often express the view that figurative language, used in exploratory ways, equips every reader for the processes of cognitive and emotional discovery. Yet just how and when this instrumental force works remains a puzzle, since any research method is inadequate to follow the words of literature through all their reshapings in the thoughts, actions, drawings, or verbal expressions of an individual listener or reader in any particular culture. If anyone could come close to employing the range of methods necessary to shadow children as they come to know literature, a mother could. And her capabilities would surely be enhanced if she could, as Shelby did, bring to the observational tasks a thorough knowledge of children's literature and of the research literature on language acquisition and early literacy habits. To be sure, no amount of social science training or enmeshment in the various research arguments on oral and written language could—or should—reshape significantly a mother's natural bias to see what is good in her own children.

Children and adults have always been and will continue to be at odds with each other—in experience, points of view, and goals for action. This self-evident point is exemplified by countless children's stories, whose plots subvert the power and authority of adults and reshape the ordinary rules of order in the world. Hence, any perceptive observer of children—both as they are portrayed in books and as they respond to books—will know that what is "good" in children's responses to such literature is never entirely clear. Should young readers let adults know they see the control and persistence that characters—so similar in stature to themselves—exert in the world of literature? Should they celebrate Peter Rabbit's disobedience, Max's defiance, and Little Red Riding Hood's divergence from the path? What if they take to heart the realization that stepmothers in literature are almost uniformly cruel and integrate this into their own relations in contemporary families formed of second marriages? What if they carry their visions of giants, goblins, demons, and dragons into their dreams? Which of their reactions to the vast selection of children's literature can we then term "good"?[2]

This book tries to move beyond and outside any urge to portray a "universal" good in the ways that Lindsey and Ashley interact with literature. What we have wanted to ensure within this book is that the representations of Lindsey and Ashley be as full as possible. Readers will find here the girls' responses—in action, design, and verbal expression—not only during times of reading with their parents but also on occasions that take them far beyond their direct reading experiences: during moments of intellectual and aesthetic discovery, as well as during emotional ups and downs. As the girls matured, they sometimes expressed directly the literary connections to their deeds, thoughts, and words. At other times, literature seemed to squeeze through without their direct awareness, to help them achieve a kind of nonvolitional intensity of insight. Through her daily, immediate, and continued association with the girls, Shelby, on occasion, could tease out the ambiguities of motive and identity that might have led the girls to frame their current world with literature's help. Together, however, we have tried to resist too great a readiness for explanation after-the-fact and to let stand instead the words of Lindsey and Ashley, as well as the immediate responses and recordings of Shelby as their mother and partner in reading.

Our joint effort gives a more expanded picture of reading with and for children than that of views currently prevailing. These urge one or another method of teaching reading or promoting children's literature and center on the moment of reading and its primary importance for the reader in making meaning from the text. The stories of Lindsey and Ashley suggest how extensive and porous that process of making and remaking meaning is. The words, images, attitudes, norms, and contradictions of the text spring up far beyond the actual episode of reading in new shapes and in other contexts and readings of different books. We see here how the initial reading of a literary text gives itself up to children's rereadings in the world. Even when the moment of reading includes interpretation and response, reading extends beyond these acts of perception to gradually achieved apperceptions. The experience of reading lives on far beyond the act of reading.

But what is it about children's literature that enables these extended readings? The urge to define or delineate what is special about the language of literature—generally referred to as poetic language—is an ancient one; there is no human society that has not, at an early stage in its history, assigned a special label to poetry. The language of literature offers more than ordinary language—ordering a sandwich, summing up the week's news, or greeting the postman—through its intricate design of both sound and sense. Literary language releases imagery and memory and calls up connections to set the mind in motion, imparting a movement that is at once pleasing and restless or seeking. It is possible to return again and again to literary language for aesthetic effects and multiple interpretations. Literary texts are thick with possibilities; those of ordinary language are thin by comparison. Each return to literary language taps into an almost subliminal awareness of the recapitulation of rhythm, word choice, grammatical form, and the dynamics of meaning. The language of literary works written or performed for children usually well exceeds vocabulary, word order, and imagery that children themselves would produce or hear in ordinary language. This fact leaves open for children (and adults) the possibility of multifarious links—to sense perceptions, other voices, different settings, and a host of other sources for building literary worlds. The language of literature is not that which tests precise comprehension or single absorptions of meaning, but that which invites several readings, dwells on partial readings, and stops in midstream for reflection and deflection into other texts—of either books or direct experience.[3]

About Audience, Voices, Referents, and Metaphors

We have written this book for parent and teacher readers, as well as for those scholars who try to puzzle their way through the research debates on such topics as inner speech, transferred learning, oral and written language acquisition, and children's facility with figurative language. Those who read this book primarily to deepen their own understanding of the role of children's literature in the minds and emotions of young children will move with ease and familiarity through the accounts of Lindsey and Ashley responding to and from literature. We have left these as they originally appeared in Shelby's notes, where the "I" is always Shelby at the moment of her notetaking. We have altered neither tense nor affective content, making no attempt to force them into linkage with our later shared interpretations and more distanced analysis. Those who read this book for data and interpretations related to central scholarly queries will, we hope, make use of the notes and citations that set the book in the interdisciplinary frames of current research in anthropology, linguistics, and cognitive psychology. Our footnotes are neighbors to our text.[4]

There is no single voice in this book. At times, Shelby's immediate concerns and reactions carry the central plot of the text—the cognitive, aesthetic, and emotional growth of her two children into and through literature in her literate family. At other times, with less immediacy, she speaks of her more distanced and comparative perceptions, informed by her knowledge of multiple pedagogical viewpoints about children's literature and by scholarly studies of children's language development and aesthetic imaginations.

This voice joins with that of Shirley, who considers the accounts of Lindsey and Ashley beyond their immediate family and cultural setting, linking them with current efforts in psychology, linguistics, and anthropology to understand what studies of the particular can tell us about what is universal in human learning. We attempt to go beyond stereotypes and simplistic explanations to analyze and acknowledge the multiple, redundant, and intricately overlapping ways in which the children of one highly literate home learned from and through literature. The environment of Lindsey and Ashley enabled them not only to read and write but also to carry the rules, roles, and language of literary texts into play—as re-creations to build their senses of being literate.

Through this peephole view of two children playing with their literate experiences, we see what we may need to look for in the panorama of the world's cultures that enables children to create, connect, and critique. The children's literature that inspires Lindsey's and Ashley's playfulness and their reiterations of social rules and roles has its analogues in other cultures that promote language-based play through different customs and artifacts. For example, among those societies that encourage verbal teasing, punning, and open-ended performance of group dramas and rituals, children produce figurative language, reason metaphorically, and resist adults' absolutes in ways remarkably parallel to the sometimes irreverent and often innovative twists of meaning Lindsey and Ashley make. The key that unlocks the world of "but what if?" lies not in any single medium, such as literature written for children, but in multiple opportunities to use verbal and dramatic means to reshape and reclaim any society's attempts to perpetuate fixed ways of seeing. Music, dance, visual art, storytelling, and festivals of parody and satire bear the same openness of interpretation and power of recounting that children's literature offered Lindsey and Ashley.[5]

There is an adage that tells us, "People know what they do; frequently they know why they do what they do; but what they don't know is what what they do does." Given here is a narrow but intense look at Lindsey and Ashley over nine years that provides insight into *what it is that children's literature does* in the home of a young, contemporary, mainstream, school-oriented family. Though at times throughout the book we leave aside the specificity of naming Lindsey and Ashley and refer instead to "children," we intend no broad generalization to all children of different families, sociocultural groups, or historical periods. This book makes no claim for the universality of Lindsey's and Ashley's particular patterns of response to a single type of cultural artifact—children's literature. Neither does it claim that the imaginative, analytical, and creative reasoning they demonstrated can come only through the type of literate environment their early childhood offered.

Their story is merely one of many that could—and should—be told, to extend and test our current perceptions of how children learn. Their account alerts us to the false contentment that may come from thinking that it is enough just to know what we do and why we do it in cultures familiar to us. Lindsey and Ashley tell us much that is new and previously unacknowledged about the enduring influence of children's literature, and, in so doing, they remind us of how much more we should expect to discover about children's learning from those rare occasions when we can undertake close-range studies of cultures unfamiliar to us. Diverse artifacts and habits across cultures, figurative language, repeated stories, and dramatic invitation create long-term influences on children's ways of building and renovating the social and mental worlds about them.[6]

Though mindful of the purposeful slant that metaphors can impart, we have let Lindsey's central frame for literature title this book. The tale of Rapunzel and the wondrous long braid of hair remained a favorite of Lindsey's throughout her early years of knowing children's literature. To Lindsey, the braid was the symbol of the enchantment of story, the beauty of the fairy princess, and the rich luxury of the world of fantasy. In her earliest years, with the slightest suggestion of a prop that could substitute for a braid—toys clipped together, scarves, or ribbons—Lindsey would announce, "I'm Rapunzel and this is my braid, Mama." Later she needed no props—only her own actions and assertions. For example, when streaking across the playground, her own less-than-lengthy hair streaming behind her during her first year at preschool, Lindsey replied to her teacher's question "Where are you going, Lindsey?" with "I'm not a Lindsey! I'm a princess."

Ashley, too, loved the tale of Rapunzel and Rapunzel's glorious hair. She prided herself on her own growing hair and tipped her head, arching her back, to exaggerate its length. When Lindsey improvised a wig made from an old pair of stockings, Ashley wore it as a cap with its long legs dangling over one shoulder. Later, Ashley begged Lindsey to twist the legs together to create a braid and tie it with a ribbon at the end. She flung it over the bannister of the narrow staircase, and many times, friends and family members were called to grasp the feet of the stockings and pretend to climb the twisted braid of nylon legs up the stairs. Still, Ashley's vision did not include the resolution of the climb. When the climbers reached the top, they were greeted not by "Rapunzel" but by Ashley, who giggled and resisted any continuation of the story line. Lindsey, however, in her own rendition of the scene, always greeted the climbers with open arms. The braid served not only as a symbol of beauty but as a link between two young people in love.

Yet Rapunzel, like other characters, motifs, and patterns in literature, assumed various meanings on different occasions of reading and over the course of the girls' self-perceptions as they matured. Though between the ages of three and seven Lindsey would stand down any contender for the role of long-haired heroine, by the time she was eight she preferred the role of prince, witch, or other more active and boisterous agent. During her eighth summer, in a week-long theater class which culminated in a performance of *Rapunzel,* Lindsey asked her directors to cast her as either the prince or the witch. She swaggered hopefully throughout the week, but when given the part of the witch, she cast off her bold stance and bent down over an imaginary cane, scowling dreadfully at all who came near. The sense of identity she derived from children's literature now moved beyond that of imperiled, passive, waiting, and eager heroine to that of powerful, brash, energetic, and even wicked agent. Her character portrayals extended beyond costume and other self-decoration to strongly identifiable postures, moods, and objects designed to arouse fear and to intrigue others.

As though braided together, literature lies within its connections to reality, children's re-creations of literary elements in ordinary events, and their criticism of life that mixes the rules of fact and fiction. We try to understand the strands of this braid as we hear and see Lindsey and Ashley reason, feel, and mature with images and words from many-voiced conversations—from the characters and authors of their books, from their friends and family, and from the multiple voices they hear in their own thoughts.

Story Rules in the World

Experiences with books carried Lindsey and Ashley deep into their own sensed experiences and affective responses. To be sure, they learned of faraway times and places, but the universal human dimensions of characters interacting within the conditions imposed by specific times and places transferred most often to their rethinking of their own everyday experiences. Here there were challenges enough: Lindsey's acceptance of a baby sister, Ashley; acquiescence to requests for participation in household chores; participation in the humor and straight talk of everyday conversation; and commitment to some understanding of adults' rules of politeness for interpersonal relations.

We will look at how Lindsey and Ashley transformed literature for their own purposes in negotiating attention, affection, and reason with adults and with each other. The story will take us beyond their frequent book-reading occasions with their parents to their spontaneous introductions of book meanings into the real world.[7] Like many parents who enjoy children's literature and read frequently with their children, Shelby and her husband, Kenny, spent many hours reading and discussing books with Lindsey and later with the two girls together. By "children's literature" we mean stories, poems, and plays, predominantly in picture book form, that are written and prepared primarily for an audience of children.[8] On the border of this published literature, we also include the oral stories told (fictional and factual), which often centered on family events of both past and present, as well as songs and bits of poetry that came less from books than from parents' childhood memories.

Books were also an integral part of the careers of both Shelby and Kenny, who were teachers. They began their teaching careers as Peace Corps volunteers in Tunisia, where they taught English as a second language. From Tunisia they returned to the United States and married. Both attended school in Utah to receive degrees and certification for public school teaching; Shelby was certified as an elementary school teacher and Kenny as a middle and high school teacher. Shelby then taught first and second grades, while Kenny worked as a counselor and finished his master's degree in educational psychology. Missing life overseas, they left the United States and spent two years teaching in an American school in Bolivia, and then four years in an international school in Saudi Arabia. While they were living in Arabia, their first daughter, Lindsey, was born. After Shelby became pregnant with their second daughter, the couple decided to return to Utah, where Ashley was born. They spent only a year there; Shelby completed her coursework for a master's degree in educational studies, while Kenny designed educational software for a local company and applied to graduate schools. He began a doctoral program in education at a university in California, and after three years of working at the university, Shelby entered the same program.

From the time of Lindsey's birth, Shelby kept copies of the letters she wrote and received regarding major events in the child's life: the game cards and notes from the shower her friends gave her; birth announcements and letters to other friends and family members living in the United States; and the letters and cards from grandparents, aunts, and friends who wrote to Lindsey regarding her birth and subsequent birthdays. Like most mothers who keep memorabilia for their children in baby books, Shelby collected artifacts of Lindsey's birth and development. But the artifacts she tended to collect were not such things as a lock of hair or a notation of the date of her first tooth; instead, she noted Lindsey's language development and commented on her interaction with books. Because both parents were teachers, and because they lived in a relatively isolated housing compound in Arabia, Shelby and Kenny sang songs and read to Lindsey from the beginning of her life. While they read to entertain, they also read to show Lindsey the multiple and faraway worlds where forests grew, snow fell, and mothers did not need to wear long skirts or cover their heads when they left their home. In Arabia there were few trips to museums, mountains, or shopping malls, but books from the school library enabled Shelby and Kenny to take Lindsey anywhere.

Soon after Lindsey's third birthday, Shelby began to focus on Lindsey's response to literature as the topic for her master's thesis. She tape-recorded the sessions during which they read together and she supplemented these tapes with her own fieldnotes and reflections on their book reading. In addition, she recorded the dramatized, spoken, and drawn renderings of written texts when Lindsey extended these beyond the occasions on which she and Shelby read or talked about books.[9] Shelby collected artifacts of every sort, solicited Lindsey's explanations of book-to-life shifts, and tried to capture to the fullest extent possible the literate environment that surrounded Lindsey and later her baby sister, Ashley, in a family where literature, art, music, and talk about numerous types of symbolic representations permeated daily life, from notes on the kitchen table to the books on the bedroom's crowded shelves.

Throughout these years of watching, listening, and recording, Shelby tried to balance the roles of parent and researcher. Early in the study she wrote:

> I am trying to keep our actions and reactions as natural as possible, since I don't want my research interests to force Lindsey into a predictable response. Most important, I don't want either one of us to lose the ownership of our lives to the study. Yet we are affected in many ways, some of them more troublesome than others.
> At dinner tonight my stepmother began to tell us of the plain fare that she and Dad usually chose for their meals.
> "Just a simple salad most nights," she said.
> But then she proceeded to explain that their salad was often gar-

nished with bits of bacon, hard boiled eggs, red and green peppers, etc.

I laughed at how quickly something simple became complicated. "That's like the story of *Stone Soup*," I said.

When they looked at me quizzically, I told the story of the soldiers who tricked an entire village into bringing out their hidden provisions. Throughout the additions of carrots, meat, and potatoes, the clever soldiers were able to preserve the thought that the soup was simply made from a stone.

When my narrative was complete, I turned and looked at Lindsey. And I nearly clapped my hand over my mouth in horror. I was thunderstruck by the fact that I had made an association between life and text, and that incidents like this would somehow invalidate my data!

I think this is a misguided attempt to preserve the sanctity of my study, but I am eager for Lindsey's connections to be original ones. Yet somehow, in allowing Lindsey to have ownership of her associations, I must not lose the ownership of my own. (June 14, 1986, 3;7)

Other effects of the study were less subtle. Lindsey was fascinated with the tape recorder and would sometimes clown during the recording and then beg to have her antics played back. Even after many recordings, the presence of the tape recorder would often dominate the reading. She would stop the story after the climax, stretch the antenna up to her height, and retell the story like a radio announcer. When Shelby switched to a very compact recorder, the impact lessened a bit, but Lindsey was still fascinated with the playback. Lindsey later asked for and got her own tape recorder, and kept it often by her side during our readings.

Another aspect of the tape recording caused changes in Lindsey's play: transcription—the transfer from tape to print of the context, texts, and talk of our reading together. Although Shelby did most of this work while Lindsey was in childcare or at night after she had gone to bed, there were many occasions when Lindsey saw her at work:

Each day I sit at the word processor, stopping and starting the tape recorder, tapping in the words and referring to the text. And now Lindsey has incorporated my behavior into her play. This morning I discovered her setting up her own office.

She had pulled her small director's chair up to her bed, which served as a desk. It held her "computer" (really a toy typewriter), as well as her small plastic tape recorder. She would play a section of *Star Wars,* and then stop the recording to bang out a message on the plastic keys of her typewriter. Back and forth she went between the recorder and her "computer," playing and typing, playing a new section and typing again, in a way more than a little reminiscent of my efforts at transcription. (June 30, 1986, 3;7)

Lindsey was also affected by Shelby's continual note taking. Shelby carried a small notebook, and when she couldn't get to it fast enough, she wrote on the edges of books, on small bits of paper, and on napkins. "What are you writing?" Lindsey would ask, and Shelby would reply that she was writing down her thoughts. Finally, one day, Lindsey challenged her mother: "What *are* your thoughts?" Shelby dropped the researcher role and returned to that of the parent. She explained that she was thinking about the story and about Lindsey's response.

At times, Shelby's note taking raised more than Lindsey's curiosity; it raised her ire against a mother who was so busy taking notes she missed an important cue in a dramatic production. One afternoon, when Lindsey was in the middle of giving her mother stage directions for a play of *The Sleeping Beauty* (Grimm Brothers), she handed her a yellow block as a spindle and fed her the appropriate lines:

"You say, 'Touch my spindle,'" Lindsey directed, intoning the lines with the wickedly shrill voice of a witch.

"Touch my spindle, little princess." As I held out the yellow block / spindle for her touch, I imitated her voice, but added the appellation.

Lindsey slowly crept forward and reached out a tentative finger. As soon as the tip of her index finger touched the block, she fell to the floor. Then she promptly got up and fell again to the couch. She regarded me with one eye.

"Now you're the prince. You kiss me on the hand." She closed her eye again and waited.

I took the opportunity to scribble down her last words but I apparently took too long.

"I don't have a kiss!" she scolded.

I mumbled something about just a minute and bent my head to my notes.

"Look. Look! WAKE UP, PRINCE!!" she threatened impatiently and kicked her foot in my direction.

I threw the notebook to the rug and rushed to her side, kissing her gently on the hand. The scolding look of the minute before vanished, and she slowly opened her eyes and stared at me lovingly.

"Will you marry me?" I begged.

Lindsey leaped from the couch, gave me a quick hug and said, "Of course!" (June 10, 1986, 3;7)

Throughout the study, Shelby tried to balance the roles of social science researcher and parent—a balance that would allow for an elaboration of the social context without disturbing the privacy of the family. The presence of tape recorders and note pads was counter-weighted with more natural storybook interaction, to prevent an artificiality from seeping into their home, creating what might have been a structure initiated by the parent-researcher and not by the child.

Later, while completing her master's thesis, Shelby wrote about the balance of roles:

Lindsey and I are again at work in the study. My work with a reading project at the university leaves me little time for writing, so I rise each morning at four o'clock to work on my thesis. Lindsey usually joins me at six. I am at the computer, my desk a clutter with letters from the past—notes and cards she received at her birth and copies of letters I wrote to family when we lived overseas. Several storybooks lie scattered around the room.

Lindsey is at her father's desk, eating her morning granola and drawing on the back of scrap computer paper. When she asks me for advice on what to draw, I suggest an elephant. She draws a large purple stain on the paper, with four legs sticking out underneath. At four years of age, she is unaware of how to deal with dimension and makes the elephant's face to the side, explaining that "when you draw, you can't make it come off the paper."

After I compliment her elephant, she turns back to her drawing and I to my thesis. But in a few minutes she is by my side with a new figure next to her elephant. "Mom, look at this fairy!" The figure is human with a recognizable circle for the head, complete with eyes, nose, and mouth. The stick arms extend out from the head and are covered with an ever-widening stroke. Lindsey explains that these are the wings. Extending down from the head and running alongside the fairy's body is a single pink line. Lindsey points to it and explains, "See how long her hair is? Just like Rapunzel's."

As a mother, I take delight in the picture she has created. As a school teacher, I label her picture with her words. And as a parent-researcher, I mentally pounce upon the textual weave of a fairy with Rapunzel hair. (March 5, 1987, 4;4)

Much more than books and other written texts lies beneath what it means to be literate and to achieve that state through an early introduction to children's literature. One characteristic of many mainstream middle-class families who are oriented toward the schools and public media is the interaction of parent and child during bedtime-story reading. Although such an aim is often not articulated, parents use the bedtime story as an opportunity for the transmission of culture. Children learn at a very early age that books are valued—that they not only provide entertainment but also supply insights into cultural morals. Early interactions with storybooks also pave the way for schooling. But these assumptions are limited by cultural constraints and values, for individual differences within families affect the actual situations of book reading and the extensions of meaning. This book is a reflection of one family's culture; it is an attempt to understand the role of literature in Lindsey's and Ashley's lives.

This case of Lindsey and Ashley takes us beyond their immediate book reading to those unexpected creative transfers that children can make within literature, and from literature to life, with their evaluative and analytical probes of criticism. Their stories also enable us to explore how literary language and its accompanying illustrations initiate and feed children's extensions of the act of reading into the reiterative and transformative experience of reading. Lindsey and Ashley did more than carry around in their heads pieces of texts, memories of scenes, and dialogues of characters merely to whip them out as new readings or everyday events called for rescripting. They intuited and reshaped story rules to test against the rules of stories they came to know, as well as the world that parents, other adults, and friends imposed or announced. Literature gave Lindsey and Ashley much more than opportunities for exposure to the texts of books that often provoked talk about real-world knowledge. Literature provided innumerable models by which they could make connections creatively and think critically—models they could store, transfer, and reshape and then use in testing the limits of rules and the subtleties of contemporary life. The necessary intertwining of these strands of creativity, connections, and criticism forces us to cease peering through the window of the carriage and to step inside, to gain a full view of the children's transformation into literate beings.

1

Living in a World of Words

Each morning of her preschool years, my daughter Lindsey and I went through our daily routine of preparing her for the day. We negotiated her outfit, for Lindsey is prone to more outlandish combinations than I, and then brushed her teeth and combed her hair. For the latter, she usually sat perched on the bathroom sink, contemplating her image in the wide mirror as I carefully guided the brush through her hair, smoothing the tangles of a night's sleep.

One morning she requested a pony tail. I swept her hair into a long strand, and then wound it in the grasp of one hand while I searched for an elastic band with the other.

"Good mother!" she exclaimed. "You're not going to cut it, are you?"

Astonished, I replied, "Of course not. Whatever made you think of that?"

"The witch cut Rapunzel's hair! And when I was a little girl, I had long hair and my mother cut it all off!"

I laughed and said, "No, honey. That was me. When *I* was little, my mother cut *my* hair."

Lindsey scowled. "No, it was me! *My* mother cut off *my* hair!" (May 28, 1986, 3;6)

Lindsey's story was a personal extension of *Rapunzel,* a book that we had read in recent weeks. My actions, the feel of my hand tightening on her hair, the other hand reaching out, had triggered her entrance into the world of story. She had called me "Good mother," a direct quote from Michael Hague's illustrated edition of the famous Grimm brothers' tale. And the story tells us that the witch *"in her wrath . . .*

seized Rapunzel's beautiful hair, wound it round and round her left hand, and then grasping a pair of scissors in her right, snip snap, off it came, and the beautiful braids lay on the ground" (Grimm Brothers / Hague).

Lindsey had also incorporated a tale that I had told her from my own childhood, for as a child I had extremely long hair which I wore in a braid down my back. My mother had ultimately tired of the lengthy routine of braiding such a mass and had cut it when I entered the third grade. These two tales had become internally persuasive to Lindsey, and she had reauthored the Grimm tale by weaving in a narrative of my life and her own. She wove tales from storybooks as well as from her family's history into embellishments of her daily life. Yet her initial interpretations depended less on speech than on actions.[1]

During her first year or so of frequent story-reading times, Lindsey acted on or out of a story more often than she talked about it. One afternoon Lindsey's father, Kenny, told Lindsey that she could read quietly in her room during nap time. He had tucked her in bed with Charlotte Zolotow's *But Not Billy,* the story of a baby boy who is called by every affectionate appellation but his own name. When Kenny passed her room a few minutes later, Lindsey was out of bed and rocking back and forth on her knees in the middle of her bedroom floor.

"Lindsey," Kenny scolded, "I told you that you could read, not play."
"I am reading!" Lindsey replied indignantly.
She jumped back into her bed and held up the page in the story where Billy is being compared to a rocking horse.
"See!" she exclaimed. "I was being a rocking horse, just like Billy."
(May 17, 1986, 3;6)

To Lindsey, reading was action and each part must be played. The words of story were meant not to lie on the page but to leap off and rock back and forth in life.[2]

Through both talk and action, and later with the addition of her own stage directions to enlist family and friends into sociodramatic play, she created occasions in which she brought literature's scenes, beliefs, and rules for behaving into daily negotiations of time, space, and privilege. She enlisted the characters of storybooks as companions, and sometimes incorporated them into her own character, moving from one imaginary world to another. Lindsey swept the fireplace as Cinderella, lay as Sleeping Beauty to await her handsome prince, dropped off the bed into a pool of tears as Alice in Wonderland, and chased about the house as Max in mischievous pursuit of his dog. In a literate household, living through the stories of sanctioned book characters effectively muffled and evaded direct conflicts between child independence and parental authority.

Lindsey's interpretations were not limited to the larger associations between storybooks and dramatic play complete with props and costumes. There were a thousand smaller, but no less significant, connections made between life and text and back again. These connections often hinged on a sight, a sound, or a movement that sparked the connection between the world of words and the world of the child. The movement of a rocking chair caused a recollection of a baby's lullaby. A word used in conversation by either parent would spark a reminder of a similar word in a text.

One spring day in California, Lindsey went bike riding with her father. It had rained in the afternoon and the wheels of their bicycles splashed a fan of sparkling water up behind them. They toured a bit of our neighborhood before crossing a small forested section of the village to the athletic fields. As they emerged from the trees, a tremendous rainbow greeted them. It hung suspended from the sky, stretching wide, embracing the earth with color.

Lindsey stopped her bike and stared in shocked silence. Since she had lived most of her life in the desert of Saudi Arabia, Lindsey had seen such magnificence only in illustrated text.

> Then she fell to the ground laughing gaily. "Rainbows aren't real! They *aren't* real! They're only in books!"
> As she laughed and rolled in the wet grass, soaking up the vision in the sky, her perception changed. Staring up at the rainbow, she cited Kenny a new litany of literary insights. "Giants aren't real. Dragons aren't real. But rainbows *are* real!" (April 24, 1987, 4;5)

What Lindsey saw in the rainbow recalled the words of literary texts to stretch her realizations of categories of meaning in fact and fantasy. Although this connection was more verbally articulated than enacted, the elements of character, plot, and theme came alive in ways similar to the rainbow's evocation of other literary objects possible in the real world: a face summons a character, an action brings plot to mind, a problem evokes a theme, and a new revelation calls for a reshaping of rules.

Literature gave Lindsey the equipment and the process to become an experimenter with her own world. The poet Horace said that literature's purpose was to instruct and delight. Literature, however, does not instruct directly; it provides readers the materials with which to experiment and to test what comes from various settings, characters, and situations. Literature sets up possible worlds to reshuffle for transit and testing in the actual worlds of children. But literature also stands ready to manipulate, and to be manipulated by, the rules within its own texts.[3]

Lindsey often had suggestions for the text that aligned with her personal sense of real-world rules. In the story of *Rapunzel* (Grimm Brothers / Rogasky), the blinded prince wanders in the forest for a year. The illustrator showed the passage of time by turning the prince's clothes into rags and giving him a beard. This transformation did not match Lindsey's vision of the perfect prince.

"He gots a beard." Lindsey said this last word with distaste.

"I know." Flipping back to the previous page, I said, "He didn't have a beard before, huh? No. Well, he wasn't able to shave himself."

I continued reading, and as the story reached its climax, with Rapunzel weeping into her beloved's eyes, Lindsey stopped me.

"Mama," she said, flipping back to the page before, "I wanna see something. Why does he not have a beard here and he does have a beard there?"

"Because he's wandered in the forest for a long, long time. Even though all we've done is turned the page, *he's* wandered for a long time trying to find Rapunzel. And you know how daddy's beard grows a little bit every day?"

"Uh huh," she replied.

"Well, if he didn't shave it, it would grow to be very long," I explained. "And perhaps the prince wandering in the forest didn't have a razor to cut his beard."

Though I couldn't imagine what the prince would do without his Gillette, Lindsey had an answer. "Well, he could have used a sharp thorn to raze it." (June 24, 1986, 3;7)

Just as a sharp thorn can blind a prince, it can also be used to keep up his appearance. And just as Lindsey adapted an object to the situation, she also turned her familiarity with her father's razor into the verb "raze."

Regardless of the original shape of the children's literature being read—poem, sketch, fairy tale, science fantasy, or catalogue of objects and places—children's memories reshape these into problem-solving narratives. In these, children attribute to animate beings some set of goals, and they place those attempting to achieve these goals in particular types of associations with collections of objects existing over a period of time within spatial limits. Children remember objects most often in their functional roles and especially when they belong to an animate being who has certain goals and intentions for their use. Children can interpret literature because they can locate its stories in their own belief system, which sees the world as inhabited by animate beings who make plans and act on them. In other words, the animate beings within literature also believe that their world contains creatures capable of thinking ahead, building future scenarios, and bringing about subsequent action.[4]

In the most memorable of children's literature, the intentions, goals, and motivations of these agents remain unstated, subject to change, and responsible for surprise endings or outcomes. The fundamental interpretive act of children is to create hopes, fears, and expectations for literature's characters. In fiction and poetry, the author needs to provide only two explicit ingredients—animate actors and arenas for action. Certain literary conventions of genre help move the actors into problem-solving modes, but the fulfillment of these conventions is possible only because children bring to their interpretation the expectation that individuals have intentions, emotions, and motivations.

One night I was listening to a cassette of King Lear and following the oral text with the written text from my Shakespeare class. Lindsey wandered in, listened briefly, and asked, "What's the story about?" I gave her a brief accounting of what I'd heard thus far: King Lear had three daughters, two who claimed undying love and a third (the youngest) who claimed a love that matched her duty, no more and no less. Lear, in astonished rage, divided the third child's rightful portion of his kingdom between the other two sisters. Later when he visited his first daughter, she treated him poorly. Disillusioned he cried, *"How sharper than a serpent's tooth it is to have a thankless child!"* (I.iv.295–296).

When I asked Lindsey what Lear would do next she replied, "He'll go to the second daughter's house but she'll treat him poorly. But then he'll go to the third daughter's house and she'll treat him nicely."

"How do you know?" I asked.

"Because," she explained patiently, knitting her fingers together, "in stories the two oldest daughters often treat their moms and dads poorly. But the third is always nice."

When I asked her for examples she replied, "Well, this is one. Hmmm . . . let's see. *The Fool of the World* [Ransome]. Except his parents treat him poorly and God treats him like He loves him. *Cinderella* [Perrault] . . . the two mean sisters and the mother treat her poorly."

"What about *Beauty and the Beast* [Mayer]?" I suggested.

"Oh, yeah! That would work. Her sisters were real mean 'cause the two older sisters don't really love their father and Beauty does." (November 20, 1988, 6;0)

In literature, children see "rule systems" and common structures that enable prediction of outcome. They see problems work out for characters who must act in situations that others have created and in which they must live. Seeing these simulated problems and their solutions in literature complements children's dramatizations—especially in socio-dramatic play—in which they practice problem resolution without having to encounter direct consequences. The metarules by which they bring in play enable them to announce it as *on* or to *call it off.*

Such supraorganizers and collecting cues come in several forms— genres, predictable scripts or characters, patterned illustrations, and expected modes of description or narration. Here Lindsey recognizes a familiar plot whose characters will replay scripts she knows from other stories. From the very minimal narrative frame that tells of a family made up of father and daughters who lived in an earlier era, Lindsey realizes that the story will be like those she knows in both form and substance. Moreover, some redemptive character will be necessary to the plot, and Lindsey can offer without benefit of direct text examination the descriptions of such characters and situations that motivate them. Added to such organizing principles or metarules, which enable quick comprehension of one literary text and its extension into another, are those that allow transformations of the fantastic of literature to the pragmatics of reality.[5]

Highly conscious that she both knew rules and could make up rules for literature and life, Lindsey often chose to maneuver her preferred outcomes of everyday events through literary interventions. Through fictionalizations of real situations, she adjusted different aspects of characters, settings, times, moods, and degrees of magic to match her own intentions and emotions.

Riding in the car one afternoon, Lindsey was munching on some rice cakes that I had brought for the ride. She happily ate her way through two or three and then dropped the last one. It rolled across the edge of her car seat and fell to the floor.

"Mama. I dropped my rice cake," Lindsey said in dismay.

I had been watching out of the corner of one eye. "Yes, I know. Just a minute."

"Mama. Mama. Can you reach my rice cake?"

Intent on the traffic, I replied, "No, honey. I'm driving. Wait till a stoplight."

"Mama? Mama? . . . Jizo Sama! Have you seen my dumpling?" Unsuccessful with the ordinary language of a four-year-old, she turned to the language of literature.

Laughing at her innovation, I pulled the car over to the side of the road to retrieve her rice cake/dumpling. "Here you are, Little Woman," I replied. (November 5, 1986, 3;11)

Lindsey was paraphrasing a line from *The Funny Little Woman* (Mosel), in which a Japanese woman loses a rice dumpling. The dumpling rolls off her table and falls through a crack in the floor. The woman follows the dumpling, giggling all the way. As she follows, she meets a variety of underground Japanese statues called Jizo Samas. She bows low before every ancient figure and begs the advice of each.

Lindsey's use of the literary reference seemed to be triggered by the visual similarity of her rice cake to the rice dumpling and the motion of the falling cake/dumpling to the floor. But her purpose in re-creating the text was to get my attention. Her conventional pleas received no real response, but by turning to literature and playful language, she had her wish for the return of the rice cake quickly fulfilled. Careful attention to the ways in which she called on literature tells us much about how she formed and recognized patterns, made analogies about the world's scenes, and created metaphors for processes and outcomes.[6]

Her personally internalized metaphors and analogies often made no sense to adults until she gave them some element of the literary reference—the character, plot, or memorable bit of dialogue or scene. Every Easter the girls and I read DuBose Heyward's story *The Country Bunny and the Little Gold Shoes*. According to Heyward, there was not just one Easter Bunny but five, and one of them was Mother Cottontail, the mother of twenty-one perfectly behaved children. Mother Cottontail trained each of her children in the assorted work of the household, and while she was away delivering eggs, the children performed their duties admirably: *"And sure enough, just as she had said, everything was in order. The floors were swept and there were two lovely new pictures painted and hanging on the wall. The dishes were washed and shone in the cupboard. The clothes were washed and mended and nicely hung away"* (Heyward, n.p.). As with past readings of the story, on this Easter the girls seemed less interested in the overriding message of the "well-behaved children" than in the glistening pictures of assorted candy in the Palace of the Easter Eggs. Still, Lindsey managed to take part of the message to heart before the week was out.

The day after Easter was the start of an educational convention in San Francisco, and Kenny and I spent the night in a hotel in the city, leaving Lindsey and Ashley in the care of their grandfather. When we returned late the next evening, the girls were already in bed, but Grandpa said that Lindsey had made a special point of wanting us to notice the two new pictures that were hung in the entryway. Quite frankly, I thought little about them until the next morning, when Lindsey pulled me down the stairs exclaiming:

> "Did you see our pictures? I hung them just the way the Country Bunny's children did!" Sure enough, these were not affixed to the wall with the tape rolls we ordinarily use but were suspended from fishing line hanging from push pins, just like those in the story.
>
> Lindsey's picture was a scene from *The Country Bunny and the Little Gold Shoes* and showed Mother Cottontail returning to her own little cottage after a long Easter night. As Lindsey explained, "You were gone for *soooo* long, and I wanted to make the house pretty for you . . . just like the bunny children." (March 29, 1989, 6;4)

Lindsey's work included no straightening of her room—her clothes were tumbled in her drawer and the remains of a tea party lay unwashed in a corner of the room; but she had never been a literal child. She took what she wanted from the message, and it came, no less, from the heart.

A World of Words

But how did Lindsey come to be able to stretch literature into socio-dramatic play that recast roles and rules of such real-life complexities as bedtime or parental absence? How, in other words, did the interpretive community of Lindsey and Ashley come about and exert influence on them?[7] As they acquired knowledge with and about books, they also learned basic aspects of awareness about oral and written language, sources of information and authority, and gradations of interpretations. Most of this learning came not in blatant directives but in redundant, subtle, often trivial, fleeting but repetitive routines of speech, gesture, or facial expression slipped in among the interstices of everyday family life. Through these rituals, they learned values that surrounded the knowledge and skills we asked them to display. They absorbed from us and their peers notions about what mattered most and least about books, proper and improper ways to handle, read, and think about ideas from print, and ways to judge their behavior and that of others around books. These habits accorded with and mutually reinforced other cultural patterns of space and time use, problem-solving strategies, varying plays of questions and answers, loyalties to certain systems of marking and classification, and preferred ways of spending leisure time. They also learned the limits of ways they could resist and control how books affected and influenced their lives. To reject books out of hand in our household would have been almost as unnatural as to refuse food, sleep, or any other regularly established daily pattern. But both girls were regularly able to negotiate precisely when, how, and what Kenny and I wanted them to read, and to alter interpretations and venture independent thoughts and discoveries. They were anything but a steady, passive, receptive audience: from an early age, they had their own notions of specific rules of illustrating, expanding, enacting, interpreting, and reshaping texts; they found expert ways to derail our agenda for reading, to deflect our line of talk without provoking our absolute refusal to share a bedtime story or take time out for one of their suggested reading tasks. Perhaps most important was the fact that as each girl developed a definition of her self as individual personality, she used books—just as she used other props of her daily environment (such as clothing, hair style, or manner of talking)—to reflect what she did or did not notice, remember, and reuse on other occasions.

Literacy is not acquired in a vacuum. Nor does it spring fully formed from our minds, like Athena from the head of Zeus. It is an evolutionary process changing from generation to generation and from life to life. An analysis of the role of words in our family life is ultimately a personal study of Lindsey's and Ashley's response to literature. Although all people resonate with the values of their community, every life is individual, every action unique, every pattern personalized. And the patterns of life in our literate school-oriented family, like those of many other mainstream families, created an environment steeped in cultural messages. Yet our personal household culture did not just *create* Lindsey or Ashley; they are not only products of our world but extensions. They will take what we give them and change it and shape it into something that is their own.

Lindsey and Ashley live in a world of literacy. It is a world where novels, textbooks, newspapers, and magazines are all an integral part of the flow of life. Books cram the bookshelves, newspapers lie between the breakfast bowls, notes broadcast messages from the refrigerator door. The study holds a mélange of textbooks, children's books, and reams of computer paper filled with fieldnotes. When I prepare dinner, I consult a cookbook, while other cookbooks stand by on the kitchen shelf to lend suggestions. When Kenny prepares the grocery list, he checks the shelf, reading labels and writing down missing items.

The mail announces its daily arrival with a loud slap as the letters slide through the door slot to hit the floor. Young and old stop what they are doing to check the mail, to skim and toss the advertisements, to share and often read aloud the letters, and then to save them as a reminder of a needed reply. Business letters and bills are mailed from the house on a regular basis. Personal letters are more seasonal: a Christmas letter which encapsulates our family's year; invitations, greeting cards, and thank-you letters to grandparents, aunts, and uncles revolve around family birthdays and anniversaries, when brief notes accompany pictures of the girls.

The television guide helps us choose an occasional evening program; the newspaper directs us to movie times and locations. We post notices of upcoming community events. Novels and plays lie on the dresser near my bed; I am constantly in the midst of some fictional tale, often two or three a week. I tend to steer clear of best-sellers, though I like a romance. I often read the type of book that's likely to be on the English syllabus for a high school class or a college literature course. By this, I mean to indicate not Shakespeare or Chaucer but rather novels by Hemingway, Faulkner, and Fitzgerald and plays by Williams, Miller, and O'Neill. Rereading is an integral part of my reading pattern, and several authors I read again and again.

Pregnancy and parenting books were ever-present at the time of Lindsey's birth. Since Kenny and I were living in Saudi Arabia, and there were no Lamaze classes, we learned breathing techniques from a book. We read several books on nutrition, the stages of pregnancy, and labor itself. We discussed several possible names and ultimately found Lindsey's name in a baby name book. I remember riding in the car reading to Kenny and reciting female names in alphabetical order: Allison, Amy, Amelia . . . Deirdre, Diane, Donna . . . Leigh, Linda, Lindsey!

After she was born, books on child development and parenting dominated my reading. The pediatrician and author T. Berry Brazelton became a constant reading companion, a wise but distant friend, as Lindsey and I progressed from his book on infants to those on toddlers. Ashley's infancy was not attended by such literary accompaniment. While the books continued to speak through our parenting, they were relegated to the reference shelves, consulted only in hours of illness.

Kenny and I began reading to Lindsey when she was four months old, though we sang nursery rhymes and lullabies to her from birth. Ashley started much earlier—beginning with the sound of my voice in the womb as I read to Lindsey. After her birth, Ashley joined in our reading, nursing through the softer narration, cooing through the songs, crying out at the voice of the dragon or witch and casting startled eyes up to see what had happened. From infancy through preschool years, Lindsey and Ashley shared innumerable stories and poems with us and with each other.

If I had to choose a book from my own childhood that I continue to enjoy as an adult, my selection would be *Anne of Green Gables* (Montgomery). Somewhere, in the course of the years, I lost the well-worn, muted green copy that I owned as a child. But after one evening's discussion of its continuing importance in my life, Kenny bought me a new edition, which we have both read since.

Reading was an integral part of my upbringing, though neither I nor my sisters can remember that our parents ever read to us. Instead, they told us stories and talked about books. My mother was from an old Southern family, and my relatives from New Orleans could weave tales that stretched long into the night. I remember sitting on the edge of the family poker games, listening to the shuffle of the cards, the clink of the chips, and the stories told of long ago and only yesterday. My grandmother could tell a story for every card she dealt—the one-eyed Jack, the black sheep of the family, and the indiscretions of carnival nights. She threw out stories like trinkets from a passing float, each rich and sparkling to the eyes of a child.

My father came from Indiana, where his father farmed onions. Though the farm was small and times were tight, my grandfather managed to build a library with books bought at school closings and acquired from families leaving Depression-era farming for the city. I remember that when all the aunts, uncles, and cousins descended on the small farmhouse, my grandfather would excuse himself from the nonstop chatter and seek refuge in Grant's memoirs, *Bullfinch's Mythology,* and the tales of Alexandre Dumas. My father remembers the many hours he spent as a boy sitting at the "library table," a long plank of wood with bookcases at both ends, reading the tales of Horatio Alger.

In my own childhood, reading was a given; books were bought, borrowed, and continually recommended. My father cut out newspaper articles and left them on the coffee table for us to read. My mother, an amateur artist, shared her books on the lives of the great masters. My two older sisters were voracious readers. I remember that my sister Karen, when she was little, once missed an Indiana family reunion because of a book. The entire clan had dressed and left the farmhouse for the party down the road. When we arrived, my mother and father, who had come in separate cars, asked each other about Karen's whereabouts. In a panic, they drove back home only to discover Karen immersed in a book. The story became legend among family members, who would proudly suggest that she hadn't even realized we were gone. "What a reader!" my dad would exclaim at the end of its hundredth telling.

Although as a young child I immersed myself in *Misty of Chincoteague* (Henry) and the adventures of Nancy Drew, I never read as much as the other members of my family, for I needed additional time to act out what I had read. I longed to be outdoors, where I could *be* a wild island stallion, or a clever sleuth with her own sky-blue roadster. My girlfriends and I built corrals, castles, and cottages in the woods near our homes and played out the abundant fantasies to be found in black stallions, kings and queens, and little women.

School, however, was a different story. In school I learned that memorization, not creation, was the key to good grades. In school I learned to fill in the test blanks with facts and forgo any personal interpretation of the work. I went through junior high and high school and on into college with the understanding that my opinion was less important than the secrets revealed in Cliff Notes. There were some exceptions to the rule—a ninth grade English course on mythology, a high school speech teacher, and a college class in creative writing. But it was only during my stint in the Peace Corps that I again began to read and think on my own. The Peace Corps library in Tunis was filled with the books of many past volunteers, and I read and reread all the books that had been assigned for memorization during my school years; but this time I read them for myself, and not to mold my interpretation to match that of an authority.

Kenny, too, was a reader. When we met in Tunisia as Peace Corps volunteers, he kept a notebook of memorable quotations, and our conversations and letters back and forth were punctuated with comments on things we had read and wanted to share. Years later, Kenny's mother sent us a box of memories. It held some Christmas decorations that had traditionally hung on their tree and two old volumes of a Childcraft set. Volume three was entitled *Folk and Fairy Tales* and evoked little response. But Volume one's *Poems of Early Childhood* caused him to sit down and stare. He turned the frayed and torn pages gently. "My mother read these poems to us at night," he whispered. For the following month, Kenny read the poems to Lindsey again and again, and she often requested "Daddy's book" well into her school years.

While my reading to Lindsey and Ashley increased over the years, the need to work on my master's thesis eliminated time for my own reading of fiction. Textbooks, dissertations, and photocopied collections of articles on literacy predominated, though I read articles on a variety of educational themes. For every book that I discussed with the head of my committee, she had two more titles to suggest. The most interesting I shared with Kenny, who was working full time designing educational software. Our positions reversed after my master's courses wound down, we moved, and Kenny began a program of study toward a doctorate in language, literacy, and culture. He would sit at his desk late into the night, reading and making notes on the word processor.

The intensity of doctoral study forced Kenny to eliminate his primary reading choice: the newspaper. An avid fan of current events, he read the *Herald Tribune* and *Time* magazine when we lived overseas. In the States he always read the daily paper and the Sunday edition of the *New York Times* from beginning to end. But in graduate school, leisure time was at a premium, though he still managed to read the *New York Times* daily and *Time* magazine weekly. He often read with a pencil or a pair of scissors in his hand, and would clip articles to show to me or to post on the broom closet door.

I read the newspaper as well, and in a preferred order. With the Sunday *New York Times,* the "Magazine" was always my first choice. I read the "About Men" and "Hers" columns and then any other article of interest. Next was the book review section, in which reviews of children's books were of primary importance. The "Arts and Leisure" section followed, and I would pay special attention to articles on dance, plays, movies, and television. The "Travel" section was next, usually for articles of places we'd been or might possibly travel to one day. Finally, I would browse a bit in the "Week in Review" section and among the front-page items, highly selective in my choice, for I could always ask Kenny for a summary of the big stories.

Once I had completed my master's thesis, I had additional time for reading. I read more current literature, moving beyond book reviews to the real thing. I mentally traveled through the New York scene with Jay McInerney and Tom Wolfe, to Latin America with Gabriel García Márquez, and to Canada with Margaret Atwood. When I began a doctoral program focusing on language and learning, I found my journeys once again limited to the classroom. Still, I determined to keep reading literature, and at night I shoved aside scholarly articles and textbooks to reflect on John Irving's *Prayer for Owen Meany* and Toni Morrison's *Beloved.*

Words embedded in meaningful text were a focus in our home, but Kenny also had a compelling interest in teaching the love of words. As an English teacher, he took particular pride in his vocabulary program. He believed that children master and use vocabulary if given an anecdotal scaffold to support memory. He spent years researching words, and filled one entire shelf in our living room with vocabulary books. One of his most cherished possessions was his dictionary—*Webster's Third New International Dictionary* (unabridged). It stood sentinel over our study, mounted on an antique stand, until it was forced to share space with a second-edition *Random House Dictionary of the English Language*, which the girls and I gave Kenny one Father's Day.

When teaching, he would start every class with a "Word for the Day." Rather than advocating memorization of a weekly list of unrelated vocabulary words, his program focused on the anecdotal context of the origin of each word and the relationship between words. An accompanying point system challenged students to find words taught in class in the context of life. They could look for words in newspapers and books, and listen for vocabulary on television or in movies and even conversations. Points were awarded for every new incident where a vocabulary word was used. Students needed to claim the word verbally, and then write down their new possession on a form they would give to Kenny.

His program became known throughout the community when we taught in an international school in Saudi Arabia. "That's my word!" students would shout at their teachers during a lecture or at their parents in the middle of a conversation. The competition for points became fierce when there were two or more students present and only one vocabulary word tossed out. The high school biology teacher asked Kenny for a weekly list of words and incorporated them into his lecture just to watch the ensuing scramble for points. The superintendent blamed Kenny when the students protested the dismissal of one teacher as "punitive" and "unnecessarily Draconian."

In more recent years, Kenny designed and wrote a vocabulary game, and I became the chief editor and typist. The creation of the game began in earnest the summer Lindsey was two years old. Kenny's study was a tangle of books, pencils, and yellow note pads. The click-clack sound of the computer keys and the buzz of the printer emanated from my study as I worked to type and polish the small pastel game cards, each filled with words, words, and more words.

Once upon a Time

While Kenny's love of words played a major part in family life, my love of children's literature created another essential support for our world of words. I taught in primary schools for a number of years in several different countries, and my first certified teaching position was in a first-grade class in the United States. Ten years later, I remembered two things about the opening day of classes: being nervous and reading the story "Snowdrop."

I read from an edition of *Grimm's Fairy Tales* that friends had given to Kenny and me. Although it was beautifully illustrated by Arthur Rackham, I had gathered other props I felt were necessary to a dramatic delivery. As my pupils leaned in close, the evil queen stepped before her mystic mirror, and I pulled my own mirror from my pocket. Holding it high, I intoned, *"Mirror, Mirror on the wall, / Who is fairest of us all?"* (p. 7). Several children began to imitate my gestures, staring haughtily into the palm of their hand and chanting the familiar words with me as the story advanced. I pulled out a bright ribbon for Snowdrop's lacings, a tortoiseshell barrette for the poisoned comb, and, naturally, a shiny red apple for Snowdrop's destiny. After I cut the apple in two, I held out one section. The children instinctively drew back. "Don't do it!" one small boy shouted, flinging his arm out to prevent Snowdrop from making her ill-fated decision. It was an auspicious beginning to my elementary teaching career, for I had been able to lure my children into the world of story.

For the next eight years I taught children in grades one through three. Moving from the public schools of Utah to the altiplano of Bolivia to the desert of Saudi Arabia, I taught children of all shapes, sizes, colors, and creeds. I covered the standard American curriculum—reading, math, science, and social studies—but my forte was literature. Though bound by school policies to teach with basal reading textbooks, I found the tales flat and uninspiring, the discussions muted. And so, like many teachers, I read literature (Andersen, Grimm, Sendak, and Steig) to my children daily. Through stories, I taught my children the themes surrounding what Faulkner calls "the human heart in conflict with itself," and the children taught me.

Anna Freud suggests, "Let us try to learn from children all they have to tell us and let us sort out only later, how their ideas fit in with our own" (cited in Coles, 1986, p. 15). This quote summarizes the attitude I took toward storytelling and discussion. I wanted to break from my own schooling and its dependence on memorization. When I read to children, I wanted to hear their voices, listen to their questions and exclamations, weigh one statement against another. My own questions were designed to bring out the children's response. I was less interested in the "What's that?" type of question (What did Red Riding Hood have in her basket? What were her mother's instructions?) than the "What would . . . ?" question (What would you do if you met the wolf? Would you tell him the way to Grandmother's house? Todd says he would call the cops! What would happen if he did?).

Over the years, my classes' literary discussions spilled beyond the temporal and spatial boundaries of "storytime" and into every aspect of classroom life. Children lined up for recess still arguing the finer details of a story. They called on a character's actions to defend and explain their own. They incorporated words and phrases from story into their own conversations. When twenty-five children fought back tears or openly wept at the death of a small spider in *Charlotte's Web* (White), when they laughed uproariously at the dirty tricks of Roald Dahl's couple in *The Twits*, and when they drew back from the apple extended in "Snowdrop," they entered a world not easily forgotten, the world of story.

It is a world of wonder, a world where young girls are as beautiful as the day, young men willing to give anything for love, and stepmothers yellow and green with envy. Goodness has power over death, treasures that would not be traded for riches are given as gifts, and evil is rewarded with a dance in red-hot shoes. It is a world I entered not only with hundreds of children in my classrooms but also with my own children, Lindsey and Ashley.

Lindsey

Lindsey was born on November 8, 1982, in Yanbu, a newly created city in the Kingdom of Saudi Arabia. Once a small fishing village on the Red Sea, Yanbu was turned into a boom town, with many newly constructed oil refineries ready to receive black gold through a pipeline from the Eastern Province. The refined products were then shipped out of Yanbu's highly secretive harbor, up the Red Sea, and out the Suez Canal to the waiting world.

Kenny and I taught in the international school, which provided an American education for the expatriate community in Yanbu. Although most of the students were American, there were also large numbers of children from Europe, India, and the Far East. Lindsey's birth exemplified the international nature of the community: her entry into the world was assisted by Filipino nurses, an Irish midwife, Dutch and Indian obstetricians, and a Swedish pediatrician.

Lindsey was also born into a world of diverse and abundant words. Two weeks prior to her birth, Kenny and I were feted at a surprise shower. "Best wishes to the new cub!" the hand-drawn poster proclaimed, in a wordplay on our last name. A card on one of the gifts said "Welcome Baby Roo," which was a pet name I had already given Lindsey. I chose this appellation after the baby kangaroo in Milne's *The House at Pooh Corner*, which seemed to describe Lindsey's vigorous prenatal kicking.

We received numerous gifts—quilts, booties, small stuffed animals, toys, and baby books, many of which were embroidered, printed, or stuffed with a storybook theme. We played party games, one of which was a "baby crossword" with clues like "Wynken, Blynken, and _____; Little _____ Riding Hood; and _____, two, buckle my shoe."

On the day Lindsey was born, my first-grade class wrote a picture book in her honor entitled "A Short Collection of WISHES and PICTURES on the Birth of Your Daughter." The substitute teacher, who guided its publication, had it delivered to the hospital. The children had written a number of messages:

"I wish your baby would be nice," wrote Anna-Maria.

"I know you are very happy to have your baby and I wish she was called Elizabeth," Kenny suggested.

Todd, however, chose the name "Shelley."

One of the boys in my class, Dengiz, was Turkish and quite new to English. He wrote, "Dear Mrs. Wolf, . . . Hi Wolf. Baby very good."

And Sagar wrote in his neat methodical handwriting, "I wish your baby would never cry." (November 8, 1982)

Friends and family sent notes and cards of congratulations. My father wrote a letter specifically to the newborn:

Dear, dear Lindsey,

How to welcome you into our world? Such a lovely little girl—so wanted and so needed to fill that special place in my heart. How I have waited for you! . . . There is so much to life and I wish I could provide a complete book of instructions instead of these few meager words to protect and help you—but do you know what? I'm sure you will manage and we'll learn from you.

I, too, felt the need to write to Lindsey. Weeks after her homecoming I wrote her a letter about her birth, her arrival home, the way she looked in the crib, and her first bath. Of her birth I wrote: "When you were born, there was an enchanted silence. Minutes before, the room had been filled with cheers of encouragement, 'Come on! Push! This is it!' Dad was holding onto my hand so tight. Then you slipped into our lives like some wondrous fish. Dad bent his face close to mine, and we looked into your eyes for the first time. We didn't need to count fingers and toes. We knew you were perfect."

A physically precocious child, Lindsey seemed to master everything weeks before the date that the baby books predicted. She rolled over at three weeks, crawled at five months, walked at nine months, and could do chin-ups on the dining room table at ten months. Walking soon became passé; she ran everywhere as her first birthday drew near. She did not seem to understand an object fully unless she had either put it in her mouth or climbed on top of it.

Speech progressed at a slower pace and seemed integrally connected to physical movement. Her first distinctive laugh bubbled out with a bouncing rendition of a Mother Goose rhyme:

Ride a cock-horse to Banbury Cross
To see a fine lady upon a white horse;
Rings on her fingers and bells on her toes,
And she shall have music wherever she goes.

At the age of four months, we began to read stories to her. And by ten months we were reading to her every night at bedtime.

"Look at that! What's that?" we would query, pointing to a picture of a baby in a book.

"Ba Ba," Lindsey would answer. At ten months her blanket, her bottle, and any baby were all classified under the rubric "Ba Ba."

But we knew what she meant. "It's a baby!" we encouraged. "Yes, kiss the baby."

Lindsey would lean forward and plant a kiss on the book baby's nose. Actually, any baby would do for this display of affection—the one in the mirror, or on the box of disposable diapers, or even on the cover of Dr. Spock.

"Good! Good!!" we would say, complimenting her on her reading. (Letter to my sister, October 1, 1983, 11 mos.)[8]

Her ability to translate two-dimensional storybook pictures into phys-ical actions and verbal exclamations increased rapidly. She would moo to indicate a cow, swipe at her hair to signify "brush," and say "MMMMMMM" when shown a banana, reaching out for its yellow shape.

Around her first birthday, I wrote to my father to tell him of her progress and thank him for a book that he had given Lindsey:

> Her language skills are really picking up. Naturally, her understanding is way ahead of her vocabulary, but she seems to pick up new words daily. She says Ma Ma, Da Da, hot, yuck, uh-oh, na-na (for banana), wolf, ba ba (for bottle), yeah, night, teeth, more, watszat (what's that?), up, and burp.
>
> "Book" is one of her favorite words and activities. We read to her every night, cuddling on the couch. Her present favorites are *Goodnight Moon* [Brown] and *The Runaway Bunny* [Brown]. You should see the latter. It is chewed on all corners and is missing a few pages and its cover! It is definitely a well-loved book, Dad. (Thanksgiving weekend, 1983, 1;0)

Lindsey's favorite book at fourteen months was Harry McNaught's *Animal Babies*. Under the spell of his illustrations and our tutelage, her repertoire of book-related animal sounds increased and she moved from commonplace domestic animals to the more exotic. She would stick out her tongue for the anteater, stand on one leg for the flamingo, roar for the lion, and stretch her neck high for the giraffe. Kenny and I created the original physical labels, but they seemed to strike a chord in Lindsey, who performed them with relish. And the cycle continued as we encouraged the performance.

In addition to the labeling activities which most picture books evoked, Lindsey began, not long after her first birthday, to play out certain parts of books. *Goodnight Moon,* read at bedtime, evoked an original dramatic response and her first trip into the imagination. I wrote to my sister: "She has begun to pretend and will fall on the ground and lay still when we say 'Night Night.' When it is truly time to go to bed, she calls 'Ni Ni' to all manner of things. She knows each of her many stuffed animals by name and will pick them up to give them a good-night kiss" (February 4, 1984, 1;3). Books accompanied Lindsey everywhere. We always had a few stuffed into her stroller on short trips around the neighborhood. Several books were essential for long airline trips leading to vacations abroad. While traveling, we bought more books. In Paris it seemed appropriate to buy her *The Red Balloon* (Lamorisse). After our trip to Sri Lanka, we bought several books by Laurent de Brunhoff, for elephants had become a big topic. The cartoon of Babar in suit and bowler could not substitute for the image of the Indian elephant which greeted us outside our hotel: a kingly creature draped in a spangled cloth of a thousand gleaming mirrors. But the sight of the elephants bathing in *Meet Babar and His Family* did remind us all of the real elephant that Lindsey and Kenny rode along a jungle river and then watched being bathed by his Sri Lankan master.

Toward the middle of Lindsey's second year we left labeling activities behind, and, rather than condensing or abridging stories, read them *in toto*. We saw connections between literature and life, and we taught Lindsey to see them as well. Most of the time these connections brought her understanding of life and pleasure in its possibilities, but there were times when she responded with fear. A month prior to her second birthday, I wrote to friends:

> Now she is a big girl, sleeping in a big bed, and Kenny and I still go in two or three times a night to watch our sleeping beauty. We have an every night ritual, which includes brushing away the "bad teeth" and sharing bedtime stories.
>
> Her current favorite is *The Three Little Pigs* [Galdone], and she has a real love-hate relationship with the big, bad wolf. She imitates him by turning the corners of her mouth down in a scowl. With a low, menacing voice she threatens, "Little pig . . . little pig . . . COME IN!!!" Oftentimes, she scares herself, and hugs herself saying, "Wolf. No hurt Lindsey."
>
> Katy, our baby-sitter, told me the other day that she had made a gigantic mistake. It seems that the wind was banging the door, and she casually told Lindsey that maybe it was the Wolf. Lindsey burst into tears and soon had Kara (her childcare playmate) crying too. Katy couldn't believe she'd made such an error. Both girls howled at the door until she convinced them it was safe. Lindsey now understands the word "teasing." (October 1, 1984, 1;11)

Maurice Sendak's *Where the Wild Things Are* rapidly became a favorite and fortified her with the intertextual ammunition to cope with her fears.[9] "Be still!" she would threaten the big, bad wolf as his cheeks filled with air. And she would shout the same words to me when I scolded or denied her something she wanted. By her second birthday she had learned that text provided some answers to life's questions.

The ability to tame "Wild Things" was a theme that carried beyond storybooks and into the narrative of our family life. Shortly after Lindsey's second birthday, we traveled to Tanzania on safari. Borrowing from both reality and fantasy, we developed a narrative that described how Lindsey, a powerful heroine, saves her mother from a hungry lion. In the story, I leave the safety of our van to get a better picture of a nearby giraffe. Concentrating on the photo, I am unaware of the fact that a lion is stalking me. Lindsey is watching, however. She sees the lion and cries out, "Stop, Lion!" The king of the savannah instantly recognizes her power. Staring at her in amazement, he cries, "Queen Lindsey, I didn't know you were in Africa!" After an abject apology, which Lindsey haughtily accepts, he helps me back into the van. I am much shaken, and can only whisper, "Thank you, Sweetheart. You saved my life!" Since its first telling, this story has been refined and embellished. Sometimes Lindsey saves me, and other times she comes to Kenny's rescue. But the compelling theme of her power remains at the heart of the narrative.[10]

Another narrative featuring Lindsey as powerful heroine was created by Lindsey and her baby-sitter. It wove together elements of *Jack and the Beanstalk*, *The Three Billy Goats Gruff*, and life in our neighborhood. Our playground had swings and a slide, as well as a large climbing structure that incorporated a wooden bridge. In the story, Lindsey saves her small friend Kara from a mean giant, who dominates the bridge. Lindsey orders him off the bridge in no uncertain terms, and then claims it as her own, so that small children are now free to play there. Lindsey particularly loved this story, since she was able to enter into the narrative physically. She had a magnificent prop (the bridge), a live actress (Kara), and sufficient imagination to supply the giant.

Physical entrée into story was not offered only by books or narrative, but often came from television. Lindsey is an avid fan of television in general, even though she is not allowed to watch cartoons, which Kenny and I call "junk TV." Instead, we are strong advocates of *Sesame Street*, as well as of *Wonderworks* and *Reading Rainbow*, and we often videotape book-related programs so that she can watch them more than once. When Lindsey was well past her second birthday, we made a video tape of Judy Garland in *The Wizard of Oz*, and Lindsey fell in love with it. I wrote to my father detailing her involvement in the story: "She can sing 'Over the Rainbow,' dance like the Tin Man, and shake our broom and threaten, *'I'll get you, my pretty, and your little dog too!'*

The other day she began screaming 'Help!' from the bedroom. Kenny and I ran to her aid only to discover her writhing on the floor crying, 'I'm melting!'" (April 21, 1985, 2;5). But playacting for power through anger or diabolical plotting must sometimes shift to plays for strength through other means—also illustrated in literary sources. As a toddler, Lindsey had an all-encompassing temper. Tantrums were tremendous emotional outbursts that tried the entire family. Once, in desperation, I put her in the shower, hoping that the shock of the water would calm her down. As the water pinged against her shoulders and back, she fell to her knees. "I'm melting!" she shrieked. If water had the power to destroy an evil witch, could it destroy Lindsey? To Lindsey's mind, this possibility with props clearly made the metaphor.

In search for more peaceful solutions to rage, Lindsey and I turned to *The Story of Ferdinand* (Leaf), the tale of an ordinarily mild-mannered bull who sat on a bumblebee. His ensuing rage causes him to be sent to fight in the bullfights in Madrid, and only his calm ability to "smell the flowers" brings him home again. On the surface level of text, Lindsey adored his anger. The question *"Well, if you were a bumblebee and a bull sat on you what would you do?"* tickled her at every reading. "Sting him!" Lindsey would crow triumphantly, and then bounce around on the bed holding her bottom in imitation of Ferdinand. But below the climactic surface, Lindsey would visibly calm as Ferdinand found his quiet way home.

Home became a crucial issue for Lindsey during this year, for we left Saudi Arabia and moved back to the States. Everything was new and different; the everyday events of this new setting were exotic to her. I was a university student. Kenny tried his hand at a number of things before settling into a job designing educational software and waiting to hear from graduate schools. Lindsey had a new house, a new bedroom, a new baby-sitter, and new friends. And perhaps most disturbing of all, a physically new mother, for I was pregnant with our second daughter, Ashley.

During this time the story *Who's in Rabbit's House?* (Aardema) became a favorite. It is an African story about a rabbit who returns to his home only to find it has been taken over by a "bad animal." The rabbit undertakes a long and arduous struggle to regain his home, until he is finally assisted by the humor and wisdom of a small frog. Lindsey's adjustment to her new environment was no less arduous. When we read the story for the first time, these connections did not occur to me. But upon reflection, as I think about the number of times she requested it, I realize that the story of the small rabbit struggling to regain his home may have offered comfort in her new world.

Ashley

Ashley was born on December 27, 1985, in Salt Lake City, Utah. Like Lindsey, Ashley joined the world of words at birth. She received gifts of literature and book-related toys from friends and family, as well as the traditional "Welcome to the World" letter from her grandfather. Her grandmother sent a United States Savings Bond to start her college fund.

Above the white wicker bassinet where she slept hung a framed sampler a friend had embroidered with the particulars of her birth— name, date, and "Friday's child" stitched across a parade of baby lambs that Lindsey named "Bo Peep's sheep." Ashley's walls were illustrated with other storybook characters as well: Jack and Jill, Mother Goose, and the cow jumping over the moon. Books waited on the shelves wedged between stuffed-toy versions of Max and the Wild Things. A rocking chair sat in one corner, large enough to hold both Lindsey and Ashley during nighttime story readings.

Unlike Lindsey, Ashley was plunged into the world of school im- mediately—graduate school. I was a master's student at the time, and Ashley's Christmas birth coincided with winter vacation. And so, at two weeks of age, Ashley accompanied me back to school in her Snugli. At home, she slept in my lap while I sat at the computer and typed out papers and exams. She nursed through stories read to Lindsey and crawled over the books and papers scattered on our study floor.

Ashley matched Lindsey in physical development, but her language skills developed quietly for much of her first three years. Her commu- nication appeared in the raising of an eyebrow, a sigh, the shaking of her shoulders as she giggled at a piece of text, and a few brief words. Unlike Lindsey, who perceived storybooks as social interaction, Ashley would drag a pile of books to a corner of the couch and leaf through them one by one. While Lindsey scurried about the house in search of the right prop to complete a storybook production, Ashley sat on her bed with a favorite book, silently studying the illustrations.

Language came to Ashley with all the speed of a time-lapse film showing the blossoming of a flower. In a few months, single-word utterances became full sentences, and the only thing she confused were the prepositions. "Down, down," she would call, stretching her hands up to be lifted. And "Just shut out!" she would warn her sister when she thought Lindsey was talking too much.

As our Christmas baby, Ashley staked her claim to every children's book in our house concerning the season. She confiscated Lindsey's copy of *How the Grinch Stole Christmas* (Seuss) and monopolized Tomie de Paola's pop-up version of *The First Christmas*. We encouraged her identity with the holiday by buying her *The Polar Express* (Van Allsburg), but when we purchased E. T. A. Hoffmann's *Nutcracker* for Lindsey, Ashley was annoyed. "It's 'bout Christmas. *I'm* the Christmas baby!" she cried.

She also adopted Lindsey's identity with several storybook characters. She slept through her part in Sleeping Beauty and picked flowers as Red Riding Hood, but her muse was Rapunzel. Once, while Ashley was bathing in the tub, I commented that when her hair was wet it was very long. "Yes," she replied, leaning her head back in the water to set the strands afloat, "just like Punzal" (June 26, 1988, 2;6). Ashley was by no means Lindsey's mimic, but she often followed the patterns set by her older sister. I once wrote to the head of my thesis committee: "Like Lindsey, Ashley uses text to get out of trouble. While vacationing at her grandmother's house this summer, Ashley picked the paint off an entire arm of one of the living room chairs. When I discovered the deed, I challenged Ashie in a tone that set her foot to a nervous tap. 'Did you do this?' I demanded. 'No,' she replied meekly. I repeated my question with more vigor. In desperation, Ashley looked up at me with imploring eyes and said, 'How 'bout, Snow White did it?'" (September 5, 1988, 2;9).

Although she could quickly draw on fantasy as an excuse, Ashley often selected nonfiction in her book choices. As an infant she had fewer opportunities than Lindsey to look at books in terms of objects and their labels. There was less time for hours of "What's that?"—"It's a cat, a cow, a fire truck . . . ," for we were reading to two children now and Ashley was often drawn in as a silent partner in Lindsey's storytime. But as she found her voice, she demanded a return to the labeling of objects, the myriad possible answers to the question "What's that?" Richard Scarry's *Best Word Book Ever* (with "more than 1400 objects illustrated in full color") was the book she requested most frequently as a toddler. She called it her "dictionary" and urged us to pore over the illustrations of pig families, fox musicians, and rabbit children playing with their toys. The double-spread illustrations of birds were her favorite, and she tested and retested her knowledge of unusual names—bittern, puffin, toucan—as well as the more common chick, sea gull, and rooster. We played countless requested games of "Find the ———," in which Ashley would scan the page and then point to the labeled fowl. Her second most oft-requested pages were those on flowers, and she carried her book knowledge out into the world, often asking me to label flowers we found on our outings, or proudly pronouncing the label herself.

As Ashley grew older she continued to request expository texts, to add to her fantasy favorites. One preferred series of books was on natural phenomena, with each volume prominently labeled "This Is a Let's-Read-and-Find-Out Science Book." Her most requested books included *Germs Make Me Sick* (Berger), *Ducks Don't Get Wet* (Goldin), and *My Visit to the Dinosaurs* (Aliki). As the children grew, we often split the family in two at bedtime, and while Lindsey and I read stories, Ashley and Kenny would often discuss the latest issue of *Zoobook,* a magazine filled with animal facts.

Lindsey and Ashley Together

After her third birthday, Lindsey became fascinated with her clothes. As an infant and toddler growing up in Arabia, she had worn only shorts, but she was now tall enough to reach most clothes in her closet and old enough to make her own decisions. Shorts became passé, and dresses became the mode. And the more dresses the better. Two or three, worn one on top of the other, usually created the desired effect.

Quite often her ensembles originated from storybook heroines. She would sit and study the illustrations of a book and then go to her closet. What she couldn't find there, she would borrow from ours. And what she ultimately couldn't find, she could imagine.

"I'm not Lindsey," became the watchword of her third year. Lindsey was Cinderella, Sleeping Beauty, Red Riding Hood. She was Curious George, Tikki Tikki Tembo, and the Funny Little Woman. She was Alice. She was Una. And she was Ida. Ida is the plucky heroine of Maurice Sendak's *Outside Over There.* Left in charge of her baby sister, Ida fails to watch at a crucial time and the baby is stolen by goblins.

Equipped with her mother's yellow rain cloak and her wonderhorn, she must enter "outside over there" to recover her sister.

The combination of pictures and words made Lindsey aware of her own position as a new "big sister," with its incumbent responsibilities. In an initial reading, Lindsey claimed that the crying baby looked "just like Ashley." And later she threatened, "If goblins stole my Ashley, I'd kill them!"

Numerous small plays emerged from this story. In one scene, Lindsey would instruct me to "be the goblins," and while she pretended to stare moodily out the living room window, I would sneak in and take Ashley away. Lindsey would follow, carefully walking backward and playing on her harmonica as if it were a wonderhorn. In another scene, she commanded Ashley to clap hands, and was frustrated by the fact that at three months old, Ashley could not comply.

But with the passage of time Ashley could assume her role, and Lindsey took enormous satisfaction in the vigorous clapping that resulted. Still, there were small frustrations. Sendak writes that the baby *"lay cozy in an eggshell, crooning and clapping as a baby should,"* and I would not allow Lindsey to take eggs from the refrigerator "for Ashley to sit in."

But apart from small denials, Kenny and I constantly encouraged Lindsey's play. It was a continuing cycle. We would borrow books from the library to read. Lindsey would request over and over again those that she liked, and we were eager to read her desired choice. As she became more familiar with a text, she would choose elements to stage, complete with props and actors. We would play parts according to her instructions and help her assemble props. And if a story seemed to be a continuing theme in Lindsey's life, we would purchase the book for her personal library. On her fourth birthday, we bought *Outside Over There* and gave it to Lindsey as a present from Ashley.

In our early storybook productions, the entire family played according to Lindsey's general instructions, taking up the roles she assigned, interpreting a prop in the same imaginative light, but making extensions of her choices along the way. If we departed too far from Lindsey's vision, she quickly brought us back.[11]

One morning, as Kenny was getting ready for work, the entire family joined him. Ashley was lying on the rug on our bedroom floor and Lindsey was dancing and practicing different faces in the bedroom mirror. With no university classes until later that day, I lounged in a chair, watching this early morning scene. As Kenny began to put on his shoes, Lindsey took off for her room.

"I need my party shoes," she called over her shoulder.

She returned with her black velvet party shoes, a welcome hand-me-down from her cousin. Since she rarely has a need for party shoes, they have become more of a toy than a necessity. She clumped back into the bedroom with both shoes on, but on the threshold kicked off one shoe. It went scuttling toward Kenny.

"Let's play Cinderella!" she cried. Then she reclined on the bed, dangling her shoeless foot over the side. "Now, I'll be one bad sister . . . then the other . . . then Cinderella."

Kenny jumped ahead in the game and addressed Lindsey as though she were Cinderella. "Let's try the shoe on you, Cinderella."

Lindsey sighed, sat up, and explained, "No! I'm the *bad sister!*"

Kenny reversed tack and pushed and shoved and tried to fit the shoe on her foot, but to no avail. He then took the shoe and tried it on Ashley's foot, but pronounced that it was "too big."

Lindsey had no objection to this bit of improvisation, and giggled as Kenny struggled to fit the shoe on her little sister. After he'd given up on Ashley, the timing was right, and he slid the shoe onto Lindsey's foot.

"Will you marry me?" Kenny begged. Lindsey gazed with rapt expression into her father's eyes.

"Yes," she sighed. And the promise was cemented with a kiss. (June 12, 1986, 3;7)

During this play, Kenny introduced two modifications. In one he tried to leap ahead in the action, but when this was not accepted, he quickly reverted to Lindsey's plan. In the second modification, he introduced Ashley as the second ugly stepsister, thus making a change in the object. Although this had not been included in her original instructions, Lindsey accepted and enjoyed the change.

When Kenny and I and other family members entered into Lindsey's play, we would follow Lindsey's lead yet introduce subtle changes. At a tea party of Lindsey and her girlfriends, I played the part of the butler according to Lindsey's instructions. Yet I changed the action by serving tea with a haughty British accent, which the girls rapidly took up and incorporated into their own conversation. Kenny changed the object by introducing an element of reality. He brewed a pot of herbal tea, which then prompted the girls to request real sugar and cream. On another occasion, when Lindsey's grandmother played tea party, she changed the objects as well by bringing down the dress-up box. Then she followed the girls' lead by wearing an elaborate hat, and a boa slung around her neck.

As Lindsey grew older, our role in her play diminished. Lindsey's school friends played more meaningful parts, leaving Kenny and me to play the occasional cameo: Boo Radley to Lindsey's Scout (in Lee's *To Kill a Mocking Bird*) or the parents of Lindsey's Ramona (in Cleary's *Ramona the Pest*). Lindsey still retained the position of director and stage manager, dragging out the broken cardboard dress-up box, assigning roles, and giving stage directions, but she had to negotiate with alternative opinions and vie for the best costuming. Her productions were not limited to storybook interpretation, but extended to other activities as well, as television characters and the movements of her ballet classes were brought into the configuration:

> Lindsey is now in kindergarten. She is bright, happy, and creative and still prefers dress-up to just about any other activity. At Halloween she was the princess from *The Never Ending Story*, with a baubled crown and a flowing white dress. She inherited a plethora of tutus from a neighbor who knew her penchant for brightly colored netting, and Lindsey now hosts neighborhood dancing parties, providing costuming for all. She has also convinced her friends that Jane Fonda is fun and there are many days when I'll come home from work to see the living room filled with twirling, jiving, miniature "Janes" singing "Do it!" (Christmas letter, 1988, 6;1)

As Ashley grew, she joined the play in more significant ways. When Lindsey staged *Peter and the Wolf* (Prokofiev), she still played director, controlling the music on the stereo and pulling out the dining room chairs to get Ashley, cast as the bird, to "climb the tree." But Ashley had her own opinions about her choice of costuming and the movements of the bird. And at one point she leaped down from the "tree" to check her position from the ultimate authority: her book. At first it seemed a dangerous choice, since Lindsey was stalking the living room as the graceful cat. But Lindsey dropped her role to check the picture with Ashley, and waited for Ashley to make her ascent into the tree before continuing the hunt.

In other productions, Lindsey no longer monopolized the star roles, for Ashley made her own needs known. "Why not just have *two*

Cinderellas?" Lindsey asked at the end of one argument, and after that most heroines were doubled in play, although Lindsey still managed to convince Ashley to be Beezus and kept the role of Ramona for herself. Besides the Quimbys, there were many games of "sisters," especially those lost in the forest. "Sister! Sister!" I heard Ashley exclaim one night. "Come in the house before the darkness comes." Her tone was dramatically overwrought, her hands clasped together. Lindsey responded in kind, "I'm coming, oh sister," leaping through the door as if pursued by wolves (December 16, 1989, 7;1 and 3;11). They learned to share the mystery and protect each other from the nighttime forest.

Although Ashley's roles increased in importance, her own response to literature did not match the intensity of Lindsey's dramatic play. To Ashley, storybook characters stayed more firmly in the pages of the book—they could be discussed, referred to, and even called upon in the context of everyday events, but their personalities could not be donned with the ease of a costume. Once as she played Little Red Riding Hood, picking the geraniums that grew like weeds in our California neighborhood, I addressed her as "Little Red." She rolled her eyes in exasperation. "I'm Ashley, Mama! I'm *Ashley!*"

Ashley's emphatic reply served as a reminder that a child's response to literature is highly individual.[12] Although Ashley was often drawn into stories that were specifically selected by and for Lindsey, she quickly developed her own ways of interpreting story. Whereas Lindsey preferred the enactment of story, Ashley more often chose verbal reflection, often making humorous comments, turning original words into risqué remarks:

> When Kenny read the exploits of Max in *Where the Wild Things Are* [Sendak] today, Ashley stopped him after he read the line, *"but Max stepped into his private boat and waved good-bye."*
> "No, Dada," she admonished. "Not like that. It's: 'and Max stepped onto their private parts and waved good-bye.' Like that."
> Kenny laughed so hard at this vision of a vindictive Max that tears came to his eyes, and Ashley laughed right along with him. Even after he explained the difference carefully, Ashley insisted that her way was better "'cause it's funny." (November, 1989, 3;11)

Ashley's comments on text were often related to humor, and she was able to laugh at her own mispronunciations or reconfigurations of words. Sendak's *In the Night Kitchen* (1970) was a particular favorite, expecially the part where the hero, Mickey, stands atop a milk bottle and crows like a rooster. As a young child, Ashley took the familiar rooster call of *"Cock-a-Doodle Doo"* offered by Sendak and transformed it into "Hot Dog Doo Doo Doo." Thereafter, she insisted on substituting her own words for Sendak's, crowing out her own independent rendition.

Ashley's interpretations also centered on the musicality of text. *In the Night Kitchen* is wonderfully musical, filled with rhymes and with bakers and small boys who chant, howl, and sing. Whenever we read the text, Ashley encouraged me to sing a good part of it, and she joined in when we reached her favorite parts, her voice rising loudly over mine. Her interest in the musicality of story language was reflected in her selection of books, for she consistently chose books of poetry over prose and made up original songs and rhymes. One morning, Ashley selected *The Jolly Postman* (Ahlberg and Ahlberg), a story of fairy-tale characters brought together through letters delivered by a local postman.[13]

> When we got to the witch's letter, Ashley took over the reading. The letter is an advertisement for "Hobgoblin Supplies Ltd©" and includes all the necessities of witchhood: *"Cup and SORCERER tea service—it washes itself!"* *"Easy-clean non-stick Cauldron Set,"* and so on. Ashley asked me if I would like a song and selected the advertisement for *"Little Boy Pie Mix—for those unexpected visitors when the cupboard is bare."* The text is accompanied by an illustration of a witch bringing a smiling-faced pie to her fellow witches seated at table. To the side is a box of the mix which features a little boy standing expectantly in a bowl and underneath are written the words: *"Finest natural ingredients. No preservatives."* Ashley sang:
>
> > Pease porridge hot
> > Pease porridge cold
> > Bake me a cake as fast as you can.
> > Roll it and pat it and put it in the baker.
> > And put it in the baker for a Mickey-cake!
>
> (March 14, 1990, 4;3)

Ashley's creation brought together three poems about food: one about porridge ("Pease Porridge Hot" is a Mother Goose rhyme) and two about cake (Mother Goose's "Pat a Cake" and Sendak's *In the Night*

Kitchen). The resulting feast of "little boy pie mix" brought forth images of other nursery-rhyme food, as well as Sendak's illustration of Mickey who was baked in a cake, with one hand rising from the batter. Like Sendak's bakers, Ashley mixed the ingredients from her store of poetry, creating her own concoction.

The blending of multiple verses was a common feature of Ashley's story interpretation and seeped into her day-to-day communication, as well as into her letters to friends and family. One day our family traveled to a local park to see the resting spot for monarch butterflies. Thousands of butterflies hung in thick clusters of bright color, while others flitted through the sun-dappled trees. When we returned home I asked the girls to write to their grandparents and aunts about the adventure:

> Ashley drew a picture of butterflies on most of her postcards, with intricate patterns on the wings to imitate the markings of the monarch. But on her Aunt Martha's card she drew two simple butterflies surrounded by a large expanse of black lines. At first she described her picture as:
>
> > "Two little babies sitting in a tub
> > Jack and Jill went up the . . ."
>
> But as I reached for my pen to write down her words, she changed tack, wanting to start again. She made several attempts and then said "OK, write this:
>
> > Two little babies named Lindsey and Ashley
> > Fly away, Ashley
> > Fly away, Lindsey
> > Come back, Ashley
> > Come back, Lindsey
> > Come back, Wolf."
>
> (February 1, 1990, 4;2)

She pronounced the rhyme in sing-song fashion reminiscent of the old jump-rope rhyme—"Johnny and Mary sitting in a tree, K-I-S-S-I-N-G!"—but with the words "fly away" she switched to the rhythm of Mother Goose:

> Ladybird, ladybird,
> Fly away home,
> Your house is on fire
> And your children all gone.

Ashley's first poetic attempt was a description of the picture she drew—two figures "sitting" in a circle of dark lines that might have been the water of a bathtub. The rhythm of the first line, as well as the image of two figures, brought Jack and Jill to mind. But she was not satisfied with this poem, for it said little about the day's adventure. In her final poem, as Ashley connected insect to insect, she linked life events to poetic experience. She knew no butterfly poems, and thus called up a familiar ladybug rhyme, replacing the nameless insect children with herself and her sister, who flew away but ultimately were called back home.

Ashley's love of rhyme combined with her need to reshape texts to match her own rhythms. While Lindsey seldom created her own poetry or sang the poems she knew, Ashley filled the house with her songs. Ashley was the poet and the comic, substituting words, blending rhymes, and creating humorous wordplays, while Lindsey was the dramatist, enacting her interpretations of story.

By the age of seven, however, Lindsey depended less on the movement of her body to express response. At night, as we crowded into bed to read, Lindsey tended to lie still and offer verbal comments about the story. Ashley, however, needed movement to express her humorous response. One night we read *The Five Chinese Brothers* (Bishop), the tale of a family of five boys, all uniquely equipped for survival. The first brother had the power to swallow the sea, and thus acquired a catch to sell at the market each day. In the beginning of the story, he reluctantly agreed to take a small boy fishing, on the condition that the boy obey his every word. When he swallowed the sea, filling up his head like a balloon, the text read:

> *"And all the fish were left high and dry at the bottom of the sea. And all the treasures of the sea lay uncovered.*
> *The little boy was delighted. He ran here and there stuffing his pockets with strange pebbles, extraordinary shells and fantastic algae."*

"What would you take home from the sea?" I asked the girls.

"I'd like some starfish and mother of pearl," Lindsey said.

But Ashley leaped from under the covers and began gathering stuffed animals off the bed. "I'd pick teddy bears and this doggie," she said with a droll look in her eye.

"No. No. They're not in the sea!" Lindsey exclaimed. "You know what I'd do? I'd get the gold coins off that pirate ship." (December 12, 1989, 7;1 and 3;11)

Each night, Lindsey and Ashley chose their own treasures from story: shimmering roles, unique dialogue, and iridescent insights into the world of life and literature. They turned the pieces of story over in their heads, assessing the quality, weighing the consequences, judging the beauty. Some pieces they threw back into the sea. But many were stuffed into the pockets of their thoughts, to be brought out at some private pleasurable moment or shared with friends and family.

Selecting the Story

Lindsey, Ashley, Kenny, and I shared in the selection of stories. There was no set turn-taking pattern; each selection was negotiated with minor discussion. Sometimes the children went to the shelves with our instructions: "It's getting so close to Christmas. Why don't we read a Christmas story?" Other times, they were on their own. Sometimes they returned with a book that we rejected: "No, that's too long. Tomorrow is a school day." Other times, the book was accepted wholeheartedly. The same occurred when Kenny and I went to the shelves. "Not *that* one!" the children might cry, or "Yes! We haven't read that one in a long time."

Over the years of our reading, fairy tales were the most requested, but books from other times and places piqued the girls' interest as well. Often they requested books that were a part of a series. At the age of three, both girls loved books by Sendak. Both went through a Beatrix Potter period at the age of four. During the days and sometimes weeks of immersion in a book or series, we would read and reread particular tales up to twenty times. As the girls grew older, their chosen books increased in length and there was less time for repetition. Lindsey, however, continued to request books connected by author or illustrator, entering a "Ramona" (Cleary) period in first grade and a "Little House" (Wilder) period during the second grade. Ashley was less prone to link her requests in a series, but preferred informational books and magazines, particularly those about animals.

How a book came to be on our shelves changed as the girls grew. During their infancy we bought children's literature discussed in parenting books that offered lists of recommended titles: *Pat the Bunny* (Kunhardt), *The Carrot Seed* (Krauss), *The Very Hungry Caterpillar* (Carle), and *Goodnight Moon* (Brown). *Mother Goose* (Battaglia) was their favorite, and the book was requested so often, dragged on so many excursions, and chewed on and torn up to such an extent that we have gone through several copies over the years.

But as Lindsey and Ashley passed their first birthdays, I drew upon the books that had sustained my years of primary teaching: *The Little House* (Burton), *Frog and Toad Together* (Lobel), *Make Way for Ducklings* (McCloskey), and any and all fairy tales. These selections led to others as Lindsey and Ashley developed attachments to particular authors and illustrators. Lindsey's love of Sendak's *Where the Wild Things Are* led to the purchase of *In the Night Kitchen* and *Outside Over There*. Ashley's fascination with Van Allsburg's *The Stranger* led to the purchase of *Jumanji* and *The Polar Express*. The entire family was drawn to the work of William Steig; the girls loved *Dr. De Soto*, while Kenny and I treasured our copy of *Caleb and Kate*.

Lindsey would often discover books in the library that she wanted. She found Trina Schart Hyman's illustrated edition of *Little Red Riding Hood* (Grimm Brothers) in the fairy tale section, and requested it so many times that I began to search actively for the famed illustrator's work. Through this search we discovered *Saint George and the Dragon* (Hodges), as well as Hyman's interpretations of other Grimm tales. Once Lindsey began school, she brought home her own library books; when she selected *A Little Princess* (Burnett) we had to renew it so many times that we finally bought a copy for our own library.

In my years at the university I took several classes in children's literature, and the books we analyzed and discussed were often added to our own family's discussions and to our own bookshelves. When I worked as coordinator of a reading project at a university, my colleagues and I continued the discussion. Teachers would approach me after workshops to discuss the books I used in my presentations and to recommend still others, saying, "Have you read . . . ?" and "You've just got to read . . . !"

Whether recommendations came from friends, colleagues, newspaper articles, or *The Horn Book*, I usually tracked the books down at the library to read and think about with the girls before we made a purchase. The owner of a local children's bookstore became accustomed to my requests for hard-to-find books and the fact that I often monopolized their large rocking chair to read through some of their latest acquisitions.

Because I spent a part of each day reading to the girls, it was critical to find books that held not only my children's interest but my own, through numerous rereadings. I had little patience for the "junk food" variety of children's literature, quick tales with easy and explicit morals that portray life as simple and sweet if only one follows the rules. I avoided stories that bowdlerize the original tale and turn Red Riding Hood's bottle of wine and loaf of fresh bread into a basket of goodies. I also shunned oversimplified vocabulary, for stories that are designed solely to match a primary reading level also tend to strip the story of any potential for emotional connection or thoughtful reflection. My choices aligned with critical reviews of children's literature as well as current thinking in reading education, for both subject areas made up a large part of my own reading and influenced the selections I made and my reasons for making them.[14]

I leaned toward tales of fantasy, with dragons to be slain and witches vanquished, and I believe Lindsey was responsible for this choice. To be sure, I began the process by selecting these books for her when she was young, but she loved them so and requested them so often that my respect for the tales grew. I read *Rapunzel* (Grimm Brothers), *Snow White* (Grimm Brothers), and *The Sleeping Beauty* (Grimm Brothers) innumerable times, yet I never tired of them. This was fortunate, for while Lindsey was starting to move beyond the castle gates, Ashley was waiting at the threshold.

Kenny's selections were often mythological tales. He regaled the girls with stories of the ancient Greeks (D'Aulaire and D'Aulaire), which they transformed into myriad nighttime performances. He was also more prone than I to read them poetry. At night I would often hear them laughing over *A Light in the Attic* (Silverstein) and *The New Kid on the Block* (Prelutsky).

"Read it again, Mama!" was the clarion call that signaled a desire for the purchase of a book, but given the prices of children's literature today, our selections for purchase had to meet high standards. Did the questions that the children asked change with each reading of the story? Did they notice new elements in the story and subtle features in the illustrations? Did the story cause them to think, reflect, and make connections between what they knew of life and literature? Enjoyment was a vital ingredient, but in order to join the ranks on our shelves, a book had to last beyond a moment of pleasure. It had to bring life closer through words and illustrations that captured the essence of what it means to be alive—to be afraid, to make a friend, to seek a goal, to vanquish an enemy, to find love.

We read to our children daily. The bedtime story was our stalwart, but we also read during other snatches of time—before school, during a bath, while waiting in line, or while taking a break from our own reading. Our stories were conversations, sometimes centered on the book, sometimes not. We talked about the words and the illustrations. We talked about what we would or wouldn't do. We laughed about an event. We more calmly resolved an earlier argument. We talked. Our lives were busy—both girls had their own school and extracurricular activities, while Kenny and I juggled graduate student schedules. But when we read a story, we came together and we talked.

Our reading provided opportunities for conversation in spaces and times separated from any drive for immediate action. The juggling of personal schedules and the maintenance of a busy household, especially one in which two adults were working, made it necessary that most of our time with the children centered around household routines. Books became the neutralizer—everyone's individual desires and the household needs were put on hold, and the entry into conversation around an artifact offered common ground to all the participants.

In large part this commonality of ground came about in our family because of the need in Lindsey's early reading (when we were living in Saudi Arabia) to leave the world of our immediate surroundings and to enter, through books, the totally different world of life in the United States. For Lindsey, therefore, the entry into expected situations of mainstream middle-class life came in books—women driving cars and wearing shorts outside the home, visiting a local zoo or a museum, putting on coat and mittens to play in the snow, going to the movies. Lindsey had traversed Tanzania on safari before she entered the wilds of a Stateside shopping mall.

Book-based revelations of what occurred as everyday events for American mainstream children were more necessary than would have been the case had she been in an environment where her own experiences with women's and men's roles and work and leisure activities matched the elements of books that portrayed such a life. In the case of fairy tales and other tales set in distant and exotic places, this same pattern of asking "What do you think?" or "What will happen?" or "How can that be?" or "What would you do?" led her to explain her own base of knowledge. Once we returned to the United States, familiarity with such queries made it possible for us to identify those features of daily life she might not know.

Kenny and I were aware that our own socialization regarding familiar elements and characters of the world that were very distant from Saudia Arabia might blind us to what Lindsey could not possibly know. This sense of uneasiness about raising her in an environment markedly removed from that in which we had spent our early years often prompted us to focus on the exploratory question "What do you think?" rather than "What is this?" In essence, we often knew—in the case both of fairy tales and of stories about boys and girls in more ordinary life settings—that Lindsey might well not know the *names* or *referents* of particular items, but we intuitively trusted that she would go to the heart of the pan-human dimensions of stories. We trusted then that the words of storybooks—or indeed what is usually characterized as comprehension—would not get in the way of the interpretation of their meanings.

Thus, the cycle of the ways we value literature, the children's intertextual play, and our encouragement and response to the girls' sometimes resistant ploys continued throughout innumerable stories. It was impossible to try and separate out who we were from what Lindsey and Ashley chose to be. We were a family of readers, and in this respect, our world and our children's worlds tightly interwove. We were not one and the same, but the infinite lines of our lives braided together to help form the strands of the girls' individual awareness of being literate in our family and of coming to know what it meant to be literate through a world of words.

2

The Sight, Sounds, and Sense of Story

For young children, entering the world of story through books is a sensory experience. They use their eyes to see the story and to picture it in their minds. Their appreciation of illustrative technique grows, and they become familiar with different authors' styles. In play they match and recreate scenes, gathering the necessary props and costumes. In their mind's eye they make comparisons between texts and between life and literature. These connections, which often seem most apparent in young children's recognition of similar visual images, also come by ear as children listen to the sounds of story—the author's voice, the changing intonation, the musicality, and the formality of story language. They hear the differences between natural conversation and the telling of a tale. They harken to the voice of genre, which joins one story and its possibilities to another.[1]

Seeing the Story

As an infant, Lindsey felt that books needed to be tasted. Her eyes told her "It's edible!" and her favorite storybooks were punctured with teeth marks. Entire sections were nibbled away. Books were also for tearing, with the library pocket a common target. Despite the simplistic admonitions of child development experts and numerous school librarians, showing Lindsey we had respect for books did not necessarily succeed in reforming her behavior.

By the time she was three, however, her eyes had communicated to her a different concept of "book." One Valentine's Day, Lindsey was arranging several picture cards on the kitchen counter. Her aunt had sent her a small collection of five valentines of the cartoon character

Snoopy, each portraying the canine hero in a variety of valentine stances. Like baseball cards, the valentines had pictures on the front and a message on the back. I commented that she had received a great many cards and asked her which she liked best.

"My book valentine," she replied.
"Which is your 'book valentine'?" I looked curiously at the pile.
"The one Grandpa sent me. I'll show you."
She ran up to her bedroom and when she returned she waved her grandfather's valentine at me. "See," she said, opening and closing the card, "it's like a book!" (February 14, 1986, 3;3)

According to Lindsey's visual interpretation, a book was anything with a cover, a back, and words sandwiched in between. The flat, two-sided cards did not meet her criteria for a book, but the traditional card form did. By the age of three, Lindsey displayed knowledge of the basic properties of a book. She could identify the cover of a book, she followed the pages from left to right, and she knew that pictures in books are right side up. She understood that books have titles and title pages. She found that stories are usually descriptive and sequential, beginning and ending with predictable formulas.[2]

One night, as I returned home from school, I whisked Lindsey into my arms and carried her into the kitchen. I plunked everything on the kitchen counter—Lindsey, books, college catalogue, and purse. As I prepared a dinner salad, Lindsey began sifting through my paraphernalia. She was particularly delighted with the "Division of Continuing Education" catalogue, an adult education listing of university courses for the spring quarter.

The cover of the catalogue was festooned with a brightly colored fish kite with streamers flying. The inside listed university classes, and the information was interspersed with numerous black and white illustrations. Lindsey studied the kite curiously and then intoned:

"The Little Crab." She opened to the first page of the catalogue, where a miniature of the cover illustration appeared, and repeated, "The Little Crab." She then flipped through the first few pages until she arrived on page 7, where the illustrations began. She began reading:
"Once upon a time there lived a little crab. He had a big apple and he lived in a house . . . where he painted."

She proceeded through the catalogue, incorporating the pictures she recognized. When she tired of the story, she skipped great chunks of the catalogue to the last page where she finished with "and that's the end of the magazine." (February 18, 1986, 3;3)

Through Lindsey's eyes, this alien catalogue with its course listings, prices, and dates became a story. The cover signaled that a title was necessary, and so she dubbed it "The Little Crab." The repetition of the cover illustration inside signaled a title page, and she announced her title once more. Her story began with book language, "Once upon a time there lived . . . ," and terminated with the traditional "The End." The catalogue pictures, rather than the words, aided her own verbalization of the story, and she selectively chose those that seemed to make sense in the context of the story, book, print, covers and other objective features she associated with reading aloud. In this performance, she used a definite way of talking—intonation, formulaic phrases, and arrangements of words she would not have produced without the book as "narrative prop."[3]

Lindsey's know-how with books extended beyond the basics of book handling and production of the outline of story genre to an eye for illustrations. By three years of age she preferred Mayer's *Beauty and the Beast* over other editions. Mayer "draws a scarier beast," she claimed. She chose an edition of *Hansel and Gretel* (Grimm Brothers) illustrated by Susan Jeffers over one with illustrations by Paul Zelinsky (Grimm Brothers). In Jeffers' version, "the house is so yummy!" Hyman illustrated "the most beautifulest Princess," and Sendak drew the "best bad boys."[4]

Once we attended a story-reading by Audrey Wood at a local children's bookstore. The noted author and illustrator appeared in a tuxedo and performed a magical rendition of *Elbert's Bad Word* (Wood)—cracking eggs filled with sparkles over our heads and answering the telephone in her carpet bag. Lindsey, Ashley, and I brought our own copies of her books to be autographed and bought some new ones as well. Later in the day, Lindsey studied the signature on *Heckedy Peg* (Wood) and then turned to an illustration of the seven children featured in the story. She commented to her sister that the illustrator "just draws the best kids I know!" Ashley pulled the book over to her seat. "Yeah," she replied. "That one's just like me!" (November 1988,

7;0 and 3;11). In the text the children are named for the days of the week, but Ashley renamed them after members of the family and neighborhood friends. If I forgot and began reading "Sunday, Monday . . ." Ashley would quickly admonish me, "No. Say 'Kenny, Shelby . . .'" When it came to illustrated stories, her preferences often centered around finding familiar faces in storybook characters.

Lindsey's criteria for favorite illustrations were sensual and highly affective. She liked illustrations that helped her envision the terror, anger, joy, or humor of the story. While she was consistently drawn to the elegant winged creatures created by Hyman or the fresh dimpled faces of the children drawn by Wood, she also felt attached to the children of Sendak's vision. Like Ashley, when she was younger the comparisons she made between characters and herself were based more on imagined physical similarities. But as she matured she made more comparisons between herself and the inner nature of the character. Lindsey saw herself as the heroine, someone who could not only ultimately attract a handsome prince but also take over a mother's responsibilities and rescue her own baby sister.

Shortly after she turned three, Lindsey began to recognize the artistic technique of her favorite illustrators—particularly those who followed similar patterns throughout their stories. One winter day we were on our way to a nearby city to see an exhibit of Ramses II, and to fill the long car ride, I had brought along a library book entitled *The Book of Jonah*, by Peter Spier. Known as an illustrator of few words, Spier depicted God's message as a strong ray of sunshine beaming down on Jonah as he works in the field.

> "Look at that light," Lindsey exclaimed. "That's just like . . . what was that book?"
> "Which book?" I replied innocently.
> "The one with the big boat. You know, where he's picking grapes."
> I knew the illustration she was referring to. Spier used the same technique to show God's acceptance of Noah.
> "You mean *Noah's Ark*? [Spier]" I asked.
> "Yeah! *Noah's Ark*."
> Later, as we read the story of Jonah, we came to the part where God sends a tremendous storm to Jonah's ship to punish him for his disobedience. The other sailors huddle on deck to cast lots and discover who is responsible for the evil that has befallen them. One

of the sailors was depicted as a balding old man with a full, white beard.

"Look," Lindsey shouted. "There's Noah!" (February 27, 1986, 3;3)

The visual image of characters is often stereotypical, and authors exploit these stereotypes to help carry a metaphorical message. In Maurice Sendak's stories, Max, Mickey, and Pierre are visually interchangeable. A downturned mouth and the dark glower of a gaze sum up the "I don't care" attitude of characters that will meet trouble ahead. As a young child, Ashley continually mixed up their names, placing Max in the night kitchen and Mickey among the Wild Things. Trina Schart Hyman's heroes, heroines, and evil antagonists all have striking similarities. For William Steig, evil continually appears in the guise of a sinister fox. A child accustomed to illustrative metaphors will quickly recognize the honesty, mischievousness, or inner beauty of a character and use the clues of costume or expression to define character and predict outcomes.[5]

Once, as she sprawled on the living room rug with her friend David, Lindsey was reading Verna Aardema's *Who's in Rabbit's House?* The illustrators of the story, Leo and Diane Dillon, used a multiple-animal technique to portray action. Like some animated collection of pictures laid side by side instead of shuffled to create motion, the reader might see six rabbits on a page. These were meant to be not six different rabbits but rather six different actions of the same rabbit. David's immediate reaction was similar to Lindsey's on first reading. "Look at all the rabbits," he said. "No, no," Lindsey explained. "That's just one rabbit doing many things" (March 6, 1986, 3;4). As Lindsey's preschool teacher wrote when she read this language story, "sometimes [children] use our words so perfectly" (May 1987). She recognized that Lindsey's understanding arose from an earlier conversation with me on the artist's style and purpose, and that Lindsey's words echoed those I had used in explanation. Lindsey was alert to the messages in pictures, and when I pointed out the varied techniques, the use of light, or the subtle clues often found in illustrations, she remembered my comments and used them in subsequent readings.

One afternoon we read *little blue and little yellow* (Lionni), a story about the adventures of two friends who are torn circles of colored paper. Little blue and little yellow discover that when they hug, their two shapes merge into one and their colors become uniformly green. They enjoy many "green" adventures until they try to return home. Both little blue's and little yellow's parents fail to recognize their children and reject the green impostor. Naturally little blue and little yellow are upset, and Lionni shows blue and yellow tears emerging from the unified green:

> *Little blue and little yellow were very sad. They cried big blue and yellow tears. They cried and cried until they were all tears.*
>
> At this point little blue and little yellow are broken up into tiny bits of blue and yellow paper, which made Lindsey giggle. But on the next page they are whole once again, and Lionni explains:
>
> *"When they finally pulled themselves together they said: "Will they believe us now?"*
>
> In the first reading of the story I laughed at Lionni's pun, as the characters "pull themselves together" both physically and emotionally. Lindsey asked, "What's so funny?" I explained the joke and she began to laugh and at the end of my reading went to show the joke to her dad. In our next reading she stopped to giggle again. "Pulled themselves together!" she chortled, pointing to the picture. (February 2, 1990, 7;3)

Insights into the messages in illustrations came from other adults and children, as well.

One morning Lindsey, Ashley, and I visited the children's section of a local bookstore and the girls asked me to read them some stories. Lindsey spotted the first selection.

> "Read that!" she exclaimed, pointing to *The Keeping Quilt* [Polacco]. The other day, Lindsey's teacher had been late and the principal had come to read them this story. Lindsey said it was a "great" book. I was eager to read it as well—I had heard it recommended by teachers in the past. The three of us sat on the floor and, leaning against one of the bookshelves, we began to read.
>
> The story is about a family of Russian Jews who pass down a well-loved quilt from generation to generation. Lindsey seemed quite taken with the story and anticipated the words I was about to read several times—whispering them softly in my ear. She pointed out features of the illustrations, particularly the fact that the quilt itself was always in color while the background of people and events stayed in muted browns and grays. I asked her how she noticed this and if

other children had seen it, too. She told me that other kids had talked about it when the principal read the story. (February 3, 1990, 7;3)

But the interpretation of illustrations is not always filtered through the eyes of the adult.

Lindsey's interpretations of an illustrator's meaning often led to possibilities neither I nor possibly even the author imagined as intended in the art. During another bedtime story hour, Lindsey and I were reading *A Baby Sister for Frances*, by Russell Hoban. In this story, Frances is thoroughly disgusted by the arrival of a newborn baby sister and decides to run away. Equipped with a goodly supply of cookies, she runs to the shelter of the dining room table. In one illustration Father and Mother were shown seated on the couch, and we could see Frances through the doorway of the dining room, eating cookies under the table. The doorway was drawn with a soft, wavy line. "Is Frances in a dream?" Lindsey asked. "No, I don't think so. Why?" I responded. "Because she's in a cloud" (March 3, 1986, 3;4). To Lindsey, a cloud signified the beginning of a dream sequence, a technique not uncommon among illustrators. Was Frances simply dreaming of running away? Although this was in all likelihood not Hoban's intention here, using certain techniques to suggest the beginning of a dream sequence is common in children's literature. Max runs away in *Where the Wild Things Are*, and Mickey dreams of falling past his parent's bedroom in *In the Night Kitchen*; these are two books by Sendak that Lindsey had read time and again. Lindsey saw potential in Hoban's wavy line, a potential that had been established by the many other illustrations she had seen in her life.

Illustrated Life

From such cues as soft charcoal lines, sharp thorns, or multiplied rabbits in action, children pick up critical features that they then recreate in their own drawings and, as was the case with Lindsey, in reenactments of the illustrations.[6]

Lindsey's real interest in drawing started midway through her third year. As with most illustrations by very young children, Lindsey needed to explain what she was drawing. Seated at dinner at the home of a family friend, Lindsey was drawing while we sipped our after-dinner coffee. She was composing an elaborate and vigorous swirl of pen strokes. "What are you drawing?" I inquired. "Saint George and the dragon" [Hodges], she answered. And pointing to some particularly dark splotches, she exclaimed, "See! Here's the blood dripping out!" (March 13, 1986, 3;4). The swirls now took new form, with the splotches of dark blood capturing her personal response to the most violent of the book's scenes—the death of the dragon.

Lindsey's drawings integrated not only her personal reaction to text but the interrelationship between text and life. Within a month of entering preschool (3;10), she began to draw recognizable figures with eyes, nose, mouth, and hair, as well as legs and arms sticking out from the head. She asked her teacher to label these figures with the names "Mommy," "DaDa," and "Ashie," as well as with the names of her neighborhood and school friends. But she transposed these characters from their ordinary habitat into a more enchanted abode. She named one large pink shape on her paper "Mama's, DaDa's, Lindsey's, and Ashie's castle."

By kindergarten she had mastered the illustration of simple figures, and arms and legs moved into appropriate position. But her female figures, including self-portraits, consistently wore long elegant dresses with heart-shaped bodices and had hair that hung well past their skirts. When asked by her teacher to illustrate the most beautiful words she knew, she included "rainbow," "butterfly," and "fairy." Her fairy had a broad red smile and golden hair. Her gown was blue, adorned by a sparkling star, and in front of her large green wings, her hands held a magic wand (September 30, 1988, 5;10). In her "About Me" book, she completed the sentence frame "For Halloween, I would like to be . . ." with the words "an empress" (October 27, 1988, 5;11). Toward the end of the same book, she drew a typically exaggerated self-portrait which she labeled with the words "If I were magic, I would fly." And in her "alphabet pages," in which the assignment was to draw pictures of objects that started with particular letters, she used "Tinkerbell" for *T*, "wish upon a star" for *W*, and "evil" with a picture of a witch for *E*.

Her initial stories also integrated her personal world with the book world. In one story, she drew her standard female character with heart-shaped bodice and hair hanging to the ground. She placed the figure in a boxlike structure and dictated the following words to her teacher: "Once upon a time there was a little girl and her name was Lindsey. And she was captured by some bad men. She got captured underground. A prince got her out" (November 29, 1988, 6;0). By the time Lindsey entered first grade, the heart-shaped bodice had disappeared, but the prince and his princess remained, as well as the witches that were forever in pursuit. In one story entitled "The Witch" and published by the imaginary "Ghost Press," Lindsey cast her best friend Amelia as the evil witch, depicting her in a black pointed hat and perched atop tombstones. In one section of the story, she wrote:

> Amelia wus macing [making]
> a stoo [stew] to kill
> little chidin becos
> she wos a bad witch.
>
> (October 27, 1989, 6;11)

Illustrations in hundreds of books influenced Lindsey's early drawing—fairies flying, princes rescuing, and witches humming over their cauldrons. She merged different texts and styles to create her own illustrations and stories. Though her figures grew more recognizable as she grew older, she steadfastly refused to look carefully at her own short hair and rather ordinary school dress, but instead created self-portraits with all the elegance in her artistic power.

Ashley, too, was intrigued by the details of costuming. The frocks her female characters wore were consistently adorned with detailed patterns—multiple small circles and tiny boxes in a rainbow of colors. The bodies of these characters were also carefully drawn. Though arms usually stuck out at hip level, faces had all the necessary features; other details included a long rope of hair, a neck, curving shoulders, and tiny feet emerging from the bottom of the gown. Her use of detail did not extend to characters other than elegant princesses. Witches and ugly stepsisters wore simple sheaths, while monsters were blobs on the page, sometimes depicted with triangle teeth. Ashley's picture of a Cyclops was a large circle with a single darkened splotch in the center, and a triangle body extending down. The text she dictated was simple, but did portray some sympathy for the creature: "Poor little Cyclops. He had one eye" (April 19, 1990, 4;4).

Even the heroic figure of a prince was given little artistic energy, often drawn as a simple circle face, with long legs extending directly from the chin, and arms sticking out at the knees. In her written text, too, princes played little part, for the world swirled around the princess and belonged to her: "Sleeping Beauty has a prince. She had a balloon and a kite. The sun was very beautiful and shining. She went to a party and she had fun. She had a party dress on and her prince" (February 14, 1991, 5;2). In Ashley's eyes, the prince was no more than an accessory, equal in status to other party favors.[7]

Although Lindsey used paper and paint and colored pens for some story interpretation, they were not her media of choice, for she always preferred to reenact directly both illustration and text. She often acted out parts of stories and, right up through her preschool years, she would reillustrate in her costuming those critical features of the illustrations in books. The visual connection between reality and the imagination was often brought to life by the motion and emotion of the gesture. The action of holding a barrette to her lips and blowing on it created Ida's wonderhorn. The physical properties of the barrette were quite far from those of the elaborate horn of *Outside Over There* (Sendak), but Lindsey's gesture bridged the gap.[8]

The barrette was not permanently allotted the position of wonderhorn but was replaced when something better came along. One afternoon, as we were leaving a friend's house, Lindsey asked if she could borrow a toy from her two-year-old host, David. She had a large plastic horn in hand and was determined to take it home. After some wrangling between the children, all agreed that she could borrow it for a short time. When we arrived home, Kenny and I began walking around the garden looking at the tulips, and Lindsey slipped into the house. She reappeared in a nightgown and announced that her recent acquisition was "Ida's wonderhorn!" I laughed, now knowing the reason for her persistence, and a few minutes later we left her berating the invisible goblins in the yard (April 6, 1986, 3;5).

Lindsey often borrowed and created these props in order to assume the character of a particular story, but her follow-through on actions or plot was not bound to consistency with one story or illustrator. Instead her costuming of one character could then remind her of certain critical features of another illustration, and she would transform herself by announcement or through behaviors that exaggerated certain illustrations of the second character whose identity she had assumed. Props transformed just as stories did.

In literature play, props serve as the connection in visual image. An image springs from story or life, and props are the vehicle to make the connection. The objects Lindsey incorporated into her play were used not only for their properties but also for their potential. The everyday functions of objects were less important than the possibilities for their use. Swirling her panties round and round in the bathtub caused Lindsey to reconstruct them visually into *The Little Mermaid* (Andersen). The distance between function and fantasy was great, but Lindsey's action brought the two together.[9]

In the same way, ribbons could be stretched end to end to create a forest path, but they could also be braided and tied to her headband to imitate the length of "Rapunzel's hair." A red bathrobe could serve as Red Riding Hood's cloak, but it could also be used to play the part of the Grinch. Chairs could be knocked over to create a forest of thorns around Sleeping Beauty, or they could be lined up to provide spaceship seats for Luke, Han, Leia, and Chewie.

Ashley, on the other hand, was more firmly tied to function than to fantasy. Jump ropes were for jumping, not for flinging over the banister as Rapunzel's hair. Poles were for climbing, not for skipping about in a fairy's Maypole dance. Lindsey lived in the dress-up corner of her preschool class; but when Ashley attended the same classroom, she preferred the outdoors, climbing the jungle gym and finding new ways to descend the slide. The rope swing was her favorite and she monopolized its use, to the dismay of several little boys who tried to get their share of turns. Once a boy approached Ashley and said, "Let's play Tarzan. I'll be Tarzan and you be Jane." Ashley took a firmer grasp of the swing and replied, "I'll only play if I can be Tarzan" (Spring 1991, 5;0). Ashley was not about to relinquish the rope to play a less active character; the first requirement of play was to meet her own desire to be physically active.

At times, Lindsey would decide on a character she wished to play (as distinct from a plot she wanted to set in action) and then go in search of the appropriate props. This sequence was particularly true of her costuming. In the first months of preschool, Lindsey made crowns day after day, and each day she created a variation on the same theme. Like Bartholomew Cubbins' hats (Seuss), her crowns became increasingly elaborate and ultimately included a train of brightly colored tissue paper, which she called her "hair." These crowns became vital props in her dramatic play and enhanced her role as princess. Lindsey's teachers encouraged her penchant for the elaborate and did not try to shift her to the Lego corner or the blocks. For her fourth birthday, they made her a sparkling diadem with multicolored streamers. Lindsey reveled in the creation, running about the room to watch the streamers fly.

Costuming in literature play was crucial, especially when she was imitating one of the fairy-tale heroines. "I'm Sleeping Beauty and you're the queen," she commanded one evening as I sat watching the evening news. She was dressed in a dark blue leotard; over this she had put on her red velvet turtleneck dress, pulled down to the level of her hips. The effect was that of a long dress, if one could ignore the sleeves dangling next to her legs. Lindsey apparently could, but as she played she was unable to ignore the fact that she was missing one vital element.

> "I have to get wings!" She threw her arms up in exclamation and ran up the stairs.
> "Wings?" I shouted after her. "Did Sleeping Beauty have wings?"
> "Yes," she called as she raced up the stairs.
> "I don't remember. Can you bring me the book to show me?"
> When she returned she had two T-shirts and *The Sleeping Beauty* in hand. In this version of the story, Trina Schart Hyman had pictured Briar Rose with a frothy blue shawl. It lapped about her shoulders like an ocean wave. On closer inspection, it was really not a shawl at all, but a spirited decoration extending from her sleeves.
> "See," Lindsey explained. "We'll take the two shirts and put them on my shoulders and then I'll have WINGS!"
> Lindsey's voice rose high in excitement. I tucked the T-shirts into the shoulders of her leotard and watched as she gyrated and twirled to create the desired effect. Satisfied, she sped up the stairs once again to gaze at herself in the mirror. (June 10, 1986, 3;7)

At other times, the sight of a toy, a household tool, or an article of clothing would spark a connection with the world of story. Lindsey's yellow sponge ball provided easy entrée into *The Frog Prince* (Tarcov), for the princess of that story drops her golden ball into a well where the frog has his home. A kitchen broom could transform Lindsey into Cinderella. And a baby's yellow comforter could be wrapped around her head, changing her into Goldilocks. The visual image did not have to be confined to a single object. It could be a series of objects, or even a scene.

One summer, while we were all vacationing with my sisters in the Grand Tetons of Wyoming, Lindsey took up a role that was perfectly suited to the environs: Red Riding Hood. We had organized our respective families for a hike in the forest one morning. When we reached the beginning of the trail, it was early and cold, with the sun just beginning to send a shimmer across the dew. Lindsey was snuggled into her red down jacket and wanted to be carried. But as we walked further and further away from the road, the small dirt path became increasingly lined with a profusion of flowers, and Lindsey leaped down from Kenny's arms to look. The whole forest seemed abloom with pink geraniums, lupine, mule's ear, and Indian paintbrush.

> After gaining permission to pick "just a few," Lindsey began to gather more and more. She soon had a large bouquet and declared, "I'm Little Red Riding Hood." She unbuttoned her jacket and freed her arms from the sleeves. She then rearranged it like a cape, flinging the coat over her shoulders and clasping it with one button at her throat.
> The scene was perfect for her play. We were on a path through a flowered forest of pines, and she could stray slightly off the path and still feel the safety of her family around her. We met no wolf, but a moose did convince us to make a detour. And although the rest of us had our hearts in our throats over the threat of a wild moose, Lindsey continued blithely to add more wildflowers to her bouquet. "Grandma will love these," she calmly assured me. (July 6, 1986, 3;8)

Lindsey had a sharp eye for the visual connections between narratives of story and other narratives in her life, and used the parallels to define the possibilities of both. A man hacking away at the ivy of our house became "ole Jack" of *Jack and the Beanstalk*. Lindsey compared her own sister to the crying baby of *Outside Over There* (Sendak). The cracked and broken shell of the snail in Lionni's *The Biggest House* (in *Frederick's Fables*) reminded her of the smashed snail we had seen on the sidewalk near our house. And hunting for frogs in a muddy creek brought to mind Lobel's *Frog and Toad Together*. Lindsey used the images in stories to help her expand into other times and places she met in her own daily life. By connecting the visions and recreating the focus, Lindsey not only made sense of her immediate world but maneuvered her awareness of metaphorical similarities of dress, place, and state to make connections beyond the moment.

Lindsey and I were gardening one day, potting new plants and transplanting those that had become root-bound. In the process, I selected a large clay pot that had been sitting neglected in a corner of the patio. I planned to use it for a large spider plant, and I asked

Lindsey to hose it out. She had hardly begun her task, when she shoved the hose aside and stared intently into the depths of the pot.

> "Hi," she said into the pot.
> I stopped my work and regarded her curiously. "Who are you talking to?"
> "Come and see, Mom!"
> At the bottom of the pot, in a puddle of water, was a small brown frog. Having a natural dislike for these creatures, I drew back.
> But Lindsey leaned in closer still and said, "Hi, little fellow. Will you get my golden ball?" (October 27, 1986, 3;11)

The sight of the frog had sparked an entrée into the world of story. She was no longer Lindsey but a princess in need of assistance. The frog, too, had the possibility of being in another world. Not only did Lindsey see the handsome prince trapped in the body of a small, brown frog, but the connections between stories and their multiple plots and places were as powerful as her ability to incorporate their rules for being into her testing and expanding of everyday life.

Echoes of Heard Voices

An author stands behind every story, a voice in the child's ear. He or she reveals the text, painting a picture in words. And within every story, characters also speak—to each other and often directly to the reader. The preschool child's emerging knowledge of salient actors and speakers in the world of story must eventually embrace the unseen author—whether direct narrator of the story or not—as well as the characters within the story.

Finding the author's voice depends on the young reader's mapping onto a set of text features some combination of indistinct clues about the distant producer of the text—ranging from no overt hints at all to a photograph on the book jacket to favorite animals of the author's that are silently included in the illustrations. Awareness that there exists a speaker other than the parent reader or the pictured characters in the book is by no means a trivial accomplishment, since the child must realize that the words on the page not only do not originate with either the parent or the storybook character but come from an unseen source. Moreover, since adult readers usually have little difficulty knowing that an author exists and recognizing that the narrator is a persona of the author, their inclination may often be to skip entirely over the issue of who, where, or what the author is, leaving the child utterly alone to find the author.

At three, Lindsey's perception of the author's voice was incorporated as character in the text. One lazy summer afternoon, Lindsey was home with strep throat, and we snuggled in bed to read *The Tale of Peter Rabbit* (Potter). After reading the part where Peter flees Mr. McGregor's garden and safely makes it home, we came to the line: *"I am sorry to say that Peter was not very well during the evening."*

> "Are *you* sorry?" Lindsey asked, as if this were my personal comment.
>
> I said no, and tried to explain the author's voice, doing a fairly botched-up job of it. I said that the author was sorry, and Lindsey asked who the author was.
>
> "Beatrix Potter," I replied.
>
> "Oh," she said, and looked at me for awhile. "Is he a bunny, too?" (June 19, 1986, 3;7)

Linguistic cues by the author often lie deeply hidden within the text and do not announce themselves directly in any way. Often only by the subtlest shift in intonation do parents signal narration or direct insertion of the author's voice, as distinct from storybook characters' words.[10]

Only after repeated discussions to tell her that texts had writers, whose likeness I could sometimes point out on back covers, did Lindsey understand that in addition to me as reader, other adults lurked about her books. These needed to be labeled, even if initially only by analogy to terms she already knew.

> Lindsey pulled the pile of new library books over and chose a familiar one. "*Over in the Meadow* [Langstaff]," she addressed the cover. "Over in the Meadow," she read the title page. "Over in the Meadow," she read another page.
>
> Then she turned to me. "Who's it wroten by?" she asked.
>
> I flipped to the cover of the book. "John Langstaff," I answered.
>
> Lindsey began reading again. "Over in the Meadow, by John Longstuck." (June 25, 1986, 3;7)

Some authors' or illustrators' names came to hang about their books as appended bits of intriguing sounds and sights. "Trina Schart Hyman! Trina Schart Hyman!" Lindsey would chant the name of one of her favorite illustrators as though it were a nursery rhyme. After her father explained that some authors had their likenesses on the inside back covers of books, Lindsey searched our weekly stack of library books, checking the back covers of those illustrated by Hyman. To her great disappointment, there were no photographs, which led her to assume the author's demise. "Is she dead?" she asked in a stricken voice. She remembered that Kenny had also told her that sometimes there were no pictures when the authors were dead or had lived a long time ago.

I calmed her fears and finally discovered an author photo while writing a paper for a university class. *The Horn Book* (1985) carried an article on Ms. Hyman, along with her acceptance speech for the Caldecott Award. When I showed the picture to Lindsey, she stared hard at the face and the short-cropped hair. "Are you sure this is her?" she asked skeptically. "What happened to her hair?" The illustrations of enchanting princesses with luxurious hair (a constant feature in Hyman's books) did not match the illustrator's coiffure. Utterly disappointed, Lindsey never looked at the picture again. Years later our family attended the 1987 International Reading Association convention, and I took Lindsey to Hyman's talk. Lindsey stared in awe at the face of the illustrator as she spoke and showed her larger-than-life slides. Lindsey later remembered Hyman's explanation of how she had represented herself as one of the dwarfs in *Snow White* (Grimm Brothers)—quietly playing with Snow White's hair and later holding her hand as the young princess lay still on the ground. "There's Trina!" Lindsey would reiterate with each reading.

Later, Lindsey and I wrote to Ms. Hyman to express our admiration for her work, and Lindsey drew her a picture of Little Red Riding Hood holding her basket of wine, bread, and sweet butter (October 19, 1988, 5;11). Trina wrote back a letter filled with tiny hearts, stars, and assorted sparkles that tumbled out when we opened the card: "I also love Lindsey's drawing—especially her heroine's beautiful, heart-shaped bodice. Tell her I apologize for not looking anything like a fairy tale princess (she's not the first kid who's been disappointed by that!)" (November 2, 1988). Lindsey pasted the little sparkling shapes to the cover of her edition of *Little Red Riding Hood* (Grimm Brothers), which was her favorite book of Hyman's, and shared the letter with all her neighborhood girlfriends.

At the same age at which she pulled Beatrix Potter into the text as a bunny, she saw Maurice Sendak, the author of *Where the Wild Things*

Are, as both storybook character and as wide-ranging label for "things I like." In the middle of her third year, she took to lugging my copy of *The Art of Maurice Sendak* (Lanes) from the shelf and leafing through its oversized pages. "Here he is walking his dogs! That's him when he was a baby. There's his dog, Jenny!" she would inform me in a recapitulation of events in his life I had recounted to her.

One autumn day, Lindsey requested a snack. I asked her if she would like cheese and, if so, what kind. She wandered into the kitchen and, opening the refrigerator door, inspected the selection of cheeses.

> "I want the Maurice Sendak cheese!"
> "The what?" I replied.
> "The Maurice Sendak!" she stated emphatically pointing to the mozzarella cheese.
> "Ahhhh!" I smiled. "You mean the mozzarella."
> "That's what I said!" (October 27, 1986, 3;11)

The word "mozzarella" was new to her, but Sendak was an entity she knew and understood.[11] Her use of Sendak's name to label a desired food item carried over from the echoes in her head—from the sound of this author's name in her verbal repertoire.

The sheer magic and memory-peg quality of fanciful or fun-to-say names enable children to acknowledge not only the authors behind the texts but also language variations that mark one kind of text from another—Mother Goose rhymes from stories, names designed to hurt versus those of more neutral delivery, and nonsense words of emotion versus words of reference. To the wonderment of discerning adults, children—apparently almost instantly—often pick up these discriminations from casual and brief exposure to cues that adults do not specifically identify for them. In children's literature, the language of rhyme covers not only words but also rhythm, alliteration, assonance, and consonance, which need not be accurately verbalized but which may be carried in the head just as young children carry the intonation patterns of certain chunks of language before they can segment or articulate specific words.[12]

Lindsey loved nursery rhymes long before she could repeat them. From age one she would drag her well-worn copy of *Mother Goose* (Battaglia) into my lap and snuggle down for a good long read. She *felt* the rhythm before she could sing it. She was rocked to sleep with it, bounced on a knee with it, twirled and danced and pranced with it. She heard many of the sounds of literature as bound together in the stream of vocal sound, and only later segmented these chunks out into words as separate units of rhythm blocks.

Often Lindsey's wordplay was not for the benefit of communication. The creation of language was an end in itself—not always an instrument for immediate results, but words and sounds as toys to be manipulated and transformed. When she played with language, singing songs and rhyming rhymes, it was usually in the privacy of her bath or in the quiet of her room—creative experimentation not meant to be shared.

Playing with language meant playing not only with character, emotion, and situations through vocabulary but also with rhyme, and just prior to her fourth birthday Lindsey learned the traditional meaning of rhyme. She begged me to play rhyming games and could create a rhyme for almost any word I gave her: "Pan—man, table—bable, alka-seltzer—talka-meltzer!" Often these rhymes were associated with stories. One day she performed a song and dance that sprang from *Henny Penny* (Galdone). She stomped and clapped her way through the house singing, "Ducky Lucky. Goosey Loosey. Cocky Locky. Ashie Pashie. Lindsey Mindsey!" On another day, while we were baking, she made a rhyming revision of Sendak's *In the Night Kitchen*. As she poured the milk into the bowl and stirred, she sang, "I'm in the milk and the milk's in me. Beat it, bake it, shake it, take it."

Rhythm is essential to rhyme, and as Lindsey listened to the rhythm of story language, she stored up the verbal movement to take out and manipulate on other occasions. In preschool she listened to story cassettes, and one of her favorites was Ann McGovern's *Too Much Noise*. One day, as she sat playing with clay, she began to chant the words of the story. Her teacher was not close enough to overhear the words exactly, but she quickly recognized the cadence of the familiar story. As Lindsey pushed and pulled the clay into a pleasing form, she shaped a rhythmic wordplay to accompany her work. Lindsey's teacher explained this event as common in the lives of the children in her class. "The nonsense words I hear all the time. [The children] love to play with words. And that, I think, goes back to the idea of vocabulary . . . just the fascination with the use of language" (June 6, 1987, 4;7). The language of children's literature is not uniform, however, but depends on genre, historical period, and author's voice, and children learn to separate out sounds to fit the specific requirements of varying literary situations.

By the age of four, Ashley was able to recognize and reproduce the different sounds of a story and a nursery rhyme. One morning we read *The Jolly Postman* (Ahlberg and Ahlberg), in which a postman delivers letters to fairy-tale characters like the Three Bears and Jack's giant. The letter to Her Royal Highness Cinderella was from the Peter Piper Publishing Company, which was begging permission to publish a small book about Cinderella's whirlwind romance. The book was enclosed for "Cinder's" perusal. I was about to read the abridged version when Ashley grabbed the book and sang:

> Hiddley Diddley Doo.
> She kissed her sisters and they were bad and they said:
> "Don't kiss me! Don't kiss me!
> My master's going to kiss me.
> Don't kiss me! Don't kiss me!
> My master's going to kiss me.
> Don't kiss me! Don't kiss me!
> I will kiss my own fairy
> He's good or bad.
> Don't kiss me. My sir will kiss you if I don't promise."

At the end of her song I asked her to read the story instead of singing the song, reminding her that she had taken this tack in an earlier reading.

> She cleared her throat and read her interpretation of the title, "Cinderella and Her Two Bad Sisters." She paused and then continued, "Once there . . . no!" She had accidently turned to the second page of the story rather than the first page. She turned back to the first page and began again, "And her bad sisters said, 'Do that! Do my job. Do that! Do my job.' Because they are ready. 'Clean up the . . . way.' And she was *so* so good at cleaning. She had to scrub the floor. And do that. And she had to . . . And she had to . . . umm . . . And she had to bring a bucket for scrubbing. And she had to do *all* the work she had to do. And the prin . . . And the fairy came and turned the dress into *everything*. And there she was . . . And she got a lizard and mouse and a pumpkin! The . . . And they were all married. The End." (February 7, 1990, 4;2)

Ashley's "song" included many elements of a traditional Mother Goose rhyme, including rhythm and repetition. Although she attempted to incorporate a bit of the story plot in the beginning of her song ("She kissed her sisters and they were bad"), the plot was soon abandoned in the rhythm of the kiss. Ashley's interpretation included snatches of other nursery rhymes, with "Hiddley Diddley Doo" replacing "Hickory Dickory Dock" and "My master's going to kiss me" standing in for "My master's gone away." Several sets of lines were repeated, as though serving as a chorus.[13]

Her story, on the other hand, called on the elements of the fairy tale. It began with a title and "Once there . . ." and ended with a group wedding and a satisfactory "The End." The sisters' voices were imperious and demanding, goading Cinderella into work. And Ashley provided an explanation for their demands by suggesting that Cinderella was "*so* so good at cleaning." She connected her story with a string of "ands," so common in young children's stories, but omitted them from her "song." She also emphasized different words in her story by drawing them out and saying them in a louder voice, while in her song she emphasized the words that fell on the beat.

Beyond the catchy musicality of literary language lie not only emotive meanings but also referential meanings that children stretch out into well-formed sentences or chunks of dialogue or commentary. While Lindsey played in her room one morning, I read *Hansel and Gretel* (Grimm Brothers / Jeffers). She was quietly building towers with her Duplo blocks and threading junk jewelry charms on her fingers as rings. She hardly seemed to be listening to the story, and I wondered whether I should continue reading. Yet when I reached the part where the wicked mother shouts at the children *"Get up, you lazybones!"* Lindsey started to laugh.

> "Lazybones. *Lazybones!*" she chuckled and slapped her thighs. "That's funny, lazybones. Their bones are lazy!"
> After her giggling subsided she returned to her blocks and did not acknowledge the story until the children arrived at the sugary house of the wicked witch. (June 13, 1986, 3;7)

Here Lindsey acknowledged that the compound "lazybones" is a reduction of a full sentence. She practiced again and again—as though in pattern practice for a foreign language—words that struck her funnybone. For days following this incident, she called all of her dolls "lazybones," and woke them up with a jerk, bringing into her own play both the malice and the medium of Hansel and Gretel's wicked mother.

Lindsey often called forth both nonsense sounds and whole phrases from literature in response to nonsense sounds she heard elsewhere. When Ashley whined about Lindsey's refusal to share her colored marking pens, her voice was a high-pitched and extended "EHHHHH!" Lindsey listened in disgust and then retorted with the words, "No more twist!" taunting her sister by imitating the squeaking sound of the wailing mice in Beatrix Potter's story *The Tailor of Gloucester* (February 9, 1990, 7;3 and 3;2). Ashley's whine and the squealing lament of the little mice who run out of thread ("twist") struck a similar chord in Lindsey's ear and prompted her match of Ashley's pitch and emotion to that of the mice in Potter's story. Both Ashley and the mice were saddened by life's events—the mice by the fact that they had no more twist to finish the last buttonhole of a coat, and Ashley by the fact that she had no pens to finish her drawing.

Lindsey also recollected chunks from stories and often used her memory of specific pieces of dialogue to announce "That's like [one story or another]!" One night Lindsey requested that I read *The Country Bunny and the Little Gold Shoes*. During the story, I sniffled and snuffled, battling my annual spring attack of allergies. When I finished the story, Lindsey was ready with her usual request.

"Scratch my back," she pleaded.
"Okay." I turned off the light and began to scratch.
"You're so snuffly, Mom."
"It's just my allergies," I explained. "They'll clear up in a few days. You wait and see."
Lindsey turned over. "You sound just like Cottontail. You said, 'You wait and see.'"
It was true. In the story, Cottontail bunny declares that someday she will be an Easter Bunny. But no one believes her. As the book explains:
"Then all of the big white bunnies who lived in fine houses, and the Jack Rabbits with long legs who can run so fast, laughed at the little Cottontail and told her to go back to the country and eat a carrot. But she said, 'Wait and see!'" (Heyward). (April 7, 1986, 3;5)

Thus, whole pieces of dialogue or description were held up for comparison and reflection. But chunks of text could also be spliced into the smooth talk of everyday conversation.

Ashley was adept at inserting story phrases at opportune moments to extend or explicate her own observations on the world. One evening, after a particularly rambunctious bath with her sister, Ashley reentered the bathroom as I was attempting to straighten up. She slipped and momentarily lost her balance on the wet floor, but I grabbed her elbow and kept her upright.

> "Whew!" I exclaimed. "That was close."
> Ashley nodded solemnly and replied, "Yeah. The floor's all slippy-sloppy in the bathroom."
> I recognized the words of *The Tale of Mr. Jeremy Fisher,* in which Beatrix Potter describes the home of the frog, Mr. Jeremy Fisher:
> *"The water was all slippy-sloppy in the larder and in the back passage. But Mr. Jeremy liked getting his feet wet; nobody ever scolded him, and he never caught a cold!"* (1906, p. 10).
> The story was a long-time favorite of Ashley's, and when I asked her where she got the words "slippy-sloppy," I expected her to cite Potter. Instead, she insisted that the words came from the movie *Bambi* and reminded me of the scene where the young deer prince is sliding around on the ice with his pal Thumper, who describes Bambi as being "kinda wobbly." (May 31, 1990, 4;5)

While Potter's words fit the situation, Mr. Jeremy's action did not—he was not slipping across the floor, but surefootedly carrying some dishes into the water-drenched larder. And although Thumper used different words to describe the young deer's antics, Bambi's actions fit Ashley's perception of a slippery fall. In her sentence, Ashley spliced together three texts: the words of one and the action of another with a third, personal text—a description of her own near-accident.

For Lindsey, sound similarities between conversation and story would often spark connections. As my father tickled Ashley's chin, he would tease, "Tickle, tickle, tickle." Lindsey wanted to join in the merriment and reached under Ashley's shirt. "Tikki Tikki Tembo—No Sa Rembo—Chari Bari Ruchi—Pip Peri Pembo," she chanted as she tickled. As she played with her sister, she played with language, and the name of the main character in Mosel's story seemed to strike just the right chord. Lindsey was particularly intrigued with the African words in Verna Aardema's stories. In *Who's in Rabbit's House?* she imitated the "Gumm Gumm Gumm" of the elephant and the "Gdung Gdung Gdung" of the laughing frog.

At lunch one day, I made Lindsey's sandwich with rye bread, forgetting her dislike of it. When she complained that she didn't like the bread with seeds, I told her to open her sandwich and simply eat the tuna fish. Her tongue made soft smacking sounds against the roof of her mouth. "Wasu Wusu . . . Wasu Wusu," she whispered. She looked at me and her tongue darted in and out. "That's what the snake said when he went into the rabbit's hole" (June 5, 1986, 3;7). In this incident she was quoting from *Why Mosquitoes Buzz in People's Ears* (Aardema). She seemed to savor the sound of the African words on her tongue, rolling them over and over, delighting not only in the sound but in the feel of the word. In the musicality of language, Lindsey connected sound, experience, and concept. Not only did she use language to communicate, but she manipulated rhyme, rhythm, alliteration, and nonsense to add to the other extensions of playing with rules that literature gave her.

In every story, one encounters not only the author's hidden voice but also the voices of the characters. Works of literature that offer predictable characters ensure an early equation of voice with certain personal features: the shrill, crackling voice of the evil witch; the deep, confident voice of the handsome prince; and the soft, musical voice of the princess awaiting her rescue. Similarly, the characters who reappear again and again in a series, such as Frances, the persistently poetic young badger (Hoban), and the irrepressible Ramona (Cleary), develop personalities that prevail across many situations and lend their voices to adoption by young readers. As Lindsey read to me, she often translated print into vibrant voice.

One morning Lindsey was seated in her blue director's chair, leaning up against the sunny window. I had asked her to go to her room and have some quiet time while I changed the baby. When I was ready to nurse Ashley, we came in to join Lindsey. She was just beginning to read *Bedtime for Frances*, by Russell Hoban. She held the book properly and read "BEDTIME FOR FRANCES" from the cover. She quickly flipped past the title page and dedication page and proceeded to the first page of the story. Lindsey read:

> It is seven o'clock.
> The little hand is on the 7.
> The big hand is on the . . . 7.
> It is bedtime for Frances.
> "It is time for bed," said father.
> "It is time for bed," said mother.
> "Can I have a glass of milk?" said Frances.
> "Yes," said father.

"Yes," said mother.
"Thank you," said Frances.

(February 11, 1986, 3;4)

Much more interesting than her close approximation of the words in the text, or her display of book-handling knowledge, was Lindsey's varying intonation to indicate different characters. For Frances, Lindsey had a high-pitched voice and used a "sh" sound liberally. She said, "Shank you" instead of "Thank you" and "glash of milk" instead of "glass of milk." For Father, Lindsey used a deep, resounding voice and held her chin tight against her throat. Mother's voice was smooth and tranquil, almost melodious.

This was only one of many times that I heard the voices of literary characters. The wolf's voice in *The Three Little Pigs* (Galdone) was gruff and deep, while the pig's approached that of a squeal. Max, in *Where the Wild Things Are,* had a defiant, commanding voice. Little Red Riding Hood had a sweet, innocent voice that included a tremor as she approached the wolf.

Lindsey's intonation was an extension of our own. When we read Lindsey stories, we constantly varied the intonation while supplying predictable interpretations of character.[14] And these voice shifts did not always originate with me and Kenny. I heard the same kinds of shifts in the stories my father told me of his childhood, in those my sister read to our children on vacation, and in those that Lindsey's teacher read to her class. I heard Kenny's father use similar variations as he read Lindsey her bedtime story:

Grandpa "did the honors" tonight, and not without hesitation. But Lindsey insisted that he read, so he went up the stairs dutifully with book in hand. After they had begun the story, I crept up the stairs and sat quietly outside Lindsey's room to listen.

Lindsey had selected *Who's in Rabbit's House?* [Aardema], a tale that was completely new to Grandpa. Yet he had no trouble immersing himself in the story. As the intensity of the story grew, and as the animals who came to Rabbit's aid increased in size, Grandpa's voice built to a resounding boom. Lindsey laughed with glee as Grandpa shouted, *"Who's in Rabbit's house?"* (November 26, 1986, 4;0)

The voices of story characters tell more than our verbal interpretations of motive, intention, and emotion.

Lindsey's understanding of the intonation of story reading spread to her everyday conversation. She would experiment with the patterns of her family, her friends, and characters from television. Although she often chose similar patterns of telling, she extended intonations in her own ways.

One morning we read Rosemary Wells's *Timothy Goes to School*. It is the story of a small raccoon's first days at school and his struggles to overcome the criticisms of the "in-crowd" raccoon, Claude. On the first day, Timothy dresses in a checkered sunsuit that his mother has lovingly made. Claude gives Timothy the once-over and comments, *"Nobody wears a sunsuit on the first day of school."* I read the line as a haughty put-down.

> Lindsey chimed in, however, and her interpretation was quite different. She scrunched her face up in the expression that children take on when they say something like, *"My* dad's bigger than *your* dad!!" and she singsonged Claude's line.
> I giggled over her expression, "What?"
> Her lips curled back in a sneer and she sang Claude's line again. (June 16, 1986, 3;7)

The story's voices vitally link the meaning behind the words to children's experiences with descriptions of character, their sense of dominant and subordinate powers, and possible sets of winners and losers.

Making and Breaking Rules

Perhaps no other concept has been more debated for its role in young children's lives than that of *rules*. Parents, teachers, and other authority figures see rules as proscriptions and prescriptions directed to children from external sources. Children learn these rules and, most important, they learn when to apply them and how to negotiate their obedience under different circumstances, with various individuals, and for goals of varying degrees of importance.

Psychologists, linguists, and others who try to understand children's learning, and especially their perceptual and productive abilities in language, focus, however, on "rules" that children themselves devise, as well as on the representations they carry in their heads. These researchers point out that children actively perceive, process, and store innumerable sounds, combinations of meaning, and occasions of uses and users of language. Children's own efforts at producing language result from their trying out their internal rules of mental representations. In the case of all neurologically sound children, their productions in language eventually come to have meaning for listeners about them, but their internal rules of combinations and symbolic representations and situational constraints on meaning are far more complex than any set of rules that adults might be able to offer on how to talk or how to learn to talk.

In short, although adults tend to focus on children learning overt rules so they may apply them and know when they are breaking them, young children are neurologically prepared to make rules unconsciously. In so doing, they must constantly reorder, reshape, and retry patterns they see emerging again and again. Moreover, as they move in their constant comparing and contrasting of objects, events, and responses, they induce certain premises that others hold and act upon.

Children's literature gives youngsters numerous voices, scripts, and settings other than those they receive from adults in the course of their daily lives. Children come to see children's literature as a part of the full repertoire or range of selections of scenarios and situations from which to infer rules—for combining sounds, for assuming character roles, for managing human relations, and for attempting to control the universe. Children's literature provides opportunities for children to learn the names of items as well as the predictable behaviors of types of characters and the features of particular environments, both textual and real-world. These features are easily observed and often receive comments from adults. But equally frequent and far less often noted by adults is the ability of children to call forth the particular rules for human relationships that are at work in literary texts and to consider how their premises relate to the patterns of interactions about them in their daily lives.

The vast majority of such premises (for example, all sisters in a family will not be equally loving, parents do not always protect their children, infants see the world from their own perspective) would never be verbalized by adults in daily life, for they would seem too complex, frightening, or suggestive for children. Children's literature often takes up themes as subtle—and as potentially radical—as the importance of intrinsic values over surface features, the pervasive need for the weaker to excel in devising strategies to overwhelm the more powerful, and the inevitability that bad things will happen to good people. Indeed, classics in children's literature often turn the tables on adult pretensions and assumptions of what is acceptable and polite.[15] Consider the tea party in *Alice's Adventures in Wonderland* (Carroll):

> *There was a table set out under a tree in front of the house, and the March Hare and the Hatter were having tea at it: a Dormouse was sitting between them, fast asleep, and the other two were using it as a cushion resting their elbows on it, and talking over its head. "Very uncomfortable for the Dormouse," thought Alice; "only, as it's asleep, suppose it doesn't mind."*
>
> *The table was a large one, but the three were all crowded together at one corner of it. "No room! No room!" they cried out when they saw Alice coming. "There's plenty of room!" said Alice indignantly, and she sat down in a large arm-chair at one end of the table.*
>
> *"Have some wine," the March Hare said in an encouraging tone.*
>
> *Alice looked all round the table, but there was nothing on it but tea. "I don't see any wine," she remarked.*
>
> *"There isn't any," said the March Hare.*
>
> *"Then it wasn't very civil of you to offer it," said Alice angrily.*
>
> *"It wasn't very civil of you to sit down without being invited," said the March Hare.* (Pp. 82–83)

Crashing tea parties, leaning on sleeping guests, and exchanging angry insults are not usually covered in the numerous books for children on manners. Carroll—and many other authors of children's literature—overstep the boundaries that the "Miss Manners" of the world so carefully delineate. In classic tales, children defy their parents, escape to powerful dream worlds, and stray off the path. They are offered wine at tea parties and carry other bottles off to Grandmother's house. They drink from still other mysterious bottles, shrinking and stretching the rules that ordinarily prevail in life but not necessarily in story.[16]

Rare is the adult who will take up these topics for discussion with a toddler or preschooler, but writers of children's literature have no such hesitations.[17] Moreover, these subtle and complex issues stand out for children whose early lives incorporate a substantial amount of children's literature, because literary language is highlighted both by context and by its own internal characteristics.

The context of snuggling down in the lap of a parent who has ceased all other activity to read with a child signals that something extraordinary is occurring. In the ordinary course of waking hours, adults rarely stop all other activities to focus on the young, unless they are offering direct nurturance or playing with them. Book-reading has special powers, since it demands total cessation of all other activities by the adult. Mothers and fathers can play with their children while they prepare meals—offering the occasional tease, adding suggestions for props, or stopping momentarily to take a turn in hide and seek. But book-reading centers exclusively around child and text, and language and lessons from this context are thus highly signaled for children as nonordinary.

Similarly, because most texts of children's literature include a greater array of voices, characters, and plots than ordinary life, children receive the widest possible exposure to alternative perceptions and responses. They hear the sounds of Gloucester mice taunting a cat, the unexpected consonant clusters of an African chant, or the endless repetition of the same formula varied only by a single word. They spot the solitary human hand hanging oddly where a bird's wing should be, and they follow a minor character who is rarely mentioned in the text but who appears on each page nonetheless, carrying some of the emotional content of the story. Those who study adults and infants communicating tell us again and again that the raised intonation, changes in pitch, and focused gaze help infants attend to the language around them.[18] All of these features combine in the reading of literature with children; the calls for their attention, intonational and postural, are marked, are set apart from ordinary language. The occasion is signaled—by the stopping of other action, the special close positions of adult and child, and the joint focus on a single artifact that bears no practical and direct relationship to surrounding or ongoing activities at the time of the reading. Evidence that children recognize these features abounds as they grow older and seek out secret hiding places for reading, choose reading over other daily activities, and delight in occasions when they themselves can read and assume the voices of cowboys, kings, and miscreants—characters forbidden them in their ordinary lives.

Adults rarely think of how their reading of children's literature offers an abundance of opportunities for rule-making and rule-breaking by children. Children can make up rules for language—rules that are highly complex and totally out-of-awareness for adults. For example, most adults are unaware of all the ways in which a sense of internal rhyme is achieved or how forms of alliteration can vary, but they themselves may enjoy the effects of these literary devices and thus choose books that offer these in their texts. Children, on the other hand, hear and see these marked or out-of-the-ordinary uses of language and often set about to show that they can make rules for the processes. They not only lift pieces to which these rules have applied out of texts, but they also manipulate their rules to create an additional repertoire of rhymes, nonsense words that follow the rules, or intoned imitations of large blocks of text that obviously "belong" in the mouths of those with greater or lesser degrees of authority, acceptance, and confidence.

Though later chapters deal with some of the larger blocks of rule-making that children gain from literary experiences, it is important to mention here in the context of the "senses of story" some of the most frequent language features of children's literature and ways they contribute to children's repertoire of language skills—both receptive (or listening) and productive (speaking).

The writing in children's literature usually comes in a special register or a style of language marked for a particular use. Certain words and arrangements of words into sentences that open, close, or mark the tone of certain characters appear in children's literature but rarely in daily life—except when adults mark their talk as playful by speaking with the special vocabulary and grammar of this literary language.[19] Between "once upon a time" and "happily ever after," the words of story describe a world where life is nonordinary—often somehow more formal and elegant than ordinary life. In the world of story, people "weep," their clothes "turn to rags," and when they are childless "it grieves them more than can be imagined."

One Sunday night we were watching TV. Lindsey, Ashley, and I were on the couch, and Kenny was doing stretching exercises on the rug beside us. He stood and headed for the kitchen.

> "Shelby, do you want anything?" he asked. "Some ice cream, some tea?"
> "No, no thank you." I replied. "I feel perfectly content."
> Lindsey eyed me sharply. "You sound just like Beauty," she exclaimed. "You should ask Daddy for a rose!" (March 9, 1986, 3;4)

Later I pulled out Lindsey's library copy of *Beauty and the Beast,* by Marianna and Mercer Mayer. The story read:

> *"Very well," said the hopeful merchant* [addressing the greedy sisters]. *"You shall have the finest dresses money can buy. But what do you want me to bring to you, Beauty?"*
> *Beauty had been very quiet while her sisters planned. She gathered her*

> *father's traveling clothes and put them into his small trunk. "Really,*
> *there is nothing I need," she said . . .*
> *"Now, you must have something you'd like me to bring you. Tell me,*
> *girl, what shall it be?" . . .*
> *"Yes, there is something I'd love to have. Please bring me back a rose."*
> (Mayer)

The formality of my language construction, the fact that I said "perfectly content" rather than a more conversational "I'm full," led Lindsey to leap into the language of literature—the diction of princes and
princesses, fairies, beauties, and beasts.

In children's literature, the link between texts is more prominent
than in adult fiction: uniform descriptions of forests and castles, resolutions that punish the evil and reward the good, and characters who
speak the same phrases. One night Kenny read *Rumpelstiltskin* (Grimm
Brothers) to Lindsey while I played with Ashley. As the peasant girl in
the story sat weeping, the infamous dwarf approached her with the
question, *"What will you give me if I spin it for you?"*

> "That's like the Princess and the Frog," Lindsey suggested, refer-
> ring to her copy of *The Frog Prince* [Tarcov].
> I asked her why and she replied, "He says, 'What will you give me?'"
> Her voice changed to the higher pitch of the princess, "I'll give you
> my crown of gold. I'll give you my necklace of pearls." (March 1,
> 1986, 3;4)

Lindsey not only equated the questions "What will you give me?" but
she predicted the words that the peasant girl would give in answer to
Rumpelstiltskin as she quickly offered her necklace and her ring. In
story, princesses and peasant girls, dwarfs and frogs speak in the same
tongue to accomplish their goals, and Lindsey had numerous opportunities for listening to their words. "Tell it again," Lindsey would say
as she summoned us to the retelling of a story. The repetitive nature
of a story in its structure, dialogue, and rhythm was not boring in
Lindsey's eyes. These routines gave her the opportunity to treasure her
possession and discover and admire new facets with each retelling. Not
only did she request multiple readings of her favorite stories, but she
would practice story dialogue in her play: lifting the words from the
page, assembling them like her other props, and carrying them with
her to her room, to the backyard, and to the bathtub.[20]

When Lindsey's grandmother arrived for a visit, she brought a collection of toys purchased on the boardwalk in Ocean City, where she lives. A dazzling array of junk jewelry was accompanied by a huge plastic doll and a very lifelike rubber frog. Lindsey loved it all, but particularly the frog (possibly taking into account my aversion to the species). At bathtime one evening, she assembled her props before submerging in the tub.

> Bringing in a towel I asked, "What are you playing?"
> "The frog prince."
> Using a bright yellow sponge ball and the frog, Lindsey was the princess. She began the story by weeping into her hands.
> "What's the matter, Princess?" She imitated the croaky voice of the frog.
> "I've lost my golden ball." Lindsey's voice was high and sweet.
> "I'll get it, but you must promise me to let me sleep on your fine, silk pillow." And with this, Lindsey guided the frog under the water toward the ball. (March 2, 1986, 3;4)

Lindsey was able to apply story language to life as well. She warned her sister to sit down in her high chair or she might "come tumbling down." When Ashley had a fever, Lindsey commented that her skin was "as hot as dragon's fire." On another occasion I asked her to stop Ashley from opening the door and escaping into the garden. "Not so fast!" she hissed, in perfect imitation of Viola Swamp, the mean "substitute" teacher in *Miss Nelson Is Missing!* (Allard).[21]

At times Lindsey's use of story language was on a literal plane—she was gleaning information from the text. One evening the girls took a bath together. Because Ashley was young and still a bit unsteady, I stayed in the bathroom with them after the shampoos were done. I was brushing my teeth when Ashley took a nose dive into the water.

> "Mom!" Lindsey yelled.
> I dropped to my knees and yanked the baby up. Ashie came up gasping for air, coughing and sputtering. I worriedly watched her face, holding her close.
> Lindsey, too, was worried and her voice was panic-stricken as she suggested, "Push the water out of him and push the air into him." But Ashley recovered quickly, and had no need for emergency techniques. (November 5, 1986, 3;11)

Lindsey's frantic advice came from *Tikki Tikki Tembo* (Mosel), the story of two small boys who take turns falling into a well. An old Chinese man with a ladder methodically pushes out the water and pushes in the air and thereby saves their lives. In her sense of urgency, Lindsey forgot the proper transformation of pronoun, but she did not forget the survival information. Even in an emergency, she reached to text for resolution.

The phrasing, cadence, and highlighted dialogue of literary language invite redundancy, repetition, and replay by children. Moreover, the comfort and intimacy of book-reading sessions plus the predictability of presentation ensure a soothing recollected affect from such language.

The Power of Prediction

Without predictive powers, we could not make our way through the world. Because the social constraints of all the groups to which we belong, whether family, community, school, or nation, will not allow any individual to be entirely unique, most of what we learn must be shared and socially agreed upon. But preparing to know what to do in all possible situations that may arise seems an impossibility if we think only of direct practice; therefore, we must learn to draw from our experiences a store of categories, skills, behaviors, and attitudes that enables us to predict how these might apply in future scenarios. The essence of children's literature is its enabling of prediction.

Children's literature and the separate, intimate domain of its reading intensify children's opportunities to figure out the world and how they will make their place in it. Such a claim sounds outrageous, since the children's literature that is often judged "classic," "best," or "most outstanding" presents plots, characters, and scenes far more fantastic and complex than the world of everyday sensation and inference available to children. Why, then, might children's literature do more to focus children's perceptual, categorizing, and inferencing abilities for recall in prediction than the immediate reality about them?

Storybooks and the set-aside time for their reading place a double stop-action on the pace of the world and intensify and emphasize domain-specific and structured knowledge. The first stop-action comes from the fact that the time for book-reading halts the normal flow of activity of both adult and child. All channels of sensation and communication between adult and child open: touch, sight, sound, and even smell and taste in detailed illustrations and descriptions, as well as more literally in "scratch-and-sniff" books. By gesture, comment, or question, children can display and investigate not only the page before them but its links to remembered sensations or experiences.

A second stop-action results from the fact that, unlike the continual and relatively undesignated pace of everyday life, storybooks frame page-by-page words and pictures to make them hold still indefinitely and stand ready for repeated revisits. Moreover, both the illustrations and the language of literature highlight the immediate fixity of the page frame and its potential fluidity and flow off the page into the child's creative manipulations.[22] Drawings and words depend on their overemphasis of particular features to gain children's attention. Just as the highly varied and high-pitched baby-talk of adults helps focus the attention of infants on speech and the nurturing actions it often accompanies, so the highly musical, repetitive, and often exaggerated language of children's literature pulls children in to focus on a limited range of phenomena. Illustrations drawn with bright colors, repeated characters and motifs, and stylized patterns of movement and displays of emotion catch the eye and hold the joint attention of adults and child for repeated examination and query.

Furthermore, no absolute answers or totally fixed resolutions of these explorations are offered in either literary language or imaginative illustration; these leave open alternative outcomes and revised pursuits of meaning. Occasions around children's literature offer experiences of a highly congenial sort that serve as a laboratory of activity in which children can use their minds for the inner equivalent of scientific experimentation. And just as the laboratory depends on the fundamental "but what if?" query, so the storybook invites circles of mutated and selective testing of not only categories by which to discriminate between and infer properties of natural kinds (to know a frog from a lizard) but also to distinguish types of social and moral judgments (to know kindness from cruelty, mischief from passivity). The predictive punch of children's literature rests in its invitation to young readers to experiment and explore the most fundamental and most complex of societal concepts and social cognition. Ironically, children's literature offers such openness in large part because it does not purport to impart primarily facts or fixed information. Its setting, characters, and scenes usually do not rely on any absolute or accurate knowledge of specific times, places, and people. Children can enjoy and understand Mother Goose rhymes without knowing the facts of the political history that gave rise to their composition. They can revel in the antics of Peter Rabbit without knowing what rabbit warrens are, how carrots grow, or what camomile tea is. It is not facts that make the enjoyment and interpretation of children's literature possible, but, instead, inferences that depend on the child's gradually acquired encyclopedic knowledge of sensations, emotional responses, and reasoned approaches.

Asking "but what if?" then follows easily from literary texts, for a maximal (though not infinite) range of objects, concepts, and social judgments is there as experimental apparatus. The range of "if-then" questions possible from literature lifts the child out of current role and world into the endless possibilities of fictional experimentation, armed with all the verbal (and visual) equipment that children's literature offers. Child becomes playwright, set and costume designer, actor, and critic of future scenarios that develop from the extensions possible within and from literary texts.

With story image and language, Lindsey chose the roles she wanted to play, as well as those she did not, and also the conditions under which she might choose to play or just become the critic. In preparation for a visit by her grandparents, Lindsey and I were cleaning the house and she was being quite helpful. We scrubbed the kitchen floor together, and though she tended to be too generous with the spray cleaner, we actually got the floor more clean than wet. As we were scrubbing, Lindsey began to polish her image in the oven door. She did some light dance steps to the satisfaction of her reflection and then began rubbing away at the grease stains.

> "Thanks for helping me, sweetie," I cajoled. "It's great not to have to do all the work by myself."
> Lindsey turned and spread out her hands with a shrug.
> "You're not Cinderella! I'm not the ugly stepsister! You don't have to do all the work!" (April 16, 1987, 3;5)

Creating a verbal analogy between our roles and those of story characters was a telling example of Lindsey's wordplay. The words "all the work" triggered a verbal connection that unleashed an entire metaphorical set of images, actions, and themes.

Years later, the themes of Cinderella still clung to issues of work. One New Year's Day, Lindsey organized a play of *Cinderella* with Ashley and their friend Andrea. Lindsey selected herself as the subservient maiden and, dressed in torn jeans and soccer shirt, she brought

breakfast in bed to the demanding sisters (played by Ashley and Andrea). As the play shifted to the dining room and Andrea and Ashley
ordered more food with accusing fingers and dissatisfied glares, Lindsey kept a calm countenance. When she spilled some milk on the table,
she stayed in character and apologized profusely, while Andrea played
her anger to the hilt.

Lindsey then draped the sisters in beads and scarves to enhance their
beauty and prepare them for the ball, quietly ignoring their superior
stares. She applied makeup—lipstick and blush, continually under the
demanding eye of Andrea, who pointed out the spots she missed and
hissed out other sarcastic remarks. She dressed them attending to every
detail—adding a skirt underneath Ashley's dress to imitate the length
of a ballgown, draping the front of her dress with pearls, and wrapping
another strand around Ashley's hand to create the effect of rings.
Ashley, in the meantime, adopted the stance of the bored nouveau
riche, her face in a pout, her eyes cast up in haughty dissatisfaction. All
three children held to the rules of the story, enacting the actions and
reactions of their character.

Work is one of life's harsh realities, but play softens the blow. As
Lindsey cleaned up her "stepsisters'" tea things, she turned to me and
said: "You know, mom. Now I can understand why you complain
about doing all the dishes. It's a pain. But it's fun when you're playing.
The next time I have to *really* clean something up, just tell me to
pretend I'm Cinderella, and I'll do it" (January 1, 1991, 8;2 and 5;0).
Rather than objecting to the idea of cleaning up alone, and whining
that Ashley and Andrea did not help, she went vigorously at her task.
Only after it was completed did she sit for a moment in her imaginary
fireplace to reflect on the day's events. Her hands lay wearily on her
dishtowel-draped lap, her eyes downcast in sad contemplation. She was
dejected and alone, overworked and unloved. But she had chosen this
role purposefully and done the work without complaint, for she knew
that though times were tough, her reward would come.

Indeed, just as the moment came for Cinderella's sisters to leave for
the ball, there was a fortuitous call from the window below Lindsey
and Ashley's bedroom. Another neighborhood friend, Daphne, was
calling to see if the girls could play. Lindsey flung open the window
and told her friend about the play already underway. She said that
Daphne could come in *if* she would agree to play the handsome prince.
When Daphne joined the game, she asked if she could play the fairy

godmother instead. "No, no," Lindsey said. "We can skip her. We need the prince more!" and Andrea and Ashley agreed. Lindsey ran for her father's sportcoat and a prince was made. Daphne embellished her attire with a hairbow for a tie and a painted-on mustache.

Cutting a whole section of the plot presented no problem for the girls. With no one to play the fairy godmother, the girls eliminated the pumpkin coach and the mice footmen. Lindsey, a child of modern times, dressed herself. Without further ado, the ball began. While Andrea and Ashley tried to capture the prince's heart, Daphne played her role cordially but with little sincere attention. Ashley looked down demurely, as any well-brought-up ugly stepsister should, but Andrea looked coquettishly over her shoulder, trying to persuade the prince to notice her. The prince remained aloof, however, until the arrival of Cinderella. Then he bowed low, bewitched by Cinderella's smile. Lindsey was dressed in simple elegance—with few additional baubles and no makeup. As Lindsey told me later, "I don't think she'd wear it, Mom."

As the play continued, they danced, they exchanged vows, and Lindsey fled the room as the clock struck twelve. A proclamation was sent throughout the land, and because there was no one to play the squire, the prince himself came to fit the shoe on all eligible females in the household. Andrea made an attempt, gritting her teeth and exclaiming over the fit. Ashley, too, had her turn, holding onto the chair for support, but to no avail. Finally, it was Cinderella's turn, and Lindsey, dressed in rags, slipped her foot into the shoe with ease. Great rejoicing followed, though Ashley and Andrea filled the air with spiteful curses. Lindsey effected a quick change and she and Daphne, her prince, were wed. This gratifying last scene, where all the pain of the past predictably becomes insignificant in the pleasure of the present, is one that Lindsey had loved from childhood.

The readings and rereadings of story language to test their predictability and transfer need not be so complicated as the enactment of an entire plot. Preparations for future uses can rely simply on the introduction of new vocabulary and its quiet storage for other occasions. Although Lindsey did not stop and question me about every new word, she often wanted to understand a particular word and its importance to the story's outcome or its apparent contradiction of her ordinary language use.[23] In reading Judith Viorst's *I'll Fix Anthony,* Lindsey asked me the meaning of "clobbered." She asked what a "crystal ball" was when we read William Steig's *Tifky Doofky.* "What's a 'float'?" she inquired as she regarded the frog in *The Tale of Mr. Jeremy Fisher,* who was waiting for a minnow to catch hold of his line.

Beatrix Potter's language raised many questions. In *The Tale of Benjamin Bunny,* Peter returns to the scene of his crime. He is nervous, and continually drops the onions that his cousin Benjamin has directed him to hold. Yet Potter tells us that *"Benjamin, on the contrary, was perfectly at home"* (p. 33), and this statement startled Lindsey. "But I thought that this was Mr. McGregor's garden!" she exclaimed. I explained that "perfectly at home" simply meant comfortable. She nodded, but did not seem at home with the answer. She asked me for an explanation in the next two rereadings (June 26, 1986, 3;7). Words or terms that defied their customary uses needed to be fixed for her, so that their role within literary texts as well as in her own daily communication might be plausible.

Lindsey wanted to be especially clear about definitions of frightening things. She was particularly insistent upon understanding the definition of a "spindle" in Trina Schart Hyman's *Sleeping Beauty.* In *Snow White,* one of her most requested fairy tales, she had several questions. "What does 'devour' mean?" she asked when the huntsman spared the child's life, thinking that the wild animals of the forest would complete a job he could not bring himself to do. "What is 'envy'?" Lindsey worried about the queen's character. "Is a 'bier' like a grave?" she asked as the dwarfs laid Snow White to rest. Time and again she requested word explanations, and she would ask the question again if she forgot a definition in a second reading. Authors of children's literature often choose the out-of-the-ordinary word or phrase rather than the simple label, offering yet another attention-getting hook for children's attention.[24]

Once Lindsey had a definition in mind, she used it. Her words reflected the musicality as well as the stylistic variance of story language. She drew people that had "cheeks like roses" and hair "as dark as the night." When Lindsey really wanted something she pleaded "I beg you!" And if she was unsuccessful in her quest, she threatened punishment: "And you shall have no pie!" Such language transformed her character, even if only momentarily (and sometimes unsuccessfully), to give her power and a role far beyond that of preschooler or just big sister.

Lindsey's incorporation of story language into conversation linked ways of talking that were often separate. In our home, the everyday demands of household maintenance ensured considerable redundancy, and direct word-referent associations were helped by the possibility of engaging our children in some of these tasks (sweeping floors, baking, making beds, cleaning bathtubs, gardening, and so on). Though Lindsey and Ashley listened to adult conversations that included abstract vocabulary, it was not our custom to address them in overly complex language. We said, "Change your clothes for the party," not "In light of the fact that you have an invitation to a friend's festivities, you should alter your attire."

Literature, however, observes no such limitations. The vocabulary and the sentence patterns are often more complex than those of everyday talk. But rather than shrink from literary language, Lindsey and Ashley requested it; when we read *Saint George and the Dragon,* they begged me to read it rather than tell it. The story is adapted from Spenser's *Faerie Queene,* and the description of the dragon exemplifies the language of the tale:

> *He reared high, monstrous, horrible, and vast, armed all over with scales of brass fitted so closely that no sword or spear could pierce them. They clashed with every movement. The dragon's wings stretched out like two sails when the wind fills them. The clouds fled before him. His huge, long tail, speckled red and black, wound in a hundred folds over his scaly back and swept the land behind him for almost half a mile. In his tail's end, two sharp stings were fixed. But sharper still were his cruel claws. Whatever he touched or drew within those claws was in deadly danger. His head was more hideous than tongue can tell, for his deep jaws gaped wide, showing three rows of iron teeth ready to devour his prey.* (Hodges)

To stop and explain every vocabulary word would have been a futile endeavor and would have broken the spell of the language as Lindsey and Ashley sat mesmerized by the approach of the dragon. Though I would often pause in stories to explain a critical word, in this case I waited for their cue. In one reading Lindsey asked me to explain "speckled" and in another reading "prey." Although a precise definition of each of the words was missing from her repertoire, she well understood that the words added up to one thing—the dragon was horrible!

In children's storybooks, the words are often packed with meaning, for the author has fewer words to describe the immensity of life. The language of story carries particularly strong weight, and words like "stepmother," "giant," "poison," and "kiss" connote worlds far beyond the confines of the letters. In our home a lie was a "Pinocchio story," brushing your teeth avoided a trip to see "Dr. De Soto," and a kiss with eyes wide open was a "Cyclops' kiss." The word "fairy" conjured up an entire universe of magical winged sisters who bring good to those who wait.

Emerging from the shower one day, I had just opened the shower curtain and reached for a towel when Lindsey appeared in the bathroom.

> "Look at me. Look at me!" she intoned in an authoritative voice. She waved Ashley's wooden rattle over me.
>
> "I am a fairy," she explained. "You are going to have a daughter. Her name will be Urana!"
>
> She remained for a moment striking a pose of fairy power, her arms held dramatically overhead. She was dressed in her new ballet shoes. Her panties bunched out from under her pink tutu. Her chest was bare, but slung carelessly over her shoulders was a white shawl clipped together at the throat with a junk jewelry charm. (June 7, 1986, 3;7)

With the words "I am a fairy," Lindsey was transformed into a beautiful being with the power to grant a woman her deepest wish. As she proclaimed the birth, she designated the child's sex; indeed, in the world of story, these miraculous births are often reserved for females. Finally, she named the child Urana, which was the most exotic name she could muster and which followed along the traditional lines of Una, Rapunzel, or Aurora.

As Lindsey held her pose, she created a story that combined crucial elements from the fairy-tale genre. How many women in stories desired children, only to receive them through the help of fairies, frogs, and fruitful longings? Snow White's mother wanted a child as white as snow, as red as blood, and with hair as black as ebony. Rapunzel's mother longed for a child, but longed for rampion more. Sleeping Beauty's mother was bathing in a pond when a frog granted her wish.

Lindsey's understanding of genre and her ability to predict the organizing frame of the coming story permitted her to make assumptions and predictions from the first few lines. It was as though her knowledge of genres of fantasy gave her an intellectual runway to take off from in her problem solving.[25] From the moment I spoke the words "Once upon a time," Lindsey was searching for similar patterns, watching for character motivation, calculating an ending. When she was a three-year-old, her incipient predictions were held in her questions. One Saturday an old Shirley Temple movie, *A Little Princess,* was on TV. As Lindsey and I settled on the couch to watch, I read her the television guide's synopsis: "A child of the Victorian era moves from rags to riches."

> "Do you know what that means?" I asked her.
> She shook her head solemnly back and forth. "No."
> "Well," I explained. "It means that the little girl was very poor and then she became rich."
> Lindsey digested this information and then asked, "Did her mommy died when she was poor?" (April 3, 1986, 3;5)

Although Lindsey was not yet familiar with the original version of *A Little Princess* (Burnett), her question was an accurate assumption. Hansel and Gretel, Cinderella, and Snow White all lost their mothers at a very early age, and eventually each character became poor and found his or her way in the world to a witch's secret cache of jewels or a handsome prince.

Lindsey's question reflected her understanding of the traditional formulas in fantasy genre, an understanding that was substantiated in a later reading of *Snow White.* Lindsey had decided to do her own rendition of the story, pulling the antenna of our tape recorder up to match her height and speaking into it like a radio announcer. She began her story with Snow White's mother:

> "And . . . she said, 'I wish I could have a child as white as snow, as red as blood, and as black as ebony.' She gave birth to a little girl. Her name is Snow White. When she was born the queen died."
> Lindsey turned to me and asked, "That what happens to queens when some child are born, huh?"
> "Sometimes that happens," I commiserated. "That's right." (June 16, 1986, 3;7)

As Lindsey grew older, her questions about genre turned to statements of fact. One night Lindsey and I read the Grimms' tale "The Clever Little Tailor" (in *Grimms' Tales for Young and Old*). The story began:

> *There was once a princess who was very proud. When a suitor presented himself, she asked him a riddle and if he couldn't answer it, she scoffed at him and sent him away. She had made it known that anyone who answered her riddle would become her husband . . .*

At this juncture, Lindsey announced that the story was "just like *King Stork*" (Pyle), another folktale with an equally challenging princess. We continued reading:

> . . . *regardless of who he might be, and one day three tailors set out to court the princess. Because of all the difficult jobs they had already managed to sew up, the two oldest were confident of success in this undertaking as well. The third was a useless young scamp, who didn't even know his trade properly, but he thought to himself: "This thing is sure to bring me luck. Where else would I find any?" The other two said to him: "Better stay home. You'll never get anywhere with that bird brain of yours."* [Grimm Brothers, p. 396]
>
> But Lindsey had other ideas: "I bet he'll get the princess . . . because in other stories when people are small and there's riddles and stuff to answer, they always get it right." (July 12, 1988, 5;8)

Lindsey's understanding of outcome was based on a knowledge of both genre and plot format, as well as mandates for character competencies. In fairy tales, characters are easily identified as good or evil, proud or humble, clever or stupid. Fairy tales have a strong focus on justice, and Lindsey held the traditional notion of justice firmly in her head: the small and meek were rewarded in the end. The patterns set in a number of texts merged to create a fairly all-encompassing outline for a certain type of story: the beautiful princess, the wicked stepmother, the rule of three often seen in the two clever elder siblings and the younger naive but well-meaning bumbler.

At seven years of age, Lindsey still searched for the "happily ever after" patterns originally set by fairy tales. She knew that Sara in *A Little Princess* (Burnett) would win out over Miss Minchin, just as Manyara, in *Mufaro's Beautiful Daughters* (Steptoe), would eventually reign over her selfish sister. She predicted that Mary would find the key to *The Secret Garden* (Burnett), and that Ramona (Cleary) would move from being a pest to being appreciated.

She then began to break the pattern of "God's in his heaven, all's right with the world" established by earlier stories. Lindsey slowly learned to accept the death of the grandmother in *Annie and the Old One* (Miles), Boo Radley's return to the isolation of his home (Lee), and E.T.'s return to his ship (Kotzwinkle). But she still resisted these unsatisfactory endings. When I told her the story and read large chunks of *Lonesome Dove* (McMurtry), we both wept bitterly at the death of Augustus.

"It's just not fair!" she later explained. "He's the main character!"

Thinking about her reasoning, I asked, "If you were the author, what would you do?"

The answer came quickly, "I would let Augustus and Lorie Darlin' get married and they would live till they died regular. They would live happily ever after." (December 20, 1989, 7;1)

Lindsey clung to the "happily ever after" ending, because in the traditional world of story, fear and loss were always overcome by beauty and love. Death held no power over the beauty of young love, and characters that did die could return with the loosening of laces, the removal of a poisoned comb, and a stumble over a bump in the road that dislodged a piece of apple. But as Lindsey made room for new literature in her world, she came to the realization that beauty existed below the surface and that immortality was only a fantasy. There was a whole world of literature beyond "happily ever after"—a world filled with alternative meanings and situations which would increasingly demand that she expand her strengths of prediction.

3

Moving to Possible Worlds

One autumn day, Lindsey and I reread *Arrow to the Sun* [McDermott]. She rarely had many comments on this story. It was as though she was so swept away by the radiant images and sparse text, she could hardly bring herself to comment verbally. Yet after this reading, she sat quietly for a few seconds and then slowly, as if in a dream, spread her hands out wide with palms up. Then she bent her elbows and her stiff hands came together, completing a triangle. With fingertips touching, she had formed herself into an arrow. Once the figure was formed, action ensued and fantasy led to practicality. She shot off the couch and into the kitchen in search of apple juice. (October 28, 1986, 3;11)

Lindsey had captured the spirit of the young Indian boy who becomes an arrow to the sun in his search for his father. Though her ultimate goal was less compelling than that of the protagonist, her pantomime still carried the excitement of journey and the angular quality of artistic form. In her search for meaning, she, too, needed to become the arrow. Lindsey had waited for the story's end before her play began. Some theorists believe that this is essential; the poetic response of the young child to literature must wait until the story is over.[1] But the interpretive expression through movement in the middle of a reading does not spoil the effect; it enhances it. In fact, it can be the child's very *participation* through movement that strengthens understanding.

While reading *Thumbelina* [Andersen], we read that the tiny child had carried a blanket to cover the dead bird and make the still form more comfortable. Lindsey got up off the couch and retrieved her own blanket, Babette. She carefully and tenderly wrapped Babette around my legs, tucking in the corners with a pat. (October 26, 1986, 3;11)

Through the physical motion of pantomime, Lindsey displayed the written emotion: her gestures were caring, her play compassionate. Thus, *motion embodied emotion,* and it was played out as it was felt. If I had asked her to store up her interpretation until the story's end, the compassion might have been lost, for in story and in life different emotions take precedence in different phases of any event. Through Thumbelina's compassion, the bird returned to life and eventually carried her to her prince. Thumbelina's compassion was not forgotten, but the joy of meeting one's true love became the overriding emotion by the end of the story. The compelling motions and emotions in a story remain stored, to be remembered and released through play.[2]

Movement Makes the Metaphor

Lindsey's and Ashley's many connections between story and movement showed that bodily actions could release symbols, as well as emotions, of story. Through motion, the girls created intertextual ties and linked "once upon a time" with the here and now. Running from a friend on the playground caused Lindsey to turn and yell tauntingly, "Run! Run as fast as you can! You can't catch me! I'm the gingerbread man!" A balloon attached to her back belt loop jounced along behind her, and jogged a memory of Pascal in *The Red Balloon* (Lamorisse). Blowing on her art paper to dry some glue caused her to "huff and puff" like the big, bad wolf. And wrapped in a black shawl, she flew through the living room like a great bird singing Sendak's rhyme, "Flapping once, flapping twice, flapping *Chicken Soup with Rice.*" Again and again the physical feel of a situation evoked a literary response recalled from illustration and literary phrasing.

In 1986, when Lindsey was nearly four, we prepared to move to California from Salt Lake City. The last days before we moved were spent packing, organizing, making lists, labeling boxes, and coping with the plethora of loose ends involved in any move. I kept getting up at odd times of the night, my head swimming with details. The day the moving men came, I woke up early to work on the computer, make final lists, and enter addresses. The excitement was palpable, and Lindsey was tremendously high as she raced downstairs, discarded her nightgown, and flew to the back porch bathroom. When she returned, her underwear had been abandoned as well. She climbed up the counter like some naked gibbon and perched on the edge, demanding her breakfast.

"Wait just a minute," I said.

Lindsey began to delight in her lack of attire and danced upon the counter. She ended up stomping in circles shouting "Break-fast! Break-fast!" in time. The heavy thud of her feet on the counter, combined with her increased height and appetite triggered a gigantic response. "Fee Fi Foe Fum," she bellowed. "I smell the blood of an Englishman. Be he live or be he dead—I'll grind his bones to make my bread!" Like the good giant's wife, I dutifully left my work to prepare a much-needed meal. (August 12, 1986, 3;9)

In Lindsey's breakfast dance, her enactment of the poem brought immediate action. The giant, with his all-encompassing power, would never have had to wait, and neither should she. Motion takes the mind to action, and action brings results.

Acting the part of the giant was a unique bit of drama, for Lindsey's characterizations in her preschool years were usually those of a young and beautiful girl. In full-fledged dramatizations, she chose to play Red Riding Hood over the wolf. She was Snow White, never a dwarf or a wicked queen. She was Cinderella, not an ugly stepsister.[3] From time to time she would take up a role that differed from the pattern of acceptable, gendered roles of wife, mother, princess, or sweet innocent child lost on the path or forced to sit among the cinders. Literary texts modeled these roles in her image, and Lindsey had the props of everyday life to support her adornment—the jewels, veils, tiaras, hoods, and magic wands necessary to create the desired effect. For Christmas and other occasions, family members often sent books, but they also sent party dresses, beribboned headbands, junk jewelry, and a dress-up box complete with flowered hats and a feather boa. When Lindsey was a little older than four, she hoped that Santa would bring her heart's desire—a tutu—and in her annual letter of request she was explicit:

December 23, 1986

Dear Santa,

I love you, Santa. I want a tutu . . . a pink tutu. And I want a wand and a crown. I would also like blue ballet shoes. I would dance in them. Doo doo doo da de da. That's how I would dance in them.

On Christmas Eve we'll leave you a treat. We'll leave apples and oranges for your good big tummy, and carrots for the reindeer.

Love,
Lindsey

Neighborhood girls had their own wish-lists, which they discussed avidly with Lindsey. Every afternoon they joined in games that set the stage for playing out female roles: big and little sisters, teachers and children in class, queens and their maids. "I'm Kundara," I heard Lindsey announce one afternoon. On another occasion, she said, "I'm Laura and Ashley is Mary." Many afternoons I heard Lindsey and a neighbor negotiating over the roles of Dorothy and Glenda (Ashley often got the role of Toto). For Lindsey's sixth birthday party, her girlfriends brought "Barbie" and all her accoutrements into our home. I occasionally allowed Lindsey and Ashley to wear makeup for dramatizations, and they rummaged my drawers for scarves and stockings which they could wear on their heads and thus imitate the look and feel of long hair.

Though I tended to live in my jeans when at home, wore old sweatshirts to do my daily fast walk, and wore a helmet when bike riding, Lindsey preferred my "dress-up" work clothes, offering me advice on color coordination and accessories. Lindsey persistently chose to protect what she viewed as behaviors and clothing choices that assured her femininity. For years, she steadfastly refused to wear anything but dresses. I remember the exasperation I felt on having to stuff her dress into a snow suit and find suitable tights to keep her legs warm. Only the possibility that boys "might see [her] underwear" called for a general shift to pants and shorts when she entered public school kindergarten. Still, she carefully created her ensemble each day, adding a belt or tying ribbons through plain buttonholes. At seven, she tried to refuse to wear a helmet while bike riding, claiming it would "mess up" her hair, and she continually managed to "forget" her helmet at school. Once home, the shorts would immediately be replaced by the long skirts or tutus in her dress-up box, and play would begin.

While a traditional notion of femininity predominated in her play, there were also occasions for throwing off these roles and adopting alternative models to get what she wanted. Lindsey recognized that male characters in literature were not confined only to features opposed to those of women. Little male rabbits were known to cry. Little boys were understood to wish for a doll. And young men of gentle spirit could serve as guides to secret gardens. But it wasn't until the end of second grade that Lindsey began to take more notice of the traditional role of men and boys, and want to emulate them. At recess, she hung out with the boys in her class who were playing soccer and ball games. "The girls just talk and walk around," she complained. And after months of talk about getting her hair cut, she had it cut "like a boy's" just prior to the onset of third grade. Her shift in gender focus spilled over into literature, and she began to take more notice of the role of princes and kings. In games, she gave the previously more coveted female roles to Ashley and took on the male roles for herself.

The season that stretched between second and third grades was a "Robin Hood" summer. We had read abbreviated texts in the past, but when the movie (starring Kevin Costner) came out, Lindsey entered Sherwood Forest with a vengeance. In contrast to movie critics everywhere, Lindsey gave the film a four-star rating. When she found the movie-based book in a local store, she begged me to buy it, but then she spotted an illustrated version for children (McSpadden). I told her she could choose one, and she perched on a stack of books and leafed carefully through them, asking me to read random passages from both so that she could hear the language. She ultimately decided on the children's version (which had more traditional language, including phrases like "by my troth" and "'Tis well said indeed") because, as she explained, it "sounds truer to the real story" (June 15, 1991, 8;7). It also had illustrations by Greg Hildebrandt, whose pictures provided realistic clues for the costuming Lindsey created in her play. She assigned the role of Maid Marian to Ashley, and, after studying the illustrations, adorned her with medieval accoutrements. Yet she reserved the role of Robin for herself, thrusting my long-handled knife sharpener into her shorts and flinging a shawl over her shoulders. She strode about the neighborhood, addressing children as "Little John" and "Will Scarlett," assembling quite a crew of "Merry Men."

In most of her early play, however, Lindsey chose the role of the innocent young beauty for herself and gave me the antagonist's role. I was the goblin, the stepmother, and the wolf. Yet Lindsey did not like the antagonist's roles to be played too realistically.[4] Once, while reading *Little Red Riding Hood* (Grimm Brothers), Lindsey stood to play the part as I read.

The text read, *"When she got there, she was amazed to find the door open, and she tiptoed in."* With this, Lindsey leaped off the couch and immediately rose up on her toes. *"She felt quite frightened, but she didn't know why."* Lindsey's mouth opened in a round ohhh.

"What's wrong?' she thought. 'I always like coming to Grandmother's so much. Why should I feel so afraid? Can it be because she is sick?'" Lindsey crept toward me.

When the time came for Red Riding Hood's evaluation of her grandmother's face, Lindsey took over.

"Grandmother . . ." I began.

"What big eyes you have." Lindsey's voice was timid and incredulous at the same time.

Although this veered from the exact wording of the text, I followed Lindsey's lead. "The better to see you with, my dear."

She was beginning to back away and would be too far out of reach for my upcoming grab. "Come closer," I demanded. *"Grandmother . . ."*

Lindsey's voice was barely audible. "What big ears you have."

"The better to hear you with, my dear."

Lindsey was getting scared. This part of the story has always been a tug on her emotions. She loves the thrill of fear but tries to deny it entry. She crept a few inches toward me and then stopped the scene.

"You're not the wolf. You're not the wolf!" she cried, her hand cutting through the air with a gesture of finality. (April 29, 1986, 3;5)

Lindsey's denial revealed her dual reaction—her attraction and aversion to the antagonist. She was drawn to the wolf, yet ultimately attempted to shut him out. But more often than not, she did let him in, for she knew that only through the wolf could Red Riding Hood reach her final resolution.[5]

Lindsey's struggle to understand this push-pull nature of the villain came through again and again in her play. She would ask Kenny or me to play the wolf, and then scream in fear and delight when we pounced; sometimes she would suddenly announce the play was off. Her preschool teacher mentioned that Lindsey was good at leading other children in play, because she understood a story's ultimate outcome. When the teacher read the above anecdote about Lindsey's interpretation of Red Riding Hood, she explained:

Knowing the outcome is such a saving grace. A lot of children who get into dramatic play don't do that, and they'll just play along, and sometimes they'll get so worked up that they don't know what the end's going to be. You can lose them sometimes in the middle, or the play just falls apart. When there is that . . . wholeness to it, and you do know what the goal is, it's so much safer for them. And

Lindsey is one child who is able to give that to other children. She likes to give the scope. She does give that sense of the wholeness of the game, as opposed to "let's just play." (June 4, 1987, 4;7)

A sense of the whole carried Lindsey through the danger of many stories. As Sleeping Beauty she approached the waiting spindle, and as Gretel she nibbled off a corner of the witch's window. In the dramatic motion of play, the danger was tangible, the consequences known, and resolution could always be assured by verbal announcement that the play was off. At the end of her fear was the ultimate destination: rescue and, quite often, marriage.

One day, she began to build an edifice with her brightly colored Duplo blocks. What began as Sleeping Beauty's castle quickly turned into Rapunzel's tower.

> "Hey, I know," she began to build in a greater hurry now. "We'll build a tower. We'll cut off the door and cut off the window and the witch can't get in . . . and we'll get married in there."
>
> I could see that she had somehow left *Sleeping Beauty* behind, and questioned her intention. "But if we don't have doors or windows, how will we get in?"
>
> "Easy!" She shrugged her shoulders and extended a hand toward me, palm up, in a way somewhat reminiscent of an Arab trader. "I have long hair and we can climb up." (She obviously did not see climbing up her own hair as a problem.)
>
> "How can I do it?" I questioned.
>
> She tilted her head to the side, drawing her hair into one strand. "Put your fingernails on my hair and climb, climb, CLIMB and then we can get MARRIED!!" (June 10, 1986, 3;7)

Weddings were Lindsey's favorite scenes to play, for elaborate costuming was assured.[6] In preparation for a wedding scene, Lindsey drew upon her most imaginative thinking. T-shirts became long skirts. Ruffles and frills were added through the transformation of scarves and hair ribbons. A brightly colored bead necklace clung to her throat, and her wrists were bangled with "jelly" bracelets. The junk jewelry charms that ordinarily hung from a necklace were worn as "wedding rings," as if one ring were not enough to ensure a proper ceremony.

The wedding that Kenny and I chose had been well below Lindsey's elaborate standards. In the winter of 1977, we had hiked up a snowy path in the company of a few friends to be married by another friend, who happened to be the judge of a small mountain town. I wore blue jeans, multiple sweaters, and an old down parka. Kenny wore the same. In the informal picture displayed in our living room, our faces emerged from ski caps and woolen scarves. My hair was damp with snow. At three, Lindsey could not believe that these were the only photos of our wedding. "This is your wedding picture?" she would ask incredulously. Friends of ours, however, had been married in style, and when Lindsey saw the large, formal, glossy photographs set in the embossed leather album—the tuxedos, the abundant flowers, and the bride all in white— she exclaimed, "Now, that's a wedding!"

Initially, Lindsey's concept of ritual in books centered around weddings. She reconceived all celebratory ceremonies as nuptial affairs. Later, she acknowledged ritual in her own life, and though the prevalence and ascendant position of weddings remained firmly fixed in her repertoire of story scripts, she recognized homecomings, family reunions, Christmases, and birthdays, as well as more routine events, such as bedtimes and mealtimes, as markers of human relationships and the passage of time.

Lindsey expected certain visual images to indicate certain ritualized occasions. In the story *Star Wars,* Princess Leia gives Han and Luke medals in a hero's welcome, and Lindsey was convinced of its nuptial possibilities.

> After introducing me to Han and Luke with a wave of her hand through the empty air, Lindsey stood in regal reverie for her wedding. She held herself very erect, with her chin high, and clasped her hands quietly in front. Suddenly, she broke from her stance to check the picture in the book and then returned to her position, but this time her hands fell to her sides, in imitation of the picture of Princess Leia in the final pages. (June 30, 1986, 3;7)

Just as visual images were integral to her acceptance of certain celebratory events in literature, so visual image and movement dominated her thematic play. To dramatize abstract themes (such as happiness, satisfaction, or security), she used props to symbolize certain entire scenes or events. A veil over a long, tattered T-shirt called up an entire wedding party; certain gestures of the extended hand, the acceptance of a ring, and a formal stance provided the potential for the full development of a castle scene, complete with king and queen on the throne and anxious prince and princess awaiting the ceremony. Dramatic play therefore combined the present with unique, selected details of sweeping analogy from past literary texts. In these details, activated in play, story and life meet, combine and recombine, and create possibilities for the future.

Along with bits of costume, jewelry, gesture, and facial expression, children may use words to announce the full scripting of sociodramatic play. In such play, to create possible worlds, children move their critical, logical, and hypothetical scene-building through their experiences with literature and their acceptance of the fact that children have limited access to "real" props, full costumes, and stable, secure environments for the full unrolling of their imaginary scripts. Thus, though they acknowledge and often announce what they perceive to be the rules and dialogues within individual pieces of literature as well as certain genres (such as fairy tales and myths), they acknowledge the limitations of bringing all of these rules and dialogues into their current play. The invitation to play *Jack and the Beanstalk* calls for certain imaginative adaptations of the available environment, in order to create a thin, high structure. Parental rules and children's real-world bumps and knocks warn against going to extremes in trying to re-create the beanstalk. Pantomime, or substantially lowered but sternly announced transitions ("So now we've climbed the beanstalk—we're at the castle now"), carry children up and over the troublesome spots for duplication in sociodramatic play.

Although Ashley joined in the enactment of text, she often preferred to balance her playtime with a variety of other activities. She built colorful block designs that stretched across our living room rug, drew pictures, colored, and played with her baby doll. She rode her bicycle, roller skated, and climbed the light-pole outside our door, pulling herself up again and again. She and her best friend, Nate, who lived across the courtyard, played "house" and "store" and molded shapes with clay. They filled bright balloons with water and tended these "water babies," carefully feeding them with bottles until they ultimately tired of them and smashed them on the sidewalk.

Like Lindsey, Nate was a child who spent long hours enacting text, with Peter Pan, Luke Skywalker, and Robin Hood being a few of his favorites. He had a rack of plastic swords, and Ashley and I contributed to his arsenal on his fourth birthday by presenting him with a knight's plastic helmet and breastplate. Many an afternoon in the winter of their fifth year, I read the two friends stories and then copied illustrations from books for them to color. Nate consistently chose illustrations of men with swords drawn in battle, while Ashley chose female figures with long hair and longer gowns. Nate carried his pictures home in triumph and his mother mounted them on his bedroom wall.

Over the course of time, Ashley and Nate's friendship became storybook romance. In their fourth year, they agreed to marry, and even after they reached and passed their fifth birthdays, they did not give up their resolution. Nate brought Ashley a ring from Disneyland, and they discussed children. The years of playing mommy and daddy and caring for water babies spilled over into their future plans. Still, as with all couples, there were disagreements. Nate's penchant for fantasy play tired Ashley at times, and if negotiations concerning coloring versus "jousting" failed, she would sometimes return home to take up her crayons in peace.

At home, though she often joined Lindsey's enactments, she did not have the same interest in long-playing productions. One afternoon, after I had picked up the girls from summer school, I told them they had to postpone their play and help me clean the house. Lindsey wrangled for a compromise, suggesting that if their friend Andrea came over they could play Robin Hood and accomplish the household duties. I reluctantly agreed, and waited for them to dress in full costume with Ashley as Maid Marian, Andrea as her handmaiden, and Lindsey as Robin. Lindsey tried to give me the role of Much, the cook, but knowing there were real tasks to be done, I negotiated for more power and took the role of King Arthur.

> I directed Ashley and Andrea out to the car to "clean out our forest hut," while Lindsey was sent to the kitchen to do the dishes and "prepare for a feast." The girls performed their tasks with much energy, until the time came to wash the windows. Lindsey and Andrea grabbed a roll of paper towels and set to work, but Lindsey stopped Ashley from joining in.
>
> "You're Maid Marian. You sit," she commanded.
>
> Ashley immediately began to cast off her medieval costume, much to Lindsey's disgust. When Lindsey tried to dissuade her, Ashley retorted, "I don't want to *sit*. I'm not Marian. I'm Ashley and I want to do the windows!" (July 11, 1991, 8;8 and 5;7)

Playing story was fine, but not if it separated her from the real action. Even doing windows held more allure than demurely sitting on the sidelines.

Though Lindsey was often moving at center stage, by the age of four she was increasingly supplementing her movement and pantomime with her own verbal analogies and metaphors from our reading. These she savored silently and pulled out to prop up her proposals to change the rules of the world, so that she could mold reality into new possibilities. Through metaphors and elliptical similes, she shortcut the step of saying "this is *like* (some literary scene, character, or event)." She simply announced the metaphors in a figurative comparison (for example, "he's a jolly postman"), and though often willing to refer her father and me to the particular literary reference from which she drew her basis for comparison, she rarely elaborated on *why* or *how* she drew the comparison.

All of literature became her frame of reference from which to draw characters, period, costume, objects, events, emotions, and other features. She expected us not to take her words at face value but to use them as sufficient evidence from which to move to correct judgments (her own) about texts and about her tests of real-world events. She was happy to link the odd with the obvious and expected us to follow her example, though almost never had the features of events she chose for metaphor been salient in our attention as we read to her.

One morning we were rushing about to get ready for school. I quickly made Lindsey's sandwich, while she got out her lunchbox and washed her apple. Ashley's preschool program was over before lunch, but each child brought a piece of fruit for snacktime. I directed Ashley to our basket of fruit to select her daily fare. She rummaged about, selecting and rejecting, and finally chose a large orange.

> "I need a great, *huge* orange for our great, *huge* snack!" she exclaimed in a loud voice.
> Surprised, and feeling worried that I'd missed some preschool announcement, I asked, "Oh, is today some special day at school?" Earlier in the month they had made "stone soup," and I thought perhaps today was another feast.
> Lindsey laughed. "No, mom, she's just being the bear from Goldilocks!" Both girls chuckled at my naiveté. (February 26, 1990, 7;3 and 4;2)

Later, I checked Ashley's edition of *Goldilocks and the Three Bears* (Brett) and found the passage that both girls had recognized so easily: *"They each had a bowl for their porridge—a little bowl for the little, small, wee bear, a middle-sized bowl for the middle-sized bear, and a great, huge bowl for the great, huge bear."* While I had been centered on the reality of school schedules and perceived responsibilities, the girls had been active in metaphorical play. The size of the orange brought about a comparison to the size of papa bear, with his great, huge accoutrements. Long after I had gotten the joke and laughed, Ashley continued to revel in her wordplay. She repeated it several times on the way to school, holding out the orange and rubbing her round tummy in anticipated pleasure.

Following a technique frequently used in literature, both Lindsey and Ashley often summed up their view of events using metaphors and similes. One night, after Lindsey and I had finished reading, she stretched out in bed and I scratched her back while we discussed some of the day's events. We had spent the twilight time planting grass seed on some of the bald patches in the front lawn. Kenny and she had dug and chopped at the hard ground, and I had followed with fertilizer and seed. Flipping over in bed, Lindsey asked me how long it would take for the grass seed to come up. I told her that I thought it would take only a few days, since grass grew very quickly.

"Like rabbits?" she queried.

Struggling to understand the connection, I repeated her question back to her. "What do you mean—'like rabbits'?"

She looked at me in frustration. "You know, *like rabbits.*" She reminded me of Americans in Paris trying to make their English understood—she raised her voice and spoke very slowly. Surprisingly, I caught her drift and thought of a discussion we had had several weeks before.

"Are you thinking of something we read in a book?" I asked.

"Yes!"

"Which one?"

"The one with the light shining down," Lindsey exclaimed.

Now I knew that I had correctly guessed her reasoning. She was talking about Spier's *Noah's Ark.* In this story, God relates his instructions to Noah via a spiritual light. During the voyage, a number of the animals have babies, including the rabbits, who have many babies. I remembered Lindsey asking me why the babies were the same size as their parents, when this was not the case with the elephants or some of the other animals. I told her that rabbits grow very fast.

Still, I did not want to jump the proverbial gun. I asked her if she knew the name of the book. She didn't. I asked her if she could find the book. Eager for the opportunity to get out of bed, she leaped to the floor. She searched through the large stack of books at her bedside.

> When she found it she cried, "Here it is! *Jonah's Ark!*"
> I laughed at her biblical confusion and corrected, "Yes. *Noah's Ark.*"
> "That's what I said," she declared. Then she proceeded to flip through the book until she had found the rabbits streaming from the ark, and reminded me just how fast they grow. (May 1, 1986, 3;6)

At times, Kenny and I seemed to accept the girls' metaphors as declared, with few questions about the reasons for their matching of an actual scene with a literary view. Just as we would not be likely in casual conversation to ask someone to explain why her friend is "a rock," we did not try to pull salient features of comparison from the girls.

One evening, after Ashley and I dropped Lindsey off at her gymnastics class, we emerged from the building to be greeted by a brilliantly blue evening sky.

> "Look at that sky," I exclaimed. "It's beautiful."
> Ashley gazed up into the darkening sky. "Yes, it's a blue and nightingale sky."
> I clasped her hand and praised her metaphor, "What a beautiful thing to say!"
> We continued walking in silence, watching the sky. But when we reached the car, Ashley turned to me and asked, "What's a nightingale?" (February 15, 1990, 4;2)

Ashley had chosen a word of beauty, a word she could only have encountered in written text, to capture the indescribable loveliness of the evening sky. *The Nightingale*, by Hans Christian Andersen, was a tale we had borrowed from the library months before, and although she had forgotten the definition of "nightingale," she remembered the beauty attached to the word. The sky was too brilliant for ordinary words with known referents.

At other times, however, announcements of metaphors and similes, whether from text to text or from life to text, drew our analytic attention. One winter afternoon, we set out with friends to go sledding in the snowy canyon near our home in Utah. By the time we arrived, late afternoon was fast approaching and the cool fingers of twilight drew across the canyon. Using our fleet snowtube, Kenny and Lindsey flew down the hill several times before I decided to brave it. The first time was frightening and thrilling, and I held Lindsey so tight she yelled, "Let go of me, Mom!"

Rejecting my more cautious approach to sledding, Lindsey asked our friend Steve to take her up for the next ride. She was instantly rewarded. They started higher and went faster, and at the bottom of the hill Steve spun Lindsey around and around on the snowtube.

> Skidding in circles through the snow, Lindsey screamed, "This is just like Thumbelina!"
> Ever the literary intruder, I ran up and said, "Why?"
> "Because it is," she said. And I failed to get any further explanation.
> (March 29, 1986, 3;4)

Thinking carefully about the incident later, I made a trip to the library and checked out a copy of Andersen's tale, making sure to get the same version we had read weeks before. In one of the first of Thumbelina's adventures, she is left on a lily pad. Andersen writes:

> *The fish swimming in the water below came to the surface and looked curiously at Thumbelina. "Oh, please help me," she said. "I must get away from here."*
> *And so the fish began to gnaw at the lily stalk with their sharp little teeth.*
> *At last the leaf broke free and floated down the stream. Away went Thumbelina, gently spinning with the current.*

A young child's movements often evoke a literary metaphor. As Lindsey spun round and round on her snowtube lily pad, she could envision herself as the tiny Thumbelina spinning into the great expanse of the world.

Matching and Mediating Texts

It is easy to recognize that children move from text to text across literary sources and that the literary works themselves may mediate the children's daily communication. It is more difficult to recognize the various types of grammatical rules, stylistics, and pragmatics that are at work as children manipulate, adapt, and negotiate matches and adaptations among several different sets of dialogues. The first of these sets takes place within the literary texts themselves. Dialogues most evident at the surface are, first, the dialogues of the characters themselves and, second, the prior dialogues that led characters to accept their current social situations. Beyond are those between author/narrator and character, which come through in the narrative, and those between author and reader, which are often generously amplified when children know something of the author's life outside the literary text.[7]

In addition, similar locations of dialogue take place within the child's life, as she recognizes that, in books, certain kinds of literary dialogues are called for by particular settings, situations, and emotions. These fit or match the dialogues in her own life, especially through the mediation of play, and the details or features of connection among book, play, and life are highly idiosyncratic. Children, at particular ages, moods, and moments, will see and remember certain details that trigger the memory of a particular piece of speech, fragment of scene, gesture, or facial expression and its connection to a recent event. These are occasions on which the dialogues of books get replayed back through the child and either remain in her head or erupt, as direct or reported speech, into the situation at hand. Thus, children in such situations are combining at least three types of dialogues: those of the remembered text; those adapted and used in the real moment; and those prior dialogues of figures in authority that caution restraint, consideration of politeness rules, or existing pragmatics.[8]

The child moving among possible worlds is thus enmeshed in the process of teasing apart how dialogues came to be within literary texts and how she can best operate within the set of social relations and desired actions of the current situation. Admitting these private replayings, and no doubt numerous reconsiderations of literary texts within children's heads, forces adults to see in the complexity of language and action how children learn by constant comparison of situations. But within these replayings—which are literary and thus both past and retrievable—children can and do draw and redraw rules, words, meanings, actions, and perceptions of adaptation. These redrawings often critique—from the child's perspective—the real world as adults control it, and literary texts that give children and small animals greater wit, power, and wisdom than adults fortify children's abilities to use literary reference to take on their real world for the purposes of reform—or at least scolding commentary.

A text that is known to a child does not remain in its original state or even in a steady, stable form; instead, the child rewrites it. Texts become transformative stock to which young readers can return again and again as they figure out their own roles, words, actions, and critiques of their current situations. In addition, literary words amplify in memorable chunks the language abilities of children, who know the appropriate emotions to express but who may yet be unable to formulate complete grammatical utterances or call up precise, politely acceptable words.[9]

Often, story language gave Lindsey the verbal ammunition she needed to define her feelings. Kenny and I had certain rules of the neighborhood that we taught her to follow. She was allowed to play only in our courtyard, and if she decided to visit a friend, she had to inform us. One day when I called to her, she didn't come. I walked out to the center of the courtyard, calling loudly and looking everywhere. Still no Lindsey. I went to three neighboring houses, but no one had seen her. Just as I was beginning to panic, Lindsey came skipping out from another neighbor's house.

> "Hi, Mom!" she yelled jubilantly.
> I was in no mood for enthusiasm. I marched her home, up the stairs, and into her room. As we marched, I berated her disobedience. "I love you, but sometimes I don't like the things you do."
> When she saw the reality of time in her room looming before her, she burst into tears. "I love you, too!" she sobbed.
> I closed the door but could hear her slump to the floor and say, "I love you. But I don't know why. You are nothing but a bother!" (October 25, 1987, 4;11)

These words were taken from *Who's in Rabbit's House?* (Aardema), and are spoken by the elephant who saves Rabbit from drowning: *"'I saved you,' she said. 'But I don't know why. You are nothing but a bother.'"* Though the situation was dissimilar, Lindsey had seen a new application for the words: they seemed perfectly appropriate for a mother who loves and punishes at the same time. She did not need to have the book in front of her to re-create the experience. She had taken the experience from the text and had made it her own, substituting a key phrase far more appropriate to her situation. For my own part, Lindsey's outcry might have led to further punishment had the words not come from text. Instead of being insulted, I was amused. Lindsey often used literature to express rather dangerous thoughts in a socially acceptable way.[10]

Literature could sometimes provide an escape from punishment as well. Early one morning I heard Ashley let out a yowl. Running into the living room, I was just in time to see Lindsey give Ashley a good hard pat on the side of her head. Her other palm was cupping the opposite side of Ashley's head.

> "Lindsey," I scolded. "Don't give Ashie such a hard pat. You'll hurt her!"
> "It's not Ashie, Mom. It's the gum baby." Quickly she put her feet up against Ashley's stomach.
> "See," she explained. "I'm the fairy stuck to the gum baby." (June 10, 1986, 3;7)

In Haley's African tale *A Story A Story,* a fairy is captured through the use of a small wooden baby covered with sticky gum. When the "baby" does not respond to the fairy's demands, the fairy slaps it and becomes inextricably stuck. In her fury the fairy slaps it again and finally kicks it, but she only exacerbates her predicament. Lindsey had used a literary excuse to take out a bit of vengeance on her sister.

Lindsey used words from text to shape and soften judgments, as well as to negotiate the inevitable conflicts with her baby sister. One afternoon I asked her to accompany me on my fast walk. She excitedly agreed, and grabbed her bike so she could "keep up." As we walked and rode through our neighborhood, I moved at a fairly fast clip, pumping my arms vigorously up and down. Lindsey, however, pedaled her bike in a leisurely way, circling around me several times. We talked the whole way, and since I was unaccustomed to carrying on a conversation during my exercise, my voice became rather breathy.

> Lindsey regarded me and complained, "Mom, I thought you said we were going to go fast. Here you are huffing and puffing and I'm just dawdling!"
> I laughed at the contrast in our perceptions. Here I was feeling fairly young and vigorous and Lindsey saw me "huffing and puffing" with the futile blowing of the old wolf. I was also surprised by her choice of vocabulary:
> "Dawdling?!" I exclaimed. "Where'd you get that word?"
> She rolled her eyes, "From Pearl, Mom. From Pearl." (February 10, 1990, 7;3)

She was referring to the female heroine in William Steig's story *The Amazing Bone.* Pearl is a pig who, though bound for more exciting adventures, has time to relax on her way home from school: *"It was a brilliant day, and instead of going straight home from school, Pearl dawdled. She watched the grownups in town at their grownup work, things she might someday be doing."* Lindsey was watching me, and seemed less than excited that someday she, too, might need to take an extra breath during simple exercise. Still, the word "dawdling" was less harsh than a point-blank remark to the effect that I was getting out of shape or that I was a "slowpoke"—a word she often used with her sister.

At seven, Lindsey was frequently able to attribute the literary source of her word choice, particularly if the word came from Steig. A wizard with words, Steig would never substitute an ordinary word when a more precise and dazzling word would do. Ashley likewise used his words, but, at four years of age, she could rarely tell me the source.

One afternoon, Ashley discovered a spider on a web underneath a corner table. Having an intense dislike for these creatures, she began to yell:

> "A spider! A spider! Go away, you spider!" she began to wave her hands threateningly close to the web.
>
> I ordered her to stop tormenting the creature, explaining for the hundredth time that spiders were good animals who did us no harm and ate pesky flies.
>
> She hesitatingly left the spider alone and turned back to her coloring. But seconds later she leaned toward the spider once more and issued her Parthian shot.
>
> "Scrabboonit!" she shouted, waving her fist in the air. (April 18, 1990, 4;4)

I recognized a key word from *The Amazing Bone,* in which a talking bone uses magical incantations to transform a threatening fox and save Pearl:

> *"Adoonis ishgoolak keebokkin yibapp!"* it went on. *The fox, clothes and all, was now the size of a mouse.*
>
> *"Scrabboonit!" the bone ordered, and the mouse—that is, the minuscule fox—scurried away and into a hole.*

I took the word "scrabboonit" to be a humorous combination of "Scram!" "Beat it!" and "Git!" and each time I had read the story in the past, I had yelled the word, waving my fist in the air. Ashley adopted both my tone and my gesture when she yelled at the spider, but rejected any notion of imitation. When I asked her where she had got the word, she said, "I don't know. I just made it myself!" Her words echo the wonder of the bone, who also questions the source of his words:

> *"I didn't know you could do magic!" Pearl breathlessly exclaimed.*
> *"Neither did I," said the bone.*
> *"Well, what made you say those words?"*
> *"I wish I knew," the bone said. "They just came to me, I <u>had</u> to say them. I must have picked them up somehow, hanging around with that witch."* (Steig, 1976, n.p.)

Ashley, too, must have picked her words up somehow, hanging around with books.

In children's reported speech, which often lacks attribution to the literary source, the child's "real" feelings are identified with those of the character (or the adult reader's interpretation of character) who uttered the original words. The bone wanted to rid himself of a fox, and Ashley had to contend with her spider. The situations were similar, and the word chosen for dealing with that situation was the same. Only the end result was different, since Ashley's spider refused to scurry away and instead held to its web throughout her verbal onslaught.

Later, however, Ashley was able to supply a citation, though in her references titles were often less accurate than focused on particular characters or actions. One afternoon, Lindsey, Ashley, Nate, and I were reading together on our small patio. Lindsey and Nate sat mesmerized by the text, but Ashley wandered about, looking at the flowers and picking strands of chives, which she nibbled. She tried to get Nate's attention, but he ignored her, his eyes fixed on the book. After several futile attempts, she laughingly spit a small piece of chive in his direction.

> "Ashley," I scolded. "Spitting is out! Say you're sorry to Nate."
> Ashley studied her friend and then turned to me with a smirk, "Well, the kids in *Viola Swamp* use spitballs, so I can, too."
> "If you like Viola Swamp so much, maybe I should send her over to talk to you about spitting," I retorted.
> Ashley swallowed her chive with a gulp and solemnly returned to her seat. (July 14, 1991, 5;7)

Although the true title of the story is *Miss Nelson is Missing!* (Allard), Ashley's reference was accurate in content. Still, when I chose to fight literary fire with fire, she backed down, for Viola Swamp is a notorious substitute teacher with a commanding voice and black fingernails. Her response to spitting would have been shriller than mine, and Ashley knew it.

We often perceive a thing against the backdrop of something else not fully perceived. On everyday occasions, when Lindsey and Ashley drew metaphorical connections to literary texts, they expected us to square or reshape the current context to fit with the frame of reference behind what they had said. They indirectly ordered us to move with them back into another text. In so doing, they called our attention to possible reshapings of the current world according to rules they had extracted from their reading of literature. The girls assumed not only that we knew their literary worlds but that we were also fully aware of and in command of the rules of behavior for the actual world. However, their indirect ways of calling us to their literary world most often put them in charge, since they had chosen the texts of reference. It was as though they commanded us to remember their text of reference and to call up the specific detail of illustration or text from which they drew on any particular occasion. But once they had commanded us back to the text of their choice, we were left to do the work of arriving at the result of the figurative comparison. They had set a puzzle for us, and we had to reach the solution by knowing both text and actual situation and creating our own system of likenesses and salient substitutions.

It was within book-reading that Lindsey and Ashley's sense of metaphor first surfaced. They recognized that in the book-reading activity, we were jointly involved in drawing, stretching, testing, and teasing meaning from the words and illustrations. To extend that activity overtly, they often moved into their actual world the strategies of metaphor and sociodramatic play, to sustain us in the mutually recognized task of making sense. For Lindsey and Ashley, the texts of children's literature often mediated that "other" perspective, not through the texts' reflections of fantasy but through the coherence of the worlds created as totalities from each text. Talk with adult readers about books often focused on prediction through metaphor—how one bit or fragment of each text might have been changed and might then, as a consequence, have shifted other parts of the outcomes.

One morning at the library, I selected *A Baby Sister for Frances*, by Russell Hoban, hoping to elicit some discussion of Lindsey's reactions to her new baby sister. Although the theme was vastly different from that of another Hoban text, *Bedtime for Frances*, which we owned,

Lindsey began to notice the similarities immediately. In the beginning of *A Baby Sister for Frances,* Father decides that it is time for bed and gives Frances a piggyback ride to her room. "That's just like the old one," Lindsey exclaimed, referring to *Bedtime for Frances.* "Frances always gets a piggyback ride to bed." Lindsey displayed not only envy (obvious in her voice) but a memory of something I had forgotten. Later I looked up the episode in her other text and found the illustrations remarkably similar. In both, Frances is perched high on her Father's back and Father is smoking his pipe with a contented smile.

We continued reading. In the story, Frances is tucked into bed with all her favorite stuffed animals. She lies in bed with eyes wide open, saying goodnight to her parents.

> "Does she close her eyes?" Lindsey queried.
> "Yes, I think she will. It's bedtime," I answered.
> "That's not like the old one. In the old one she can't close her eyes.
> She can't get to sleep." (March 26, 1986, 3;4)

Although her assumption did not play out in this episode from Frances' life, the question held true for the character in general. In *Bedtime for Frances,* the heroine has a severe case of child's insomnia, complete with imaginary tigers, giants, and spiders. Following these occasions, we read on as though to test the accumulated information that lay behind the similarity claims she had made. Such perceptions led not to a simple cause-and-effect relationship but instead to a sense of the interdependence of features and actions within texts, as these played themselves out in the lives of characters.

This testing of overt givens within texts models the possibility of improvising in children's everyday worlds. Here, the term "improvisation" means the negotiating, masking, and speaking in other voices that children perform or utter spontaneously in response to events in their own lives. Within improvisation—the extemporaneous performance or utterance that meets an immediate need or comments on an immediate scene or situation—children can demonstrate their acknowledgment of what are for them at particular moments the internally coherent rule systems in both literature and life and of the highly personalized mediating process through which the dialogues between the two take place. The transformative nature of their talk reflects multiple voices of text and life in a dynamic dialogue—worlds talking together.[11]

Any dichotomization of life and literature is, then, much too simple to capture the interweaving of social and cognitive knowledge Lindsey and Ashley displayed in their various zigzags between literature and current experience. They "read" texts differently at different times, and they "reread" them back into their world with varying and various intentions and expectations of rules, in order to explain and explore that world. They brought to bear textual rules of operation as they themselves tested or affirmed their own understanding of standards currently at work in everyday situations.

One afternoon, Lindsey and I were immersed in the final chapters of Laura Ingalls Wilder's *Little House in the Big Woods*. Laura's cousin Charley goes to the fields to help Laura's father and Uncle Henry cut and shock the wheat harvest. Charley, however, does hardly any work at all, and instead tricks the men by raising several false alarms. They stop their work to run to his aid, thinking he has seen a snake. There are snakes in the woods, but Charley is only teasing them and laughing at their futile attempts at rescue. He deludes them three times, but when they hear him scream yet again, the men refuse to leave their work. Charley continues to scream, jumping up and down, but still the men stay with the wheat. When the boy's screams persist, the men finally decide to see what is happening. They are shocked to discover that Charley has stepped on a yellow-jacket nest and has been stung dozens of times. After Charley has been truly rescued and wrapped in mud packs, Laura's father tells the story to Laura, ending with the words, *"It served the little liar right."* That night Laura is troubled by the incident and lies in bed thinking:

> She thought about what the yellow jackets had done to Charley. She thought it served Charley right, too. It served him right because he had been so monstrously naughty. And the bees had a right to sting him, when he jumped on their home.
> But she didn't understand why Pa had called him a little liar. She didn't understand how Charley could be a liar, when he had not said a word. (1932, p. 211)

I was curious as to whether Lindsey understood what Laura was troubling over, and asked her if she thought Charley could be a liar. "Sure," she replied. "It's like the boy who cried wolf. He cried for help when he didn't need it and that's a lie. You don't have to talk to lie . . . You could scream!" (January 26, 1990, 7;2). In her explanation, Lindsey reached far back into her literary past to call up a text that had been quite popular in her second year of life, "The Boy Who Cried Wolf" *(Tales from Aesop)*. The patterns of the sheepherder who cried for help once too often were a good match to Charley's behavior, and the punishment was equally harsh.

To be able to improvise to meet immediate needs, and without hesitation, Lindsey had to be able to reconsider and replay the texts of children's literature in her own private speech. She thus had a repertoire of direct discourse, as well as a set of context rules about the situations in which the bits and pieces of discourse originally occurred. Such perceptions and modulations of social convention are the often brief and elusive specifics of which abstract social norms and moral judgments are made.

Making the Rhyme Reason

As the girls grew older we spent more and more time with poetry, particularly a book of poems called *Sing a Song of Popcorn* (de Regniers). The book is a fine collection of poetry, loosely linked according to topic ("Mostly Weather," "Spooky Poems," and so on). Lindsey and Ashley were instantly drawn to the section illustrated by Maurice Sendak, and their favorite poem was "The Jumblies," by Edward Lear. Lindsey began to incorporate some of the poem's language into her own expressions, with particular attention to the verse that contained the following lines:

> *And when the sieve turned round and round,*
> *And everyone cried, "You'll all be drowned!"*
> *They called aloud, "Our sieve ain't big,*
> *But we don't care a button! We don't care a fig!"*

One night, a dispute over treats was effectively defused through Lear's words. Ashley had accompanied me to the doctor's office when I had gone in for my annual physical exam. I had promised her a treat, and we had splurged and eaten two large cream puffs. Since Lindsey had been in school, she had missed out, and Ashley was determined to make her suffer.

"We went to Doc Doc's and had a treat!" she taunted. When Lindsey made no response, Ashley tantalized her with: "A BIG treat, and I ate it all up!"

Ordinarily, this might have stirred a dramatic discussion of "unfair" and "Why didn't I . . . ," but instead Lindsey walked away with the words, "I don't care a button! I don't care a fig!" (February 2, 1989, 6;3 and 4;2)

Lindsey's choice of words was particularly well calculated, for I was standing nearby. She knew that if she used the word "stupid" or "mind your own beeswax" (also in her repertoire), I'd follow with a quick scolding. Instead, with a literary shrug of her shoulders, she neatly ended the discussion, deflated her sister, and avoided punishment as well.

Ashley, too, had begun drawing on literature to join the verbal repartee and to avoid using the direct judgmental language that could lead to punishment. Once, during a particularly violent argument, Ashley came screaming down the stairs with Lindsey in hot pursuit. Ashley accused Lindsey of pinching her and Lindsey denied it.

"You did!" Ashley glared at her sister and then turned to me. "She pinched me!"
"I didn't," Lindsey pleaded innocence.
"You did!"
"I didn't!!"
"Liar! Ninnyhammer! Dimwit! Dunce! To jail at once!" (December 21, 1989, 7;1 and 3;11)

Ashley was quoting lines from Harve Zemach's story *The Judge*. She recognized the potentially punishable use of the word "liar," but she softened the blow by making the author of the word not herself but a safely distanced and approved writer.

Reworking in the head and replaying fragments of language from texts often took Lindsey and Ashley away from the syntax and meanings of the original. There were other rules to be followed as well, particularly in poetry. At ages three and four, Lindsey challenged both Silverstein and Seuss when they altered a word to force a rhyme. In *How the Grinch Stole Christmas,* Dr. Seuss writes:

> *Then he slithered and slunk, with a smile most unpleasant,*
> *Around the whole room, and he took every present!*
> *Pop guns! And bicycles! Roller skates! Drums!*
> *Checkerboards! Tricycles! Popcorn! And plums!*
> *And he stuffed them in bags. Then the Grinch, very nimbly,*
> *Stuffed all the bags, one by one, up the chimbley!*

"Chimney! You mean chimney!" she would cry. But at seven she laughed and appreciated this dialect item as the stretch of a word to make the rhyme: "He just does it to make children laugh."

Such judgments of what should be literal or reasonable did not move at a predictable developmental pace, since different rule systems held sway on different occasions. There were times when, through her early years of elementary school, Lindsey still questioned the rhyme pattern and suggested alternatives. In Lear's poem "The Jumblies," she stopped me when I read the chorus:

> *Far and few, far and few,*
> *Are the lands where the Jumblies live;*
> *Their heads are green, and their hands are blue,*
> *And they went to sea in a sieve.*

"No! No, Mom! Isn't that wrong? It should be, 'And they went to sea in a sue.' See, *blue, sue!*" (February 2, 1989, 6;3). Here a call for rhyme pattern overruled any drive for a "real" word that connoted a common kitchen item. Moreover, Lindsey's focus on end-rhyme overcame any awareness of the rule here of alternating lines of rhyme. To Lindsey, the word meaning was of considerably less importance (particularly in a poem of total nonsense) than her perception of the rhyme pattern. After I explained the pattern—"few, blue" and "live, sieve"—as well as the meaning of the word "sieve," she said she understood. But in all subsequent readings, she chose to echo softly with her own pattern substituting a familiar—but in this context nonsense—word, as I completed the chorus. The rescripting of poetry illustrates her juggling of three sets of rules: first, some poetry has to rhyme; second, the meaning of poetry does not have to lie exclusively in the precise original text; third, the formal framing of the genre can override the sense demands.[12]

Ashley, too, was interested in making rhymes, and her creations were often compilations of the many rhymes she had heard in text. One afternoon she and I sat on the sofa to read a story during a break in my studies. She requested *Old Mother Hubbard,* a version of the Mother Goose rhyme done by Alice and Martin Provensen. I opened the book and had barely made it through the first line *("Old Mother Hubbard went to the cupboard to . . .")* when Ashley stopped me. "Let me say it," she commanded. And then she sang:

Old Mother Hubbard
Went to the cupboard
Eating her curds and whey.
Along came her doggie,
And snapped off her nosie,
And frightened Miss Mother away.

(February 12, 1990, 4;2)

Her verse was a blending of three Mother Goose rhymes, whose chosen parts may have fed her inspiration. The first was the original "Old Mother Hubbard," while the other two seem to have been "Little Miss Muffet" (about a little girl who ate curds and whey and was frightened away) and "Sing a Song of Sixpence." Ashley had only recently been read this version of "Old Mother Hubbard," but she was very familiar with the latter two texts, particularly "Sixpence." We had sung this song with and without the book since she'd been an infant, always ending the final line with our fingers scissoring through the air to "snap off her nose."

As she composed her verbal poem, Ashley called on and transformed the trio of verses to make them "reasonable" to her, according to several sets of rules. She spliced them together in a series of rhymed couplets followed by two sets of alternate line rhymes, in order to describe the picture on the page—that of Old Mother Hubbard and her dog heading for the cupboard. Although the text of "Old Mother Hubbard" was long and unfamiliar to her, the rhyme pattern was the same as that of "Little Miss Muffet" and allowed Ashley the poetic license to use curds and whey in lieu of a search for a bone. Still, there was no spider in sight, and Ashley conformed to the rule of taking objects from the picture on the page by replacing "Along came a spider" with "Along came her doggie."

In the fifth line of her verse, Ashley interjected her third rhyme, from "Sing a Song of Sixpence," to slip in her own interpretation of the power of dogs to snap off noses. The word "nose" was stretched to "nosie" to make the rhyme. Finally, she reverted back to "Little Miss Muffet," albeit substituting "Miss Mother" for Miss Muffet, to show a dog's ability to frighten people away. Ashley was frightened of dogs herself. They were not allowed in our housing complex, and her own brief encounters with dogs had been unpleasant. An exuberant black labrador had once chased her across an entire school playground, knocked her down, and licked her vigorously from head to toe. Her short legs had pedaled against the dog's chest and she had screamed in fear until Kenny and the dog's owner managed to pull off the dog. As it happened, the dog had been merely playing, but Ashley had doubted his friendly intent and had talked about the incident for weeks. Thus, it was perfectly reasonable to her that the "doggie" would be the agent of Mother Hubbard's ill fortune in losing her "nosie," but this claim to reason had to accommodate the necessary inclusion of end-rhyme.[13]

Transforming Life and Text

Connections between life and text flowed back and forth, washing over one another and blurring distinctions. Relations between text and reader can be described as relations between dialogues of the memory and dialogues of the moment: between those of literary characters' past experiences and current talk, and those of the child's memory of the story and of the countertexts (concerning politeness, conformity, age appropriateness, and so forth) of daily life.

As I read to Lindsey, she attempted to match texts to what seemed salient to her at particular moments of what she knew of life, and vice versa. One morning, Lindsey and I were seated on the living room couch watching "Sesame Street." I was nursing the baby and Lindsey was eating her breakfast. The morning was particularly somber, the sky gray and ominous. A flash of lightning sparked about my neighbor's house, and thunder quickly followed. Suddenly the television became a blur of cackling images, and "Sesame Street" succumbed to the forces of nature. "What happened?" Lindsey cried. I explained that I thought the storm was responsible and that sometimes during storms televisions didn't work. Rain began splattering heavily across the window, as if in confirmation of my explanation. I asked Lindsey to turn off the annoying cackle and we would read a story. As she touched the power button, another flash of lightning lit up the sky, attracting her attention.

"That's just like in *The Girl Who Loved Wild Horses* [Goble]!" she exclaimed.
"What is?" I asked, as my eyes searched the sky.
"'Member the storm in the story . . . and the girl was riding so fast?"

"Would you like to be riding a horse in the rain like the Indian girl?" I wondered.

"No . . . I want to play outside for a hundred days without a coat," she replied.

"It might be cold. You should probably wear a coat." The mother in me spoke these sensible words.

"I don't like to," she replied adamantly. "It's not even fun!" (April 24, 1986, 3;5)

Lindsey used the images in stories to help her define new concepts in reality. As she learned something new about the power of storms, she was able to clarify her understanding by relating to a fact she already understood. Just as a storm had the ability to drive an Indian girl and her horses far from home, it could also drive "Sesame Street" from our television.

Even more important, perhaps, is the transformation of character that gratified Lindsey's own desires and had little to do with the fictional character's true desires. Whereas the Indian girl wished to be free to run with the wild horses, Lindsey wished for another kind of freedom—one that would release her from the continual admonitions of an ever-watchful mother and allow her to play outside for a hundred days without a coat.

This transformation draws on all aspects of life and text, blending daily facts with fiction. Multiple texts form layers and intermingle with life's texts, like featherbeds piling higher and higher on the bed of a princess—and still the small kernel of meaning is felt. And that meaning is not taught but created. This creation of meaning comes through social combinations and interactions: adults and children, children alone with memories and reconsiderations of past situations, and children negotiating desires, role relationships, and social meanings in the immediate moment. Children are the agents who choose the texts to be included in their featherbed piles. Adults' perceptions of literary texts (and attention to features other than those that children choose) often bar them from noticing that children achieve *apperceptions* or potential recognitions of their own understanding of some element of literature in a totally new and unpredictable context. In addition, children's visual, logical, musical, and linguistic insights can exceed those of adults, since children, when they read literature, may be motivated by their quest for transformative powers to make the external world conform more fully to their wishes. Of these, adults usually have little or no awareness; for in these matters, they serve not as guides, explicators, or promoters—but only as agents of coincidence and resource for the child's building of a domain of expertise.[14]

One afternoon, we read *The Tale of Peter Rabbit*. Lindsey had been read the story many times and also had the story on cassette, but this was the first time she showed any interest in the disappearance of Peter's father.

> *"Now, my dears,"* said old Mrs. Rabbit one morning, *"you may go into the fields or down the lane, but don't go into Mr. McGregor's garden: your Father had an accident there; he was put in a pie by Mrs. McGregor"* (Potter, p. 10).
>
> When I read these lines, Lindsey asked, "Put in a pie? How do they do that?"
>
> Lindsey had recently been interested in where hamburger, ham, and chicken comes from. She had even asked us questions like "What animal does asparagus come from?" So when she asked about Peter's father, I answered very matter-of-factly that some people liked to eat rabbit. I said that I thought Mr. McGregor had killed the rabbit and his wife had baked him in a pie.
>
> Lindsey looked totally horrified, and her expression then became one of disbelief, but she made no comment. (June 19, 1986, 3;7)

Lindsey understood the fact that some of her common foods came from animals, and when the process was safely distanced she could stomach the final result. But when it came to the parents of characters she loved, the process was too horrible to be believed.

I continued reading. Peter proceeded to ignore his mother's instructions and run directly to the scene of the crime. After hearing that Peter had stuffed himself on vegetables and been caught in the act by Mr. McGregor himself, Lindsey offered her own story:

> "When I was a little girl I had a baby bunny. He ran to a stranger's garden and the stranger killed him with a pie! His name was Cunderly . . . and he was a cute little bunny," she explained with some sadness.
>
> But when I sympathized over the loss of her rabbit, she shrugged it off. "That's okay, Mom." (June 19, 1986, 3;7)

This re-creation of the story with herself as the main character who *owns* a runaway bunny—and who is presumably an analogue to Peter, who might well be ground up and put in a pie—indicates her ability to pick and choose key features of the story and manipulate them according to her own set of "safe" rules. In her story, her rabbit dies, presumably by being *hit* with a pie—a gentler death and also a process more understandable to her than his being cut up, cooked, and served in a pie. The real world for a three-year-old contains plenty of warnings about being "hit by a car," "hit on the head," and so on, but the horrors of cut-up and cooked bodies remain in the domain of fairy tales. When I offered my sympathy about the loss of her bunny, she reassured me that in her story she had everything under control.

Lindsey continued to exert control over the story as we read. Peter escapes Mr. McGregor briefly but can't find his way out of the garden. During his tearful search for an escape, he comes across a cat:

> *"A white cat was staring at some gold-fish, she sat very, very still, but now and then the tip of her tail twitched as if it were alive. Peter thought it best to go away without speaking to her; he had heard about cats from his cousin, little Benjamin Bunny"* (Potter, p. 46).
>
> Referring to Benjamin, Lindsey asked, "Where is he? Did Mr. McGregor eat him too?"
>
> I explained that Benjamin was in another story, that he had only given Peter some advice. Lindsey wanted to know where the other story was, and I promised that we would get it from the library. (June 19, 1986, 3;7)

In tying up the "loose" connections she saw regarding the demise of Benjamin, Lindsey gained a sense of order in the story and a promise of closure on the fate of characters within the story. She was learning to come to some understanding of how texts link up with one another: the questions elicited in one text could be answered by another. A few days later I got *The Tale of Benjamin Bunny* from the library, since Lindsey was eager to meet Peter's cousin who knew so much about cats. "Is this Peter's cousin?" she said as soon as I showed her the book (June 26, 1986, 3;7).

Years later, Lindsey's love of Beatrix Potter was surpassed by Ashley's. For her fourth birthday Kenny and I bought Ashley a new set of Potter's books, since Lindsey's were quite shabby. The collection contained a few books we had never read before, including *The Tale of the Flopsy Bunnies*. The first evening we read the book, we began by studying the cover; Potter's illustration showed a mother and father bunny, upright and dressed and walking with a number of baby rabbits.

> "Who's that?" Ashley inquired.
>
> "I'm not sure," I replied, and called Lindsey over for her expert opinion.

Busy with her own affairs, however, she gave the cover a quick glance and said she hadn't the slightest idea.

"Maybe it's Peter," Ashley suggested excitedly. "He's bigger now and married!"

Ashley's guess was accurate in concept, but not in character, for the father was Benjamin, who had indeed grown up and was now married to Peter's sister Flopsy. The tale is another adventure involving Mr. McGregor, who captures Benjamin and Flopsy's baby bunnies while they lie asleep in the rubbish heap near his garden. He carefully loads them in his sack, planning to take them home at the end of his work day. Benjamin and Flopsy come to their rescue with the aid of Thomasina Tittlemouse (an acquaintance of Peter's), who gnaws a hole in the bottom of the sack. Together the animals restuff the sack with rotten vegetables. Unknowingly, Mr. McGregor carries it home.

"What do you think he wanted to do with the rabbits?" I asked the girls.

Ashley looked worried, but Lindsey turned from her play casually and said, "He wants to put them in a pie!" (January 7, 1990, 7;2 and 4;1)

Even though Mr. McGregor had other ideas (he wanted to sell them for rabbit tobacco), Lindsey's concept was true to the flow of text from her memory. Animals in pies had now become a matter of course, and Mr. McGregor's habits were no longer horrifying but predictable.

But when Lindsey was between the ages of three and four, such had not been the case. Lindsey began then to reshape texts of children's literature not only by rescripting them on the spot and altering contexts and rules of relations to suit her preferred outcomes, but also by making it clear when she did not wish to consider bringing certain elements of texts into real life. While rereading *Rapunzel* one morning, Lindsey voiced her own hesitant but ultimately rejected link between life and text. After the witch wrenches the newborn child from the arms of her distraught parents, she lives with the child deep in the forest. But, as the story explains, *"The witch was never unkind to Rapunzel. Indeed, she gave her almost everything the child could have wished for. And Rapunzel grew to be the most beautiful child in the world"* (Grimm Brothers). Indeed, the picture that Hyman paints is that of a lovely blond-haired child sitting at the witch's feet. She is holding a ball of yarn, winding it from the hands of her witch-mother, and she is smiling up at the old woman.

> "Look, she's smiling at her," Lindsey said in a dreamy voice. Then she laughed, "How 'bout if you were a witch?"
> "Can you imagine?" I said.
> But Lindsey did not want to imagine. "Now read it please, Mama." (June 24, 1986, 3;7)

Since Lindsey knew this story well and also was familiar with the dastardly habits of witches in other stories, she could not entertain for very long the fact that I might be a witch. Witches were all very well within the pages of a book, but moving their characteristics (even when one story might portray a kind witch) into one's own mother was a thought not open for discussion.

In the world of story, however, the discussion refuses to be quiet. Sensitive issues, such as jealousy, power, sibling rivalry, divorce, death, and mothers who assume witchlike characteristics, are all themes to be explored either openly or symbolically. Authors and illustrators use text as an opportunity to explore these issues on a more personal level. Selma Lanes describes Maurice Sendak's love for his dog Jennie, whom he immortalized in several of his stories. A week after Jennie's death of cancer, "Sendak wrote an old acquaintance, 'My best friend, my dog Jennie, has died'" (cited in Lanes, p. 153). Sendak later acquired a golden retriever and two German shepherds; although he began to put them into his illustrations, they never replaced Jennie in his heart. Lindsey was well aware of the death of Jennie, for we had talked about Lanes's book and she was used to seeing Jennie appear in numerous stories.

One evening we read *Outside Over There,* and the picture of Sendak's dogs recalled our old discussion:

> "Does he have . . . Are his two dogs still alive?" Lindsey questioned.
> "Jennie?" I had no information on the destiny of Sendak's other dogs.
> "Yeah," she replied.
> "Jennie's not alive."
> Lindsey questioned me about his other dogs again and then returned to Jennie. "What did . . . how did Jennie die?"
> "I don't know." I hadn't read Lanes's book in a while and couldn't remember.

Lindsey was persistent. "Can you tell me what you think . . . that she died?"

"She might have died from old age," I speculated, "because she lived for a long time and . . . she certainly lived through many stories. Can you remember some of the stories that Jennie was in?"

"No," she mused. "'Cept 'Max and the Wild Things.' Maybe he wants to draw them in books . . . 'cause, ummm . . . 'cause I think he . . . he likes that dog the best."

"I bet you're right," I agreed. "I think if I could draw the way that Maurice Sendak could draw . . . I might put you in all my books . . . 'cause I like you the best."

Lindsey looked a little panicked, "If I died . . . If I died of a disease?"

"Well, I don't know if I'd just wait until you died of a disease, which you probably won't," I reassured her. "But, I might do it just 'cause I love you." (April 26, 1988, 5;5)

A single illustration called up multiple dialogues: past conversations between Lindsey and me, intertextual connections in Sendak's books and biography, and discussions of life and death and of how we express our love and sorrow. These themes reappeared again in another book of Sendak's that we read six months later.

In the fall of 1988 the children's book world was greatly excited over the publication of Sendak's new book, *Dear Mili,* a previously unpublished story by Wilhelm Grimm. I was eager to see it. Lindsey and I were visiting a local children's bookstore, when she discovered the display. "Look!" she cried, opening the book to the first page, "there's his dogs!" We bought the book, and during our first reading I brought out our copy of Lanes's *The Art of Maurice Sendak* to explore the implications of her comment.

Flipping through the pages, I found a photograph of Sendak walking his dogs. "It says that there's Sendak with Erda, Agamemnon, and Io. And look at his new storybook. There's some of his dogs."

Lindsey's eyes played back and forth across both books and she tried to identify the dogs in the storybook. She pointed her finger. "Erda. No. Ag . . . Agma . . . I can't say it."

I pronounced the name. "Agamemnon."

Lindsey compared the features of the dogs. "Yeah. Can't be Erda so . . . this dog . . . "

I read the name. "Yeah, it says that this dog's name is Io."

"Io," Lindsey sang the name.

> I picked up her tune, "Io! Io!" and then returned to the subject at hand: "And there he is walking his dogs, and he sure likes to put his dogs in his storybooks, doesn't he?"
>
> "Yeah," Lindsey replied.
>
> "They must be important to him," I suggested.
>
> But Lindsey's only comment was, "Mm-hmmm." (October 10, 1988, 5;11)

After her failure to find matching features and to confirm her sense of match between the dogs and their names, I moved to a higher claim: if he likes to put his dogs in his storybooks, they must be important to him. But she had already made this statement months ago and was ready to move on to other domains.

The first passage of *Dear Mili* describes the main character as a good little girl who says her prayers before going to bed and before getting up. I asked Lindsey about the kind of prayers she herself said.

> "I'm not telling," she quickly replied.
>
> "Are they private?" I asked.
>
> "Yeah." She closed the door to further questions.
>
> I tried to respect her feelings. "I think it's probably good to have private prayers."
>
> My tone was empathetic. Lindsey quickly nodded and replied in a conspiratorial tone, "You can't tell them, or they won't come true."
>
> "Oh." At first surprised, I finally saw the connection. "Are they kind of like birthday wishes?"
>
> "Yeah," she replied. (October 10, 1988, 5;11)

Here Lindsey asserted that if you tell your prayers, they won't come true, presumably on the analogy of birthday wishes. Straight if-then claims that tried to apply the rules of the real world (even the world of birthday wishes) to literature often proved useless in literature.

In *Dear Mili,* a young child is sent into the forest by her mother, who is desperately trying to protect the child from a fast-approaching war. The mother tells her daughter to wait deep in the forest for three days and then return home. The child is protected by an unseen guardian angel, who gently guides her to the home of Saint Joseph. Joseph is an old man, with a gray beard flowing down the front of his simple robe. He has been expecting the child, and she stays with him for what seems to be three days. Each day she plays with her now visible guardian angel in a garden of Sendak's spectacular vision. At the end of the third day, Joseph gives her a rosebud and tells her that when the rose blooms they will be together again.

The guardian angel then leads her back to her mother. But upon her return, the child discovers that her mother is now an old woman. Not three days but thirty years have passed since she entered the forest! They spend one happy evening together, but in the morning they are both found dead, and lying between them is Joseph's rose in full bloom.

> "Who was that woman?" I asked Lindsey, as we studied the illustration of the old woman with her arms outstretched to greet the child.
>
> "I don't know," she replied. "Mary, maybe."
>
> I didn't understand the connection. "Maybe. Why Mary?"
>
> Lindsey set out a tentative hypothesis. "Because she's old. If her husband's old, then she's old."
>
> I realized she was talking about the Virgin Mary. "You're right. That could very well be."
>
> But after reading on, we discovered the woman's true identity, and I commented, "So the old woman is her mother."
>
> Lindsey mouthed the words first and then spoke them aloud: "The old woman is her mother!"
>
> I tried to explain. "Yeah, it said that even though the little girl had thought she'd only spent three days in the forest with Saint Joseph, she'd really spent thirty years! And all that time her mother thought that her dear daughter was gone."
>
> Her look was incredulous. "That was her mother?"
>
> And minutes later, when she left to play outside, she turned and asked again, "That was her mother?!" (October 10, 1988, 5;11)

The aspects of story that were unbelievable at the first reading became commonplace in subsequent readings. Just as Lindsey's horror about the demise of Peter's father had lessened, her surprise over the passage of time in Saint Joseph's garden ultimately gave way to acceptance. In the world of story, the impossible is transformed into the possible, and those who are separated in life may be rejoined in death.

Making Life Play

Enjoyment and mastery are the consequences of play. When the task or skill to be mastered is obvious (say, dropping a ball in a wastebasket—a game for a two-year-old), children can do the task again and again until they decide to alter the rules of play. They may then choose to turn the wastebasket upside down and try to get the ball to stay on the flat bottom of the basket. Alteration of the rules of play draws the attention of a parent who may have grown tired of watching the repetitious drop-the-ball-in-the-basket game.

The same was true in Lindsey's and Ashley's literary play. Like the illustrator Trina Schart Hyman, who explained that she *was* Little Red Riding Hood as a child, Lindsey preferred this particular role to all others throughout her third year of life. We helped her assemble her cape, boots, and basket, and not without hesitation allowed her to pick more than her fair share of our garden's flowers. Kenny and I repeatedly played the roles of grandmother, wolf, and woodcutter: we lay prone on the sofa, leaped from behind doorways, and raised our rifle to shoot. When Lindsey said she was going to be Sleeping Beauty, Ida, or Curious George, we welcomed the new character.

Play with a verbal script as well as props requires the assignment of social roles and a mutual understanding of setting by all involved. Sociodramatic play, unlike the quickly constructed metaphor, calls for mutually internalized chunks of scripts and frames of behavior. Sociodramatic play thus can come about only when all participants agree that they have some shared experiences that they will reshape into current drama. All the players have a meta-awareness that they must play by two sets of rules: those of the previously shared experience or text that forms the basis of the new current script, and those of the sociodramatic play now under way. Often children introduce such play by saying "Let's pretend," or they may simply announce a new role for bystanders: "You be the witch." Here the imperative announces to both participants that they share the text of witch, even though some negotiation may be necessary regarding which text and hence which witch.

Sociodramatic play begins with an announcement of counterfactual conditions—of a state of affairs that is not real or literal. Mothers become witches, playmates become doctors, and baby sisters become bedridden grandmothers waiting for Little Red Riding Hood. Such play becomes possible only when participants are capable of the meta-communication which signals that play is "on," that counterfactual conditions are at work, and that roles assigned by age and gender are no longer in place. These shifts create an environment in which children can make their own connections, so long as they announce the rules of such linkages. Similarly, they experiment in a problem-solving and causal environment, in which certain events (such as overstepping one's role as authority figure vis-à-vis a reluctant younger playmate) will lead to or cause other events. The fundamental conditions of hypothesis building and if-then reasoning fall into place in a relatively safe environment. One can step away from the experiment simply by announcing the play is "off."[15]

It is easy to overlook the simple if-then notion that underlies socio-dramatic play and to fail to consider how children learn to use expressions of conditionality. In book-reading, children can add to their "What's that?" questions to identify objects, characters, and events, and to ask questions of the "but what if" variety. They need to test their predictions and hypotheses about the world. In everyday talk, though every assertion is not proved by "logical" talk, many hypotheticals are tested by action. In book-reading, the merger of action and talk about text enables children to check assertions of both text and adult reader and to add their own rules of logic and statements about sequences, expected associations, and causes and effects.[16]

Kenny began regaling Lindsey with stories from Greek mythology when she was four years old. As they traveled in the car or stood in grocery lines, he spoke of the adventures of Odysseus, the dangers of Scylla and Charybdis, Odysseus' close brush with death in the care of the Cyclops Polyphemus. Lindsey stood in awe of these gigantic myths, but the telling was often not enough.

One night she sat sprawled on the living room rug, explaining how Odysseus had made the Cyclops drunk with wine and then blinded him with a stake kindled in the fire. As she reached the part where the hero escapes, she begged Kenny to play the part of the sheep, and eagerly clung to his stomach as he crawled about the room. I immediately took up the remaining role, and staggered about as the blind Cyclops, running my hands along the "sheep's" back to try to prevent my enemy from escaping. Lindsey ducked her head and quickly shifted her hands to avoid touching my own, and she and Kenny made it safely to the hallway. Triumphantly she waved a fist in victory and taunted me from the stairs: "Ha ha! You silly Cyclops!" (June 4, 1987, 4;7)

Later, as I tucked her in bed for the night, she asked me to retell the story, but I was eager to shift to calmer, nighttime images and instead read her Edith Hamilton's story "Pygmalion and Galatea," a childhood favorite of my own. Pygmalion, sculptor and misogynist, creates a statue of a woman more beautiful than any in life. He names her Galatea, and Lindsey laughed in delight with the name, asking me to say it again and again. Then she rolled it about in her mouth, savoring the name, repeating it several times.

Poor Pygmalion. As an ultimate irony, he falls in love with Galatea. But his kisses, his embraces, his gifts of little birds and bright flowers evoke no response from the cold, hard beauty. A wretched man, Pygmalion goes to the temple of Venus and prays that he might find a maiden with the form of his beloved Galatea. The goddess of love is touched by this devotion and makes the flames of her temple fires flare three times as an omen of her favor. Pygmalion returns home, reflecting on the message of the flames, and embraces his love.

> As Pygmalion kisses Galatea, I kissed Lindsey, and just like our young hero, I started back in surprise. Instead of the cold reality of the statue, Pygmalion discovered a trace of warmth, a slight response. Could it be? Pygmalion touched Galatea's lips as I touched Lindsey's. Yes, they were warm!
>
> Lindsey stared at me with pleasure. "I'm coming to life, aren't I? I'm coming to life!"
>
> I assured her that indeed she was and ended the story with the wedding of Pygmalion and Galatea. Lindsey leaned back against her pillow and sighed. "And they all lived happily ever after." (June 4, 1987, 4;7)

The very fact that we sometimes filled the ordinary with the extraordinary (standing in grocery lines discussing the adventures of Odysseus, reading mythology as a bedtime story) was essential to Lindsey's response to literature.

Our role in her play was another important ingredient. We eagerly took an active role in Lindsey's interpretation and added the flavor of our own meaning. When Lindsey signaled the onset of literature play, we took up our assigned roles and improvised the missing elements. When we told a story, we capitalized on opportunities for pantomime. It was not enough to read about a kiss, when a real kiss could say so much more.

This does not mean that our lives were constantly the stuff of books, for we also said quite ordinary things. ("Lindsey, watch Ashley while I write this check for the groceries," and "No. You can't have gum. Put it back.") But our family's love of literature could not be ignored.

Instead, it must be actively woven into the context of Lindsey's and Ashley's responses.

A young child listens to story and for days and years after, meanings come wherever the child's life experience converges with multiple texts—worlds in dialogue, in an active process of constructing and testing. The meanings are individual, rather than conforming to expert or single interpretation, for they connect to the social world of the child, reaching out to hold a conversation with her community. Out of the child's world and the words of the text, new visions emerge. These visions are themselves experiences and form a kaleidoscope of connections—fragments of language, visual imagery, emotion, and will. The myriad bits of life and text merge together to create dazzling new patterns. And the patterns of understanding constantly shift and change to accommodate new insights and new needs to test rules of text, practice, and belief formation.[17]

Lindsey's and Ashley's interpretations of story often evolved into play. Literature play occupied a broad spectrum, ranging from small, insular wordplays to elaborate productions complete with cast, costumes, and stage directions. In play, the girls evoked the sounds, movements, and images of texts, enacting themes of personal importance. Casting a text in play was therefore a means of living the symbols of story.

Their interpretations were never limited by their language, for they could express their understanding through pantomime, gestures, nonsense words, or announced sociodrama. In the story of the Cyclops, Lindsey clung to her father as Odysseus held to the belly of the ram. By living out the narrative, Lindsey could dramatize the excitement and fear that the hero felt in his precarious position. Her derisive words ("Ha ha! You silly Cyclops!") show one aspect of her understanding. But it was the triumphant wave of her fist that captured the power of his victory as Odysseus made his escape and yelled his taunts at the Cyclops. The power of Odysseus over his enemies shines through the intelligence of the trick. The theme of a small but crafty man pitted against a large and powerful giant is an old theme in story, and Lindsey well understood its meaning. And through her dramatization of the story, she was able to send a personal message: "I may be little, but I, too, am powerful."

As Lindsey lay in bed listening to the story of Pygmalion and Galatea, she was able to anticipate the ending of a text she had never heard.

Before Edith Hamilton revealed the climactic transformation of Galatea from statue to life, Lindsey knew the outcome. "I'm coming to life, aren't I? I'm coming to life!" she whispered. The essence of the narrative, that love is the great restorer, was one she knew well. Sleeping Beauty was awakened with a kiss, and Snow White was brought to life by the love of her prince. The use of the personal pronoun in Lindsey's words was yet another example of the intimate ties between the narrative of story and the narrative of her life.

Ashley rarely led the daily clamor to get to the dress-up box and did not direct the afternoon performances, but she thundered up the stairs after her sister and created her own lines for her parts. Like Lindsey, she connected literature to her explanations, her excuses, and her explorations in life. Like Lindsey, she lay in bed at night and moved her life into and out of books. Through the written language of stories, and the children's construction of story through play, Lindsey and Ashley traveled beyond the boundaries of their actual world and entered the many possible worlds of literature.

4

Wings of Meaning

The American poet Wallace Stevens once jotted in his notebook the provocative line: "There is no wing like meaning." When we attempt to understand how young children learn to comprehend what meaning is and where it comes from, we have to acknowledge that although we may be able to describe the beauty of the feathers, we have only feeble means to describe the flight.

The connections children make "in their heads" can only be inferred through the observable behaviors they display. We label such pieces of evidence and develop theories about their possible links to mental maneuvers. Our observations accumulate around the names that children give objects, categories they recognize, deductions or hypotheses they make, and inductions they draw. Our very naming of the processes children exhibit becomes the foundation of our own ways of making some sense of the verbal, visual, and action flights they take. But our methods tell us little about the emotions that power their attempts to make meaning, and we worry that their creative or out-of-the-ordinary trials may escape our own labels and categories entirely. These we try to capture by attributing "rules," "frames," "schema," or some kind of set pattern to these behaviors, and then we attempt to put these patterns in context. We try to figure out when children are likely to apply the rules we intuit they are following.[1]

Our efforts to describe the ways in which Lindsey and Ashley made meaning with and from books have led us to see their behaviors as reflecting several elements. The first is the extent to which the girls grasped certain unstated rules about how texts make meaning within themselves—through connections between illustration and text, through coherence within the text, and with clues that help explain events that are inexplicable according to real-world processes. Closely tied to these rules were those of their own direct interactions with the text. How far could they go in revoicing characters, changing outcomes, and rescripting plots? Becoming familiar with genres and their dictates regarding plot, character, and other critical elements strongly influenced the girls' sense of control over the rules by which literature worked. But the ways in which motivation, intention, and belief affected characters' actions were grasped with far less certainty. Here the girls saw themselves vacillating in interpretation and reshuffling elements of action to match their own often-changing views of why characters behaved as they did—in both books and life.

With these tied-to-text and time-of-reading rules, however, came another set of patterns for carrying the world of literature into their everyday lives. Here social activities and interactions, as well as their own handling of certain metarules for play, facilitated their use of books to mediate their understanding of the world. The girls were able to transfer their understanding from books' content and rules of composition to problem-solving activities they encountered daily. In other words, transfer for them was not the shift of a given, right, or uniform bit of thinking from one situation to the next. Problem solving through the use of knowledge gained with books depended instead on emotional orientations, evaluations of the girls' possible limits of power in particular situations, and constant comparisons of one situation with the next. In life, as in the literature the girls read, in order to recognize and solve a problem, they had to notice the pertinence of information and experience, possibilities of adaptation, and processes of application. Above all, solutions in both literature and life called on their abilities to make connections, find creative interpretations, and consider critically the merits of storing outcomes for future use.[2]

Theories of children's development which posit that their learning moves through increasingly complex stages to full development as an adult have been applied to cognitive, moral, social, and linguistic development. A close study of children's literature demonstrates children's flexibility outside the scope and sequence of knowledge that adults might think developmentally appropriate. Such theories of development, when applied to ways of drawing meaning from literary texts, also fail to recognize that children's derivations and extensions of the sense of such texts may sometimes exceed those of adults. The pull of fantasy, flexibility of roles, irreverence for manners, and disregard for logic grounded in daily routine free children to experiment with meaning in ways long ago locked up in "decorum" and "mature reason" by most adults. It is no accident that a favorite theme of children's literature is just this limitation of emotion and imagination that afflicts adults. Children relish the strange links authors make between vivid hard circumstances and the powers of curiosity, persistence, and humor to accomplish tasks adults either ignore or consider impossible.[3]

Fear and Loss

Texts carry children into situations and emotions bound in a framework of story, where characters speak their emotions, fall prey to their emotions, or hold certain feelings for only brief periods of time. But these possibilities also play themselves out in daily life, where situations persist, certain characters and facts of life hold power over children, and adults can grapple with reality apparently only by realigning, extending, abbreviating, or ignoring certain emotions. Meaning may then become a whirlwind in which children both experiment fully in their readings of literature and search gradually for some stable sets of patterns, in order to gain a sense of control and a measure of respect from others for "growing up." To do so, they must sometimes dare to inquire into the secret abyss of intention.

Lindsey and Ashley were primarily concerned with the emotions adults tend to label "fear" and "love," and it was these they wove most often through their interactions with literature and its intrusions into their daily lives. Conjured up within stories or shifted from books into their interrelations and interactions, these emotions often shaped renarrations of literature. Far more directly than the adults around them, the girls used written texts to control, push aside, explain away, hold in absolute terms, and gradually to compare, modulate, and reshape sadness, joy, fear, delight, repulsion, and attachment.

Fear was fascination. Giants, dragons, monsters, and evil queens all held power over the girls. Their questions and comments reflected the push-pull nature of their fear. Lindsey hated the Jabberwocky (Carroll), hated Jack's giant (Cauley), and hated the Grinch (Seuss), but she requested these books over and over again. At other times, these texts were conspicuously absent. Often at night, after the lights were out and her door was closed, Kenny and I would hear Lindsey rummaging about in her room. Her door would open and we would hear a loud clump. Then another and another. Her door would close and we would hear her bedsprings squeak in final surrender. Curious, we would creep up the stairs, only to discover several of her "scariest" books lying abandoned outside her door (March 11, 1986, 3;4).

Between the ages of three and four, Lindsey never allowed the *Three Little Pigs* in her bedroom at night. Nor did she accept *Tales from Aesop,* with its frightening wolf in the story of the boy who cried "wolf" once too often. One night she took up a Walt Disney story that depicted a particularly ferocious bear and hurled it out her bedroom door to land at the bottom of the stairs (3;4). A long-time favorite of Lindsey's, Margaret Hodges' *Saint George and the Dragon,* was moved to the bookshelf in *my* bedroom (3;6).

At the same age, Ashley was even firmer in her rejections. She hated the frighteningly transformed prince in Mayer's *Beauty and the Beast* and refused even to be in the room when I read it to Lindsey. She also took a particular dislike to a small stuffed toy that her grandmother had sent her. It was a large soft shoe, filled with children and their nursery rhyme mother. Although I explained innumerable times that the mother was "the little old woman who lived in a shoe," Ashley thought she was a witch. I hung the shoe full of children on the wall, but Ashley removed the "witch" and hid her in the depths of the hall closet. Months later I found her while searching for some toothpaste, and returned her to her rightful place. Within a day, she was back in the closet. According to Ashley, the children could stay but the "witch" had to go.

Control over the emotions called up by literature came initially through the girls' attempts to distance the books they found objectionable and to ensure that these books did not invade their nighttime solitude.[4] But Lindsey also attempted to control the vehicles of oral interpretation—my facial expressions and modulation of voice. I read the roles of wicked witch and menacing giant with fearful panache. One night I gave a dramatic rendition of *Saint George and the Dragon* from a text with a particularly horrifying dragon illustrated by Trina Schart Hyman. As the dragon rose from the earth, my voice rose to match his size and terror. Lindsey clutched my arm and Ashley jerked away from my breast to stare at me wide-eyed.

"You're scaring Ashley!" Lindsey admonished with no reference to herself. "Talk the dragon in a normal voice."

I lowered my voice, but the text increased in intensity. During this section, Lindsey began nervously fiddling with her blanket and finally turned to her own tape recorder. She pressed the fast forward and rewind and finally "play" but the recorder was empty and soundless. I asked her if she wanted me to continue reading.

"Yes. But in a normal voice," she reiterated.

On strict orders from Lindsey, my tone had been very calm, but it could not mask the menace of the vocabulary. As the story finally closed on a more mellow note, Lindsey begged for a taped story. "Something funny," she pleaded.

I placed a version of *Curious George Rides a Bike* [Rey] in her recorder, knowing that would fit the bill. I tucked her blanket close around her and then left to put the now sleeping Ashley in her crib. As I passed Lindsey's room on my way to my own, she called me.

"Mom!" Silently she stretched out her hand and gave me *Saint George and the Dragon*. It was not necessary to ask why. Curious George was a better bedtime companion than Hyman's flame-breathing dragon. (July 17, 1986, 3;8)

By age five, Lindsey no longer flung books out the door or begged me to ignore the story's course and the illustrator's portrayal of demons. Instead, she herself would take over the story, or she would retreat to a place of safety to hear it out. She would sometimes cower in a corner of the bed clutching my bathrobe as a story built in suspense. She stood in mortal dread of the character Blue Duck in McMurtry's *Lonesome Dove,* and urged Augustus to "kill him quick!" She shivered as Boo Radley approached Jem on a moonlit summer night, in Lee's *To Kill a Mockingbird*.

When we read the Caldecott Honor book *Lon Po Po: A Red-Riding Hood Story from China* (Young), we were sitting in the middle of a busy bookstore, in full daylight, but fear still swept Lindsey into the story. The tale begins with the plight of three small children who live with their mother. As with all good storybook mothers, this one decides to leave the children at their most vulnerable moment and go visit their grandmother, Po Po. When we reached this point in the story, Lindsey cuddled closer to me and looked scared.

"This is just like *Heckedy Peg,*" she whispered, recalling the initial scenario in one of her favorite books (Wood), where a mother leaves her children alone and a witch shows up at the door. In Young's story, it is the wolf who appears; and though the oldest child is hesitant, the two youngest rush to let him in.

Throughout the story Lindsey sat mesmerized, staring at the wolf's wild white eye while Ashley clutched the buttons of my sweater. When the eldest child's plan to defeat the wolf was slowly revealed, Lindsey smiled in a self-satisfied way and even winked at me once, as though she and I had instigated the plan. As the wolf crashed to his doom, Lindsey and Ashley both laughed aloud, as victorious as the children in the story. "That was good!" they both exclaimed at the end. (February 3, 1990, 7;3 and 4;2)

As Lindsey gradually accumulated methods to control her fear (especially in response to loss), she came to realize that literary devices could exert control. Books with scary plots resolved the crises of their central characters; an element of trust in the text emerged as a key source of inner control. The drama of a book's tracing of loss and building of fear invited Lindsey as listener in as an active audience member. For her little sister's benefit and to heighten her own involvement, Lindsey often "played along" with exaggerated expressions of fear, anticipation, and suspense.

Though tied to fear, loss was more often a clue to a part of some whole that would lead to a complicated situation or problem in need of resolution in the book and of reconciliation with facts of the real world. Aware of a character's loss of a limb, loss of a garment, or loss of memory, Lindsey used traces of this bit to sort out causes, consequences, and corollaries. She stared at the decapitated Jabberwocky, the dragon's missing claw, and the prince's thorn-pierced eyes. When she observed Rapunzel weeping into her hands at the loss of both prince and hair, she asked: "Why is she covering her eyes? So she won't get her eyes pricked out too?" (June 24, 1986, 3;7). Lindsey interpreted Rapunzel's gesture as protection against physical loss, rather than despair over the loss of her true love. She centered on the immediate rather than the ultimate outcome. In stories, love (as well as sight) was always restored; but it was the horror of the moment that somehow had to be overcome in order to get to "happily ever after."

Both Lindsey and Ashley questioned the sudden and unexplained disappearance of a character. One of the girls' favorite books of poetry, *Sing a Song of Popcorn* (de Regniers), included a poem by Ogden Nash entitled "Adventures of Isabel." The poem was illustrated by Maurice Sendak and describes the victory of a small girl who deftly defeats her enemies without so much as a ruffle in her attire. Ashley delighted in

Isabel's calm defeat of a bear and a giant, but continually questioned the disappearance of the witch:

> *Isabel, Isabel, didn't worry,*
> *Isabel didn't scream or scurry.*
> *She showed no rage and she showed no rancor,*
> *But she turned the witch into milk and drank her.*

Ashley stared in wide-eyed wonder at the illustrated glass in Isabel's hand, and then demanded to flip back a few pages to the introduction of the section where Isabel had a firm grip on the witch's nose. Then she turned back to the "milk page" and asked, "She's in there!?" Lindsey, too, questioned Isabel's feats: "She ate the bear?! How did she do that?" and "*How* did she cut off the giant's head?" (February 2, 1989, 6;3 and 3;2). Her skepticism about part-to-whole relations and about causes and consequences of losses seemed unusual to me at first. How could Lindsey, who so readily accepted pumpkins turning into carriages, and children and grandmothers escaping from inside a wolf, not accept the powers of Isabel? Yet neither author nor illustrator provides an explanation for Isabel's abilities; she has no magic wand, fairy godmother, or woodsman to help her. She is no robust stalwart; she is but a little girl with a fairly ordinary knife and fork. Isabel's sudden transformative powers come with no observable evidence to justify her as agent, or any of her instruments as magical. Thus, for Lindsey, her actions merited explanation; to Lindsey's mind, more information should resolve this apparent-but-clearly-not-everyday possibility.

Loss did not have to be violent to make an impression. Lindsey worried about the clothes Peter lost in Mr. McGregor's garden, and the galoshes Mr. Jeremy lost in his struggle with the trout. She fretted about the loss of the Who's Christmas (Seuss). When a loss was final and death came, Lindsey felt that neither she nor the characters could pursue alternative outcomes. By the age of four, Lindsey usually tried hard to retain power over literature's solutions and to bring her own agency to the rescue of ill-fated literary characters. She cried when we dragged our Christmas tree out of the house and asked if we couldn't just "plant it in the forest like the little boy's dad did" (January, 1987, 4;2), a solution that appeared in *The Little Fir Tree* (Brown). She wept bitterly over Charlotte's death (White). Later, when we spoke of death, she cried and said, "Oh, Mommy. When we die we won't be able to come back like Snow White."[5]

Years later, when the girls experienced the death of their grandfather, I asked them to write letters to Grandpa for Kenny to place in the coffin. Lindsey wrote:

> *Dear Grandpa*
> *You are spashl to me. And I love! you varre moche.*
> > *Love*
> > *Lindsey*

Ashley wrote a series of lines and circles which she translated as: *"Have a nice trip, Grandpa!"* (January 8, 1990, 7;2 and 4;1).

The week of his death was very unsettling. The girls were devastated, both by the incomprehensible loss of their grandfather and by Kenny's absence as he traveled to a distant state for the funeral. Lindsey wrote about her feelings in her diary:

> I feil sad
> bkas my
> grandpa died
> and inside
> I feil Terrible

Having no easy answers to their persistent questions of where their Grandpa was now, I shared with them Robert Munsch's sweet and sentimental tale *Love You Forever,* with its well-known verse:

> *I'll love you forever,*
> *I'll like you for always,*
> *As long as I'm living*
> *my baby you'll be.*

Lindsey and I were very tearful during the reading, while Ashley watched and listened sadly.

"Where's Grandpa?" Ashley cried at the end of the story.

Lindsey leaned over and explained, "Well, his spirit's up in heaven, and his body's where Dad buried him."

I listened with wonder at her summation of all that the family and the neighborhood children had told her. "But where is he for you?" I asked.

She tilted her head to the side in reflection, "I guess in my heart." And then she sang:

I'll love you forever
I'll like you for always,
As long as I'm living
My grandpa you'll be.
(January 9, 1990, 7;2 and 4;1)

The final resolution of the irresolvable problem of death—the ultimate loss—came for Lindsey through literature and her remaking of it to lament her own loss.

Beauty and Love

Beauty was an aesthetic quality that softened the pain of fear and loss, and Lindsey was quite susceptible to beauty. She had a designer's eye for costume and was easily swept away by the frills of a gown. Cinderella's ball gown was at the top of her aesthetic list, but she appreciated the simplicity of Red Riding Hood's cape, as well. The epitome of beauty was a fairytale heroine drawn by Trina Schart Hyman and endowed with a long, luxurious mass of "Rapunzel hair." Even the words that described such beauty made an impression. After her birthday, I helped Lindsey write a thank-you note to Anna, the woman who cared for Lindsey and Ashley while I worked. Anna had jet-black hair, which she wore in a long braid down her back. Although the purpose of the letter was to thank Anna for her present, Lindsey dictated: "I love you, Anna. You have hair like the darkness of the night. My hair is the lightness of the sun. I hope my hair will be long as yours when I grow up" (November 11, 1986, 4;0). Beauty was often the harbinger of love, and Lindsey was in love with love. She smiled with pleasure at the joyful union of princess and prince, and once confided that waiting a hundred years for a kiss was "worth it." Physical beauty was often the predominant attraction in young fairytale love, but there was also the sound of Rapunzel's singing, which enchanted her prince, and Rapunzel, in turn, fell in love with his gentle and persuasive words. The beauty of a song, a whispered promise, a long golden braid falling from a tower on high—all these led Lindsey to anticipate that love would come in the story.

Yet love was not always romance, nor was it always associated with beauty. The sometimes predictable behaviors of princesses and kings did not carry over into themes of friendship, loyalty, and substance beneath a truly ugly or shabby exterior. Lindsey received several gifts from her grandmother for Christmas, but her favorite was a small velveteen bunny that was accompanied by one of the newly illustrated editions of Margery Williams' story *The Velveteen Rabbit*. Lindsey was much less interested in the story than in the bunny. She carried it with her everywhere for the next few days, and slept with it at night. There were even times when she demanded the bunny in preference to her blanket, Babette, which was the love of her life. One night while we were reading, Babette lay abandoned at the end of the bed, and I attempted to include her in the circle.

> "You know," I said, "the story of *The Velveteen Rabbit* is a lot like the story of Babette. She was new and pink and very fluffy when you were a baby. Now she's pale and a little shabby. You've loved her a lot, haven't you?"
>
> "Yes," Lindsey answered, reaching for Babette and rubbing her reflectively against her face. "I made her real."
>
> For years, Lindsey had claimed that when she grew up she was going to marry Babette, a sweet and silent partner, but now that's been replaced by the handsome prince. (December 29, 1986, 4;1)

True love implies loyalty, commitment, and continuity—enduring through hardship and beyond appearance. Even a handsome prince is not totally won over by surface charm. True love often meant a struggle, and Lindsey could see time and time again, in texts, the relationship between tough decisions and love. While we were reading the story of Una's search for the Red Cross Knight (Hodges), Lindsey broke in with a comparison to *Star Wars:* "Luke traveled to save Princess Leia. He fighted Darth Vader" (July 17, 1986, 3;8).

Though often unable to justify their moral understandings verbally, Lindsey and Ashley felt no hesitation at announcing their judgments and at putting themselves into literary characters' places in role playing and in pronouncements about the worth of characters. In expressing their sense of "right" and "wrong," they often referred to a combination of positional dictates (queens "should" have certain characteristics, parents "ought" to carry out particular obligations, and so on) and universal standards linked to fairness (especially for those whose size, age, gender, or state of health dictated special needs). In daily interactions that threatened their choice of activity, they could accept from literature a higher standard of morality than they might otherwise have adopted. Shifting roles or announcing the perspective of another could swing their reasoning about tasks around to that of adults; Lindsey pretending to be Cinderella assumed kitchen clean-up jobs far more willingly than Lindsey as real-life older sister. Judgments about the reasonableness, morality, and fairness of storybook characters centered around behaviors or expectations that the girls, in their daily life, talked about as "paying back hard work," "not being mean," and "saying thanks"—conventions, duties, and goals that Kenny and I dropped into our household conversations from time to time.[6]

One morning, Lindsey and I read Robert Munsch's story *The Paper Bag Princess*, which turns traditional costuming inside out (the princess wears a paper bag), reverses rescue protocol (the princess rescues the prince), and upends the happily-ever-after ending (no wedding). I got the book from a friend, but Lindsey had already heard the story at school.

"You did! Did it surprise you when you first read it?" I asked.

"Mm-hmmm. 'Cause she's wearing a *paper bag*, and look at her crown!" Lindsey laughed and then grew serious. "I don't like the prince."

"How come?"

"All he says is: 'Why are you wearing a paper bag? I'm not going to marry you unless you wear something *sensible!*'" Lindsey's voice assumed a haughty tone.

"You're kidding!" I exclaimed. "Well, what do you think about that?"

"I think he's mean!"

Indeed, the story indicates exactly *how* mean, after Princess Elizabeth defeats the dragon with her wit:

Elizabeth walked right over the dragon and opened the door to the cave. There was Prince Ronald.

He looked at her and said, "Elizabeth, you are a mess! You smell like ashes, your hair is all tangled and you are wearing a dirty old paper bag. Come back when you are dressed like a real princess.

"Ronald," said Elizabeth, "your clothes are really pretty and your hair is very neat. You look like a real prince, but you are a bum."

They didn't get married after all. (Munsch)

"She's right!" Lindsey exclaimed. "I mean, he didn't have the right to say that!"

"What do you think he should have said to her?" I wondered.

"Oh! Let's go home!" (June 17, 1990, 7;7)

In the ensuing discussion, Lindsey suggested that the princess had defeated the dragon with "her ideas" and admired her "thinking strength," words that were quite a distance from traditional notions of royal or maidenly characteristics. Her parting shot as she left the room was, "He didn't deserve her!"

Still, the ultimately happy ending where true love leads to marriage continued to hold sway. In the summer of Ashley's fifth year, her best friend, Nate, and his family moved away. The two had played together daily for almost three years and had plighted their troth many times, both in play and in serious conversations. On the family's last night, we had them to dinner and exchanged parting gifts. Nate's mother, Leslie, gave Lindsey a small figurine of Robin Hood and a plastic sword encrusted with a ruby marble. She gave both Ashley and Nate a picture of the two of them pressing noses together, Nate's hands gently holding Ashley's shoulders. And she gave our family William Steig's *Amos and Boris*—the story of two friends who must eventually part.

Our gifts were also literary in nature. Kenny gave both Ashley and Nate a book on frogs to celebrate the many shared family nights of frog "hunting" in a nearby creek. I found books for the girls to give as well. Lindsey gave Nate a set of *Nate the Great* books, by Marjorie Sharmat, while Ashley gave him a copy of Judith Viorst's *Rosie and Michael*—again the story of two friends—which she asked me to inscribe "To my best friend, Nate" before signing her name on the inside cover. I knew I couldn't read the story to the children without becoming tearful, so Nate's father, Jacob, volunteered. As he read of the two loyal friends, Jacob substituted the names Rosie and Michael with our own children's. Ashley and Nate both sat quietly listening to the story, their eyes searching the pictures. When Jacob reached the end, he stopped several times, trying to control the emotion in his voice, and both children looked up at him anxiously and then to each other. Ashley held on to the end, giving Nate and his parents a tight embrace and waving them goodbye as they left for their car, but as we turned back into the house the two of us burst into tears. We were sitting on the couch weeping, when Lindsey tearfully joined us.

"Don't worry, Ashley," she consoled. "He'll come back when you're sixteen. Just like a prince in a story. He'll come back and you'll get married."

Ashley looked up at her sister hopefully. "Are you sure?"

"I'm sure," Lindsey replied. (July 17, 1991, 8;8 and 5;7)

The sureness of love was fixed firmly in Lindsey's heart and Ashley's hope, for in times of loss the greatest consolation came from the world of story.

Fear and loss, beauty and love weave themselves through children's literature from illustration to dialogue, but they do so along with goals and intentions. For children to ground emotions in literary texts and in their own everyday behaviors, they must learn to bring under their control a belief system that incorporates notions of intentionality. Sages and simpletons, both in and outside literature, try endlessly to help us understand motivation and intent—the unspeakable forces behind the meaning of what is said and done. Tethered too often to a specific time and circumstance, intentions separated from their origins do not hang steady or secure; even the words of author or character that may profess to explicate them can be untrustworthy. The issue is not whether children can or will feel and be able to identify with particular motivations behind the words, emotions, or actions of story characters. Instead, the question is: Can children acknowledge that characters' intentions exist within the belief systems of the characters before they accept what the author imposes on the story through action and plot?[7]

Within literature, authors have to intend to mean when they write, illustrate, and shape literature, but these precise meanings lie neither in their heads nor in their words and illustrations. Authors of children's literature move children into worlds in which the characters' belief systems and the authors' genre frame provide clues for figuring out the possible intentions of those who have feelings and mental representations and take actions within the story. But these are only hints, and as such they leave open several injections of intentions by readers. When adults and children read together and practice deciphering possible intentions (of authors and characters), the experience has substantial carry-over to the real world, where messages are not always intentioned or intentional and may receive such assignment by all but the speaker or actor. Neither the child nor the adult reader can "read" all possible intentions of the writer or illustrator, and rarely does anyone know if and when there can be an exact match between the intentions of the author and those perceived by the reader. What children can and do understand from literary explorations of intent is that someone acting as an author—a maker of meaning—worked through a set of rules and belief systems to create this representation of characters, situations, and outcomes. These did not just appear, as many aspects of daily life seem to; they come about through specific meaning-making efforts—planned, scripted, corrected, and put out purposefully for interpretation by others—by readers who bring their own screens of emotion, experience, and expectation to their various and varying readings.[8]

Literary texts offered Lindsey and Ashley relatively free-wheeling domains in which to give voice and action to their own intentions. Agent and subject merged in their empathy for the characters of the stories we read. The range of situations that literary characters met permitted wide exploration of altered roles and allowed the girls to experiment by putting characters who seemed to have less power into more dominant roles. During one reading of *Sleeping Beauty,* we came to the passage in which the princess is entranced by the merrily spinning thread and approaches the spindle with unsuspecting delight. Lindsey, however, gave Briar Rose a new and more powerful voice.

> "No, no," she interjected. "She should tell her, 'No, wicked witch, I won't touch the spindle. It's sharp!'" Her tone rang with authority.
> "Don't you think the witch would be able to put the spell on anyway?" I asked, playing devil's advocate.
> Lindsey leaped to her feet. "Not if it was me! I'm too fast. She'd *never* catch me." (February 22, 1990, 7;3)

Powered by her sense of the affect operating in situations, she reshaped and reconstituted the rules of the texts to give characters different intentions that would lead them to altered outcomes. She also placed herself and her own qualities into the text to produce an altered outcome that, when explained, bore little relation to the presumed intent behind the warning of the now powerful Briar Rose.

It appears that empathy—the sensing of affect *with* characters—led the way to some sense of necessary action to alter their situation; internal motivations that could lead the characters out of their dilemma rarely received direct explication. Though on the surface fear and love seemed dominant motivations, the challenge behind these (which soon came to be somewhat predictable in frame stories or those of a particular genre) was to determine other sources of motivation and possible ramifications of intention to reorder the world internal to the text.

The Play of Story

These reorderings come through deliberate play with story, as children create their own texts from those in which they participate or those they hear orally. Individual reconstructions offer an entrée into a world of books and of people that values story as a treasure to be shared. If possession were denied, the text could not continually evolve and grow, forming links with other texts or disseminating fragments of epigrammatic wisdom or thematic allusion.[9] When Lindsey was three years old, I gave her a test on book-handling knowledge designed by Marie Clay (1979b), a New Zealand educator. When I gave her the test, I had to consider several factors. Although it was designed for five-year-olds, I thought it might still be a valuable tool for assessing Lindsey's understanding about books. I also thought that the majority of the test questions would be out of the range of her present under-standing and perhaps prove frustrating. Both these predictions turned out to be accurate.

In handling Clay's children's book *Sand* (1972), Lindsey displayed an understanding of the cover of a book, she followed the pages from left to right, and she knew that pictures in books are right side up. She showed substantially more discomfort, however, in the more formal administration of Clay's test than in her own responses to the book. We were seated on the bed in my room and had reached the mid-point of the test. On this page there were several words written with im-proper letter order and a picture of a boy sitting in the waves.

> When I asked her, "What's wrong with this page?" she began studying the picture, ignoring the words.
> She finally said, "He's getting his shorts wet!"
> On the next page, the same letter-order problem was displayed with slightly different questioning. "What's wrong with the writing on this page?"
> She responded, "I don't know."
> I then pointed to the question mark and said, "What's this for?"
> She again responded, "I don't know," but this time her voice was in a whisper.
> Then her face brightened. "I'm going to get my *own* books!" she announced and promptly jumped off the bed. I tried to get her to come back to the story, but she refused, running off to her bedroom. I could hear her rummaging through her books and then she ran back to join me. She leaped onto the bed with her copy of *The Three Little Pigs* and began reading aloud. I tried to coax her into contin-uing with the book *Sand,* but she took it firmly and placed it face down on the bed. I gave up, and encouraged her lively reading of *The Three Little Pigs*. Then we went downstairs for a snack. (February 1, 1986, 3;3)

Here Lindsey showed her need to play out the situation according to familiar expectations of our story and talk times. The text on *Sand* came not with an invitation to create worlds but with specific questions and limited answers. Yet the story of *The Three Little Pigs* came in a malleable form, one that she could structure and restructure according to her own reading. Lindsey's attachment to this story typified her relationship to all the texts she created; it was stronger because it was hers.

Both Lindsey and Ashley learned early the power of language to draw in adults. When Lindsey said she was going to "devour" her breakfast, she was sharing a word from *Snow White* that we had discussed the day before. When she cut her knees, she asked for "sticking plaster," a remedy prescribed in Potter's *The Tale of Mr. Jeremy Fisher.* As the girls played with words and tried them out in conversation, they not only gained an understanding of literary words and phrases but they lured adults into their conversations and games.

After a trip to the playground one night, Lindsey was in high spirits, and as we walked in the door, I held her giggling in my arms. I carried her to the wooden kitchen chair and began to peel off her running shoes and socks. When her feet were bare she looked at me with a devilish grin and invited me to smell her toes. This was an old game. I would smell her feet and then make horrified faces, scrunching up my nose and shouting "PU!" This slight humor would be enough to send her into hysterical laughter, and we would play it again and again. In the beginning of the game Lindsey would try to convince me to smell her feet, telling me that they were sure to smell good. I would pretend to be skeptical but then acquiesce.

This time, Lindsey began by telling me that her toes smelled "very pretty." I refused to take the bait. She then escalated the definition of her sweet-smelling toes.

> "These are pretty as roses," she said invitingly. I still declined.
> Then she played her ace in the hole.
> In her most persuasive voice she suggested, "They're RAMPION!" Her voice held a sing-song seductive quality.
> What could I do? I inhaled the scent of her playground toes and after a moment of facial agony, fell off the chair as though dead. She laughed so hard the sound of her cackle startled Ashley, who proceeded to cry. I had to leap from my prone position to comfort her, and then carry the still-giggling Lindsey up to bed. (June 30, 1986, 3;7)

The word "rampion" held all the tantalizing power of the fairy tale. It represented irresistible temptation, and by using this word Lindsey knew she could draw me into her game just as the plant drew Rapunzel's mother to the garden. A single word has the power to draw in the adult who also knows the story and can revel in the linking of two who share its play in new and special moments.

Such claims for play with literary texts often came not only through metaphors but also by assertions of absolute authority over different components of individual texts. Lindsey frequently corrected us in our reading, and she was especially bound to the original pronunciation we had given different new words. When Kenny first read *Jabberwocky*, he gave the *i* in "slithy toves" a long vowel sound. Lindsey would not tolerate a short vowel pronunciation from me, and quickly substituted her version for my edification. And she once became angry with Kenny for not conforming with my pronunciation of an African word from *Why Mosquitoes Buzz in People's Ears* (Aardema).[10]

The ability to recite sections of text also gave the girls the chance to play directors of a process over which we as adults might otherwise have claimed mastery. Lindsey loved the repetitive nature of many stories, for it offered her the opportunity to engage actively in the reading. Examples abound, especially in the Mother Goose rhymes and stories like *Tikki Tikki Tembo* (Mosel), *The Three Little Pigs* (Galdone), and *Who's in Rabbit's House?* (Aardema). Reciting text and asserting authority over its "correct" performance helps explain one of the mysteries, and indeed irritations, for adults: the insistence by children that their favorite texts be read again and again. Adults' goals in reading—to gain information and learn something new—conflict here with young children's notions of text. Children seem to know that most fictional stories intended for children give relatively little in the way of facts. But for young readers, these stories offer the chance to gather the texts into their repertoire with such a level of knowledge that they can then rework and reshape the rules according to their own playfulness. Just as toddlers have been known to lie in their cribs and practice again and again the same phrases or to alter these only slightly to include new sounds, new words, or parts of words, so children work to get into their heads not only the full texts of certain portions of literature but the totality of the rules that make the texts adhere.[11]

On a literal level, Lindsey often would not accept what the book said. In *Mr. Rabbit and the Lovely Present* (Zolotow), she rejected the idea of blue stars. "Stars are white!" she explained. And the idea of blue grapes bothered her enormously. "Those grapes are purple!" she cried. Although she was constantly willing to accept fantasy, she was unwilling to depart too far from what she knew, according to certain of her own labels and categories. Even more often, she challenged books that deviated from the predictable text patterns (style of illustrations or generic conventions) she saw in books. Through such challenges, she determined the limits of story conventions and possible boundaries for stretching these conventions.

Not only direct challenge but also wide-sweeping play with stories outside actual book-reading episodes aided Lindsey and Ashley in figuring out their own repertoires of key rules that make stories work. Both girls moved characters in and out of the text, held conversations with them, and gave them instructions and advice. In Lindsey's sociodrama of *Cinderella*, the protagonist steadfastly refused to do all the work (3;6). In Lindsey's play version of *Charlotte's Web*, the large gray spider lived on and on (4;0). In her revision of *Hansel and Gretel*, the stepmother was "nice" and the children found themselves in the forest "on accident."

One day, after reading the tale of the two children and their vengeful stepmother, Lindsey suggested a scenario for our walk:

> "You want to play Hansel and Gretel?" she asked. "You be my mother. Your name is Abra and you're a nice mother."
>
> "Well, get up lazybones!" I shrieked in my best imitation of the wicked woman.
>
> "No! I said you're a *nice* mother!" Lindsey reminded me with some frustration. "But we need some bread!"
>
> We went to the refrigerator and selected some English muffins. On our walk, Lindsey skipped ahead tossing bread crumbs in high arcs, which had little resemblance to Hansel's strategic placement of crumbs along the path. (June 13, 1986, 3;7)

A strict adherence to text denies the child the authorship that is an inherent part of ownership. The child's occasional attachment to precise wording or sequence does not mean that the story is immutable. It is simply a reflection of the child's sense of play—with roles and rules inside and outside books—that ultimately leads to reshapings of stories.

Both Ashley and Lindsey inserted story phrases to extend or explicate their comments, to analogize their stance or feelings with those of a character in a story. In their revoicings of the characters in stories we read, the girls displayed their awareness that written texts give authority beyond that of the personal claim.

Early one evening, Kenny and Ashley accompanied Lindsey to her gymnastics class. Ashley staked out an unused mat and began to practice her handstands. For the first several attempts, Kenny caught her feet and held her steady, but Ashley ultimately rejected his help. "I can do it myself," she insisted. Then with a smirk toward her father she threw out her stomach, flung her hands to her hips, and quoted, "'I'll do it myself,' said the Little Red Hen. 'I'll do my handstand myself!'" (February 8, 1990, 4;2). In her declaration, Ashley substituted the words "do my handstand" for the original words of the Little Red Hen, who insisted on eating the bread by herself. Ashley invoked text as the authority to drive away the father that she knew was not likely to budge from his protective role during her potentially dangerous antics. The situation in life was not perfectly analogous to the one in the text (her father had not refused help, as had the Hen's companions), but a strike for independence was present in both cases.

Lindsey and Ashley also used language from literature to create verbal art—to make their language "pretty." Letters, in particular, were occasions for elaborate and metaphorical compliments. On Mother's Day, Lindsey dictated the following to her father to write on a bright piece of orange construction paper, which served as a greeting card: "Dear Mommy: I love you. Your voice is like snowflakes falling like feathers from the sky. Happy Mommy's Day!" (May, 1987, 5;6). The story of *Snow White* (Grimm Brothers, 1974) opens with the lines, *"Once in the middle of winter, when snowflakes were falling like feathers from the sky, a Queen sat sewing by a window . . ."* Lindsey had requested and listened to this story so often, it was not surprising that a piece of text had worked its way into her own text. When I complimented her on her beautiful letter she commented, "Yeah, it's pretty, huh?" Taking up writing herself gave her more play even than her usual spoken adaptations of literary texts. She had, like the authors she knew, chosen the out-of-the-ordinary word or phrase to do more than just "say" her ideas.

Sharing the Story

Children can bank their literary insights and then spend them to gain mastery of a social situation, whether in the home or in school. Children who live in a world of words that are written and read can use their understanding of story in order to become members of their network of family and friends and to prepare themselves for meeting new challenges.[12]

Lindsey once used story to participate in a social event and impress the older boys in her childcare home. Lindsey's daycare mother, Beth, said she had a "funny story" to tell me. Evidently, the older boys in the group had been swapping stories of their reading. Nicholas, who was approaching five, took out a book and began to read. All the older boys were impressed with his decoding skills.

> "That's nothing," Lindsey challenged.
> She pulled over a book that she had heard many times and read it from cover to cover. Although she was reading from her own interpretation of the text rather than in the conventional sense of decoding, Beth said that Lindsey "really had the boys buffaloed."
> "Wow! She's only three. How'd she do that?" they all exclaimed. (April 9, 1986, 3;5)

Through reading, Lindsey had gained status in a world of older boys who normally excluded her. Although the adults in her world rarely excluded her, at times the conversation would do just that, and Lindsey often used literature in order to participate. Time and again she joined in adult conversation to offer her literary opinion. An adult conversation on the origins of "Aunt Nancy," a traditional teller of African-American folktales, led Lindsey to give a faithful recounting of the tale of Ananse the Spider Man, the main character in *A Story A Story* (Haley). Another conversation centered on the movie *Out of Africa*, and spurred Lindsey to inject her own evaluation of the book *Outside Over There* (Sendak). Once, when Lindsey was bending over a pot of turkey giblets boiling in water, she whispered, *"Bring me her lungs and liver as a token"* (November, 1989, 7;0). She was quoting the wicked stepmother from *Snow White* (Grimm Brothers / Heins), and turned to give me a conspiratorial wink. Being an "insider in the network" includes inside humor, unspoken messages expressed as winks and chuckles, and the multiple voices of the "here and now" and "once upon a time" meeting together to talk.[13]

As the children made connections in text, they linked with their social world—a world where these connections were used by adults as well. One afternoon, our friend Jacob came by with his son Nate to talk about Nate's progress in school and to borrow some children's books for a trip they were planning to make. Lindsey perched on the windowsill of her room to listen to our talk, but I immediately cautioned against the danger of her position. "Lindsey," I warned, "you'd better get down from there before you fall backwards out your window into outside over there." Lindsey giggled as she jumped down from the sill (May 30, 1990, 7;6). The words "outside over there" come from the text of the same name by Maurice Sendak—a story about a girl named Ida who, in her anxiety to save her baby sister from being kidnapped by goblins, falls backward out her window into a dream world. Although Lindsey was in no need to go to the rescue of her sister, her position near the window and the possibility of falling were real. The words of the everyday ("fall backwards out your window") were so similar to those of the story, they seemed to establish a frame into which the words of the text could fit. My literary metaphor made an explicit match between life and text for Lindsey to think about and act on, and thus softened the direct order. While we both knew that Ida was unhurt by her fall, the words suggested a "proof" that children could indeed fall out of their windows, and Lindsey knew that if she were to fall she would not be able to float across the sky like Ida, but would instead come to a harder fate.

As I spoke these words and Lindsey acknowledged them with her giggle, we heard the world of the text, a mother's caution, the implied catastrophe, and the social softening of a warning. When the words of literary texts slid into the language of the everyday, they became the symbols of a community—a community that referenced, cited, and valued literature. The book was an authority that, when invoked, joined adult and child not only in the actual reading of a story but also in cooperative agreement concerning (some) day-to-day situations.

The everyday world had rules, and these often emerged directly in the form of parental admonitions, friends' objections, and ritual events (for example, having friends over meant letting the guests have first choice, and keeping one's room clean was a daily responsibility). The call to story—and thus the cooperative agreement that tacitly held around reference to literary text as authority—often helped Lindsey avoid or at least delay work and occasionally ameliorate an unavoidable punishment. One Sunday morning, the girls were engaged in a quarrel, alternating between crying and yelling. I was upstairs working on my studies and had interceded several times before I lost my temper.

"If you girls have so much time to argue, then you probably have time to do some housework!"

I flung the dusty kitchen rug out the door and sent Lindsey up the stairs for the vacuum cleaner. I stationed Ashley at the sink to do the breakfast dishes. Both girls eyed me resentfully, but I ignored their pleas and went back to work. After a while, I realized that it was much too quiet and descended the stairs again, expecting the worst.

Instead, they were both happily scrubbing the kitchen floor.

"I'm Laura and Ashley is Mary," Lindsey explained. "We're playing *Little House in the Big Woods,* and we've got to get the cabin clean for our mom!" (February 18, 1990, 7;3 and 4;2)

In this case, the girls knew that no pleas of "Do we have to?" or distractions by literary reference would mitigate my irritation. Instead, between them, they made their tasks acceptable by moving into the rules of the Wilder girls' world, where children obeyed their parents instantly and rarely squabbled. Getting the cabin clean was far more engaging than doing the breakfast dishes. Lindsey and Ashley often teased apart how the dialogues of literary texts could be transformed to operate with acceptable emotions within sets of social relations and for their own desired outcomes in current situations.[14]

In addition to providing status, an entrée into an adult conversation, an excuse, and even a softened punishment, possession of stories gave the girls the opportunity to take control and thus to reshape others' rules into their own. Like a treasured possession, the literature in their lives was something they were willing to let others take a peek at if such sharing brought a rescue.[15]

One afternoon, Lindsey and I walked to the public library for the semiannual book sale. I was hoping to find some inexpensive books, but we arrived too late; the shelves were stripped of books and two long walls of metal cases labeled "Children's Books" stared vacantly back at us. The one children's picture book I saw was found by another child. It was Aardema's *Who's in Rabbit's House?* and the child's mother was berating him for wanting a book he hadn't looked at. She snatched it from his hands and hissed,

"You haven't even looked at it. How do you know if you want it if you haven't even read it?"

Another woman standing nearby softly joined in. "It's really quite good. I'm a school librarian and my kids really like it."

The scowling mother looked as though she just might devour the librarian. Fearing violence, I entered the fray. "It really is a good book. My daughter has this book and it's one of her favorites."

Lindsey smiled warily up at the woman. "It's about a rabbit," she informed.

Facing the literary awareness of the three of us, the woman's scowl yielded to a social smile.

"Here," I said, seeing that the cover was missing. "Let me see if it's all here." I flipped through the pages of the book and found that the last few pages were gone as well.

"Oh!" With disappointment I told her that the book was incomplete. She had really been right all along.

Lindsey stared sympathetically at the boy. The librarian explained, "Without the end, you won't be able to find out who's in rabbit's house."

We murmured our "Too bads," and moved away. Lindsey stayed behind staring at the boy, who held the book disconsolately at his side. I called her to join me, but she remained rooted in her position. "Lindsey!" I called once more.

She looked at me briefly and then turned back to the boy. "It's a caterpillar!" she whispered conspiratorially and then she skipped over to join me. (April 23, 1987, 3;5)

At the time, I laughed at her uninhibited desire to relate the climax of a story that she knew so well. But later I saw that a sense of pride in knowledge of text can allow the child to connect with a community that values literacy. And most important, it is a gift—a treasure to be shared and an investment on which to build.

Knowledge and Wisdom

We grow by inferring, comparing, and searching for the nuances of possible motives, new opportunities, and turns of intention. Through literature, children safely encounter a wide array of possible characters, motivations, and outcomes of actions and emotions. There they learn the rules of written texts, and then they gain license to bend these rules according to the rules of other texts. Throughout all readings from literature, and in the process of reshaping, reusing, and retelling, readers go beyond knowledge to wisdom.

Literature for Lindsey and Ashley provided a safe arena for exploring cases in which knowledge was unified and fixed within apparent emotional states, or capable of being fragmented, separated, and reoriented with possible new forms of unity and unification. For them, the deriving of rules for how books went beyond the given and immediate ranged from reconciling text and illustration to figuring out that books did not "just end."

Within books, text and illustrations "go together." Moreover, within illustrations, the expected course of change in a character's state or age conforms with the text and not with the expectations of the key feature of the character. For example, a young prince may "age" within a few pages, even though the central features of youth, optimism, romantic love, and filial commitment remain. Personality or character features hang on despite altered outward characteristics. Characters also have animacy, belief systems, and feelings, and can both create problems and plot their resolution. A character chosen by the author as the story's focus is both subject and agent of his or her destiny, and the usual weaknesses of age, innocence, or ignorance need not limit feats of wit or prowess. A young girl can therefore be brought to near ruin by a boastful father, further victimized by a greedy prince, taken advantage of by a dwarf, and still keep her crown and year-old son by guessing Rumplestiltskin's name.

Furthermore, characters can have appearances that belie or mask their inner qualities. One morning, Lindsey and I were reading the story of *The Princess and the Pea* (Andersen). I asked Lindsey to tell me a bit about the story before I began reading. In one of the illustrations, there is a great number of princesses, whom the young prince dismisses in his search for a "real princess." When Lindsey turned to this page, she asked:

"Are they pretend princesses?"

"They might be," I answered. "I think the story says something about them being *maybe* pretend princesses. Do you like any of those pretend princesses?"

"No," she replied. "I don't like her. I don't like her." She chanted a litany of rejected princesses. "Or her. Or her. Or her. Or her. 'Cause they're all ugly."

"They're all ugly?" I was rather surprised by her assessment. Although Galdone's figures are caricatures with exaggerated features, some of the princesses seemed to pass muster.

Lindsey was emphatic. "Yes," she cried. But when I asked for an explanation, she would only reply, "'Cause." (April 8, 1986, 3;5)

The first time we had read the story and turned to the same page, Lindsey had asked, "Are these the ugly stepsisters?" It was as if all princesses, like Cinderella, came equipped with at least two ugly stepsisters. In Lindsey's younger years, surface and internal qualities had to match. In her understanding of the rules that worked in books, if characters were ugly in character, they were also ugly in appearance.

One afternoon we read *Mufaro's Beautiful Daughters* (Steptoe) with one of Lindsey's neighborhood friends. In the story, one of two African sisters, Manyara and Nyasha, was to be chosen to marry the king. Although both girls were equal in beauty, only Nyasha had a good heart. Disguised as a starving boy, the king tested the two girls, begging for a small portion of food. Lindsey was very eager to share the story and attempted to reveal the story's secrets to her friend.

> Pointing to the picture of Nyasha, she exclaimed, "Guess who gets to be queen!" She then pointed to the "bad sister," clapped, and shouted gaily, "And she's going to be the servant!!"
>
> True to Lindsey's prediction, Manyara failed the test:
>
> *She had never been in the forest at night before, and she was frightened, but her greed to be the first to appear before the king drove her on. In her hurry, she almost stumbled over a small boy who suddenly appeared, standing in the path.*
>
> *"Please," said the boy. "I am hungry. Will you give me something to eat?"*
>
> *"I have brought only enough for myself," Manyara replied.*
>
> *"But, please!" said the boy. "I am so very hungry."*
>
> *"Out of my way, boy! Tomorrow I will become your queen. How dare you stand in my path?"*
>
> Lindsey grew very excited at this point, "Well, she's . . . she's . . . anyway she's going to get . . ." She ultimately began to yell at the storybook character, "We'll show her!"
>
> "You think she'd be a very good queen if she refused a hungry boy food?" I asked.
>
> "No way!" Lindsey replied adamantly. "If I did that I would . . . I would give the little boy, like, two bags of *whatever* he wanted!" (September 25, 1988, 5;10)

The rules of story for Lindsey were such that when true love was tested, the inner beauty of generosity and caring won out over a surface beauty of no substance. Understanding the reciprocal nature of love, she projected a moral image of herself as one capable of giving love, not simply demanding it by right. And she expected characters in story to do the same.

Slowly Lindsey came to accept that the surface beauty of characters did not necessarily correlate with the beauty of the character. While she understood that the "bad sister" was attractive, she was still reluctant to give her much credit.

> "You don't think she's pretty?" I asked following one of Lindsey's negative comments.
>
> "Yeah. She has these things sticking up in her hair. Yuck!" However, Lindsey loved the hair adornment of the "good sister."
>
> Interested in her assessment, I asked, "Do you think that people who act ugly can be beautiful on the outside?"
>
> "Mm-hmmm," she answered, with some hesitation.
>
> "Do you know anyone who's beautiful on the outside but ugly on the inside?" I continued.
>
> Lindsey got the point and shouted the name of her archenemy, a neighborhood girl whom Lindsey had often characterized as "pretty on the outside but mean on the inside." (September 25, 1988, 6;10)

Lindsey accepted that the uncertainty in the unfolding of the story rested, in part, on the fact that characters who were physically beautiful could turn into characters who behaved badly.

Part of this unfolding lies with the authors "behind" the texts. They can exert their will over the lives and activities of characters, themes that are pursued from book to book, and situations that characters meet. Thus, favorite rabbits can be immortalized (*The Tale of Peter Rabbit*, Potter), childhood fantasies commemorated (*Little Red Riding Hood*, Grimm Brothers), and older brothers exorcised (*Peter Pan*, Barrie). But authors and illustrators are also "real" people who can make mistakes—can forget characters, confuse features of situations, or ignore certain elements of a story that children believe "should" be there.

During one evening's bedtime story hour, we read *The Water of Life*, an old Grimm tale retold by Barbara Rogasky and illustrated by Trina Schart Hyman. The story tells of a young prince's striving to discover the water of life in order to save his dying father. The prince is blocked at every turn by his two evil elder brothers, but with the aid of a dwarf, who reveals the location of the sacred water in a nearby castle, the prince succeeds.

Following the dwarf's instructions to the letter, the prince taps on the castle door three times with an iron rod and immediately meets two roaring lions. At this point in the story, Lindsey repeated the comment she had made in every reading of this tale—that the lions' faces and bodies should be switched. In the illustration, the lion who is lying down is roaring more ferociously than the lion getting to his feet, and Lindsey always found the rage inconsistent with the position. She would place herself in the role of the illustrator.

> "If I drew the picture, I would switch those lions. That madder lion should be standing up!" she explained.
>
> "You're right," I conceded, but since it was an old discussion I didn't pursue it and continued to read:
>
> *Everything happened as the dwarf had said. The prince knocked three times with the iron rod and the castle gate flew open. In the courtyard lay two lions with their huge mouths open and their sharp teeth glistening. He threw each a loaf of bread and they quieted down.*
>
> *The prince walked into the castle. He came to a big hall, where many enchanted princes sat around a long table. They did not move, nor did they speak. The king's youngest son took the rings from each one's fingers, and picked up a sword and a loaf of bread that lay near them on the floor.* (N.p.)

While I read, Lindsey studied the facing page—an illustration of the many enchanted princes sitting frozen at the banquet table. In the past, we had had long discussions of this page, in an effort to seek out each prince's individual enchantment. One prince had tree branches growing from the top of his head, another had a full set of antlers, still another had the head of a frog. With every reading I had worried about the rings. Although the tale later explains how the prince uses the bread and sword to his benefit, the rings are never mentioned again. "Why doesn't the author tell us what happened to the rings?" I wondered aloud. But Lindsey was puzzling over the unexpected presence of all those enchanted princes, and announced her conclusions: "Hey, Mom! I figured something out!" she exclaimed. "Those princes are the ones that didn't listen to the dwarf." Her voice slowed and dropped to a whisper as she enunciated the following sentence word by word, "They—didn't—leave—the—castle—before—the—clock—struck—

twelve!" (January 30, 1990, 7;2). Although the author gives no clue that this is indeed the case and although Lindsey's observation had not come up in previous conversations, it made perfect sense. I told her that this is what happens to characters in fairy tales who don't follow instructions, and reminded her of all the princes caught in the thorns around Sleeping Beauty's castle. She nodded solemnly and said, "You gotta have good ears to get what you want." Here her wisdom extended beyond the actual knowledge of the story.

Storybook characters have limited abilities and opportunities to say all that is "behind" their emotions, actions, and wills. Whereas the three little pigs refuse a wolf entrance by calling on the hair of their respective chins, the mouse dentist and his wife in Steig's *Dr. De Soto* allow the entrance of their dreaded enemy, the fox, with the simple words, *"Let's risk it!"* Since characters cannot say all they feel, believe, or intend in the words of the text, readers must speak for them, suggest alternatives, and redirect their actions. The text is primarily a frame of plot and characters with intentions and wills, but within these givens, the reader must move to assert that what is said means more than what is said or may mean in another way—especially if the reader considers particular features of an illustration or remembers a detail.

In Hyman's version of *Little Red Riding Hood,* Lindsey differentiated between intention and action. As Little Red Riding Hood is preparing for her trip to her grandmother's, her mother gives her a long verbal list of *dos* and *don'ts.*

> *"Promise me that you won't daydream and stray off the path, and don't run, or you will fall down and break the bottle, and then there will be no wine for Grandmother. And when you get there, please don't forget your manners! Say 'Good morning,' 'Please,' and 'Thank you' nicely, without staring 'round about you or sucking your finger. Don't stay too long, or else you will tire Grandmother. And when you have had a nice visit, come straight home"* (n.p.).

"She's not going to promise," Lindsey said.

"She's not?" I asked, pretending shock that any child would lie to her mother.

"No."

But the story words suggested that Red Riding Hood would indeed promise. I continued reading: *" 'Yes, mama,' said Little Red Riding Hood."*

"But she's not!" Lindsey warned.

In the text, Little Red Riding Hood retorts: *"I promise. I will do just as you tell me."*

Lindsey stopped me. "But she . . . but she *won't* promise." (April 29, 1986, 3;5)

Lindsey knew that the words were empty and that Red Riding Hood would ultimately stray off the path, forgetting all her mother's admonitions. Because of this look beneath the surface, the punishment came as no surprise. Indeed, Lindsey could create an even more disastrous end for Red Riding Hood in her play.

One day, Lindsey and I were out in the garden gathering fresh flowers. We searched the garden for promising blooms, clipping the long stems of the tulips and daffodils. Lindsey held out her hands for them, and after admonishing her to "be gentle," I laid them carefully in her palms. With the addition of several branches of bushy greenery, her arms were soon filled to overflowing, and I could barely see her face behind the foliage.

"I'm like Little Red Riding Hood . . . because she picked so many flowers too!"

When we went into the house, she helped me arrange the flowers in the vase.

"Now I'm a different Little Red Riding Hood," she exclaimed.

"How are you different?" I asked.

"This is a movie, see." She leaned closer in a conspiratorial way. "And in this movie Little Red Riding Hood died . . . 'cause she ate her flowers and she didn't have ipecac!" (April 28, 1986, 3;5)

As a toddler, Lindsey had once eaten a purple flower and had experienced the distasteful consequences of ipecac, a medicine that causes vomiting. It seemed only right that Red Riding Hood, who was so bent on making mistakes, should suffer a similar if not worse fate.

If readers have experiences they bring to texts, authors also have experiences that lead them to write the texts of children's literature. However, young readers must learn not to expect a match between authors' lives and those of the characters in their texts. Much to her surprise, three-year-old Lindsey discovered that Beatrix Potter was not a rabbit, nor was Trina Schart Hyman a fairy princess.

Authors do not write exclusively about their own lives or elements directly known to them, and they may well be influenced by other agents (their own children, their dreams, the experiences of others).

Thus, when authors do not seem consistent within their own themes—across books, or in their portrayal of characters within stories—young readers may need to explain the authors' sources, their inspiration, or what appears to be their temporary misguidedness.

In the story *The Jolly Postman* (Ahlberg and Ahlberg), a postman delivers letters from and to fairy-tale characters. Goldilocks writes a letter of apology to Baby Bear, the Big Bad Wolf receives a letter of complaint from Red Riding Hood's lawyers, and a publishing company writes to Cinderella to ask permission to *"publish a little book for younger readers in celebration of your recent marriage to H.R.H. Prince Charming."* Lindsey, however, had a different idea:

> "It should have been wroten by her ugly sisters," she commented. And when I asked her why, she explained, "'Cause her ugly sisters have to do *something* nice to her."
>
> "Yeah, maybe so," I replied. "But they're such bad characters, do you think they'd want to portray themselves? Could you write about yourself being so bad?"
>
> "Mm-hmmm," Lindsey decided in the affirmative, "but I wouldn't *publish* it. I'd just give one copy to Cinderella and never any more copies!" (February 7, 1990, 7;3)

At other times, when contradictions or complexities appeared, Lindsey assumed that the author held the answer in his or her head.

When reading Maurice Sendak's *Outside Over There*, Lindsey and I puzzled over the meaning of Ida's *"serious mistake."* In her attempt to rescue her baby sister from the goblins, Ida *"climbed backwards out her window into outside over there."*

> "What must Ida feel like, I mean, if she's going backwards out her window into outside over there?" I questioned.
>
> "I don't . . . I don't know," Lindsey replied.
>
> "Can you imagine?" I persisted.
>
> Lindsey struggled for an answer. "Uh-uh. Well, I can but I want . . . Maurice Sendak—did this?"
>
> When I replied in the affirmative, she asked, "Is Maurice Sendak still alive?"
>
> "Oh, yes," I assured her.
>
> "Mmmmm," Lindsey mused. "Where's his house? . . . Can we go to his house? 'Cause I want to say . . . I wanna ask him about this. We can call him and we can . . . What's his phone number? Can we check up in . . . the . . . in the phone book?"

Again I reassured her. "We could try. If you saw Maurice Sendak, what would you ask him now?"

"*Why* is she climbing backwards out her window?" she replied. (April 26, 1988, 5;5)

A couple of years later, she tackled the question once again. We read the story, and I reminded her that when she was younger she had wanted to find out Sendak's number and pose her question.

"Did he answer? Did you find out?" she asked excitedly.

When I replied in the negative, she looked disappointed but then shrugged and outlined her own analysis. "This is hard, Mom, but maybe he's trying to explain that she did something wrong in a different way. I mean, she shoulda been watching her sister. Remember when I . . ." and she recounted a tale of one of her own transgressions. "If he just said she's bad, it'd be boring. Maybe he just wanted to use words that are exciting." (February 24, 1990, 7;3)

Characters within stories have certain intentions that can change as children mature and ascribe different motivations, incentives, or goals to the illustrated figures. Children discover that not only characters but authors, too, have intentions, and that authors choose their words carefully to communicate. The words "outside over there" carried metaphorical weight, and were "exciting" as opposed to "boring."[16]

During book-reading episodes, the managing of social relations and questioning of the apparent ways of operating within books benefit from the stability and sense of security that literary texts offer. Yet accumulated knowledge of books and their ways also enables children to see that security does not lie in a single answer, resolution, or even pattern of genre, author, or character. Instead, security comes from drawing out, up, and away to a comparative and distanced view that implants the wisdom for dealing with the certainty of uncertainty. It is customary for those who tout the benefits of literature for young children to talk about how literature enables children to test their propositions about real life. With literature, they have a safe point or base of comparison from which to ask questions that might not emerge in daily life. This is true as far as it goes, but for Lindsey and Ashley it does not go far enough. By the age of three, each book was a life—within its covers and within the genre frame of story, and often within the motif or character series of which the book was a part. Each story had rules that, within its confines, determined the characters, their problems, and their ways of overcoming or abandoning their problems.

These could, however, be adjusted by the girls, who had gained mastery over the rules that operated in the text itself and in its direct reading. But extending or transferring the experience of reading books into social life depends on yet another set of premises. These follow from what is given within the text and from the reader's powers to reshape these, shift them about, see their irregularities, and question or amplify them. For Lindsey and Ashley, the transfer of texts to life came both in sociodramatic play—where they could manipulate the rules and roles—and in attempts to reconcile the sometimes immovable real-world rules with their growing realization of the flexibility of literary texts.

Lindsey spent the summer of her sixth year living in her overalls and playing the part of Scout in Lee's *To Kill a Mockingbird*. We began reading the book on a summer vacation, as the four of us were driving up the northern coast of California. Kenny and I took turns reading and driving, with the girls listening and playing with toys or coloring in the back of the car. The long car hours permitted us ample time to immerse ourselves in the text, though it took us nearly all summer to finish the book. During this time, our normal reading of fairy stories and other children's tales diminished, for Lindsey was eager to discover the fate of Tom Robinson and whether Bob Ewell's threats would ultimately prove dangerous to Scout. I read the entire tome with the Southern accent I had had as a child, and Lindsey quickly learned to imitate the intonations. She had me dig out her seldom-worn overalls and left off borrowing my high-heels so that she could wear her own, more serviceable sneakers.

After I refused to begin the story again for the benefit of her neighborhood girlfriends, we rented a video tape of the movie and they all watched it, with Lindsey serving as commentator—helping them negotiate the more difficult transitions and explaining missing elements. She then enlisted her friends to play major and minor parts, and I could hear the soft, slow drawl of their own Southern accents floating out of Lindsey's room. "Now, in this story of Scout and Jem . . ." Lindsey would begin and her voice would trail off to another adventure that took the children far from Macomb, Alabama.

Months later, after the book had faded from play, she and a girlfriend created a fort in the backyard near our house. They stocked it with writing materials and played school with a vengeance, taking one long continuous spelling test. One afternoon, in their absence, some neighborhood boys discovered the cache and destroyed it all—ripping their papers into confetti and breaking their pencils in half. Lindsey was enraged by their behavior, and as she railed in her frustration, her voice slipped back into a Southern drawl. "It's just not fair, Mom. Why . . . why, it's just like what the white people did to the black people!" (January, 1990, 7;2). Lindsey had been learning about Martin Luther King and Rosa Parks in her first-grade classroom, but the accent was unmistakably Scout's.

The role of Scout was an unusual choice, for Macomb's tough little fighter contrasted harshly with the roles Lindsey tended to play as a young child—roles incorporating beauty, grace, and inner strength. Her own very real worries of powerless childhood were lost in the power of play. In real life, Lindsey's hair was short and prone to tangles, but in play, she could weave a wreath of brightly colored ribbons that fell well below her shoulders. In real life, she squabbled with her baby sister, but in play, her compassionate treatment of weaker story characters exemplified unselfish grace. In real life, her parents sent her to her room for displays of temper, but in play, she was able to defeat or at least escape from the tyrannical characters that lurked at the forest edge.

When we read *Beauty and the Beast* (Mayer) in Lindsey's seventh year, she was less preoccupied with Beauty's appearance than with her willingness to help:

> "If I were Beauty, I would love to go to the country. It wouldn't be so bad to help with all the work!" Lindsey commented.
>
> Knowing Lindsey's general dislike for any kind of clean-up, I was more skeptical. "Really?!"
>
> "Yes, I love the country," she mused, though we've never spent any time in the country. "I could ride horses and brush them."
>
> "I don't think riding and brushing horses is all the work there is in the country!" I countered.
>
> "Well, I could get them hay and water—and that's work. And I wouldn't mind it at all! It doesn't really matter that my sisters wouldn't help . . . I'd have my brothers and I'd be helping my father. It's nice to help your family." Lindsey remained emphatic over her ability to help her family without complaint. I decided it was too late to point out all the shortcomings I saw in her argument, and continued reading the story. (January 24, 1990, 7;2)

A few days after this conversation, Lindsey abandoned her younger sister and went to play with her friends. She and her two girlfriends thundered down the stairs from her room and raced out the door, leaving Ashley squalling behind them. I caught them at the garden gate, and called Lindsey back.

"Don't you think you could include Ashley in your game?" I admonished.

Lindsey assured me that the game would simply not work with a little sister in tow.

After extended discussion, I remembered her utopian vision of herself as Beauty and reminded her of our conversation. "What do you think Beauty would have done in this situation?"

Lindsey looked exasperated. She clasped her hands together and mimicked the insipid voice of Beauty. "She would have said, 'Oh, come with me, dear, sweet little sister.'" Lindsey rolled her eyes. "I can't do that *all* the time, Mom. I gotta be with my friends sometime!" (February 10, 1990, 7;3)

Roles can be altered and slipped on and off as easily as costumes. Vision need not necessarily match reality. Knowledge must sometimes expand to include hard-nosed pragmatism.

Particular texts, too, lent themselves to constant reevaluation. What was initially understood at one point could be reformulated into an alternative interpretation. One night, just as we were beginning to read *Hansel and Gretel* (Grimm Brothers), Lindsey stopped me.

"Wait, Mom. Guess what? I've figured something out. I think the *witch* and the *stepmother* are the same person."

When I asked her why, she sat up in bed. "Because of what they say. When the mother wakes up the children she says, 'Wake up, you lazybones.' And the witch says the same thing when she wakes 'em. And at the end of the story, when the children go home and the witch is dead, the stepmother is dead, too."

"And look," she continued. She leaned over and flipped the book closed to reveal the front cover. "They even look the same." She flipped back and forth between the picture of the witch and the stepmother. "Look at how mean . . . their faces!"

She stared at the pages pensively, and then remembered the description of the witch in the text. "Well, do they both have red eyes? No! Hmmmm, well, maybe they're friends."

Ashley chimed in, "The witch . . . the mother . . . they mean." (February 7, 1989, 6;3 and 3;2)

When illustrations do not match the text, or when they appear to jump beyond or outside what is given in the text, they tell more than the written words do and invite young readers to constitute words, ideas, emotions, and explanations. Children can then test their guesses about causation and consequence against what is to come in the text. They can move beyond what is obviously knowable to judge relationships and inner qualities. The word "lazybones" was the key link, however. At three years of age, Lindsey had played delightedly with the word, scolding all her dolls with it; but when she was six, the word as spoken by the two wicked women triggered an association that linked not only repetition of vocabulary but repetition of character.

A year later, Lindsey and I reread the story *Hansel and Gretel*. For the first time we read from an edition illustrated by Anthony Browne (Grimm Brothers), known for its modern interpretation of an old theme. The children are dressed not in German peasant clothes but in the shirts, sweaters, and dresses of our own time. Gretel wears Mary Jane shoes and her hair is cut in a bob; Hansel wears striped pajamas out into the garden to gather his stones. But these are the least of the surprises. "Hansel wears glasses!" Lindsey exclaimed, staring at the bespectacled boy.

The stepmother is depicted a modern-day shrew, staring at the television, grimly waking the children with the traditional words. As she leads them off into the forest, she wears spike-heeled boots and a leopard-skin coat, and has a cigarette jammed between her lips.

> "Would you want to have her as your step . . . as your mother?" I asked Lindsey.
>
> "Uh-uh," she rapidly replied.
>
> "Why not?"
>
> Lindsey's answer was matter-of-fact. "'Cause she's so mean."
>
> "Hmmm," I continued. "Wonder what happened to their real mother?"
>
> "Maybe she died."
>
> "Why would she die?" I questioned.
>
> Lindsey listed the possibilities, "Maybe she got sick. Maybe she died of hunger. Maybe she got a disease!" (April 9, 1990, 7;5)

Lindsey did not need to elaborate on her dismissal of the character. This stepmother was not in the least desirable. She stood haranguing the children, scolding and lying to them. In her explanation for the loss of the true mother, the modern word "divorce" did not enter into Lindsey's interpretation. Instead, her quick explanation made links with other fairy-tale heroines who lose their mothers; Cinderella's, Snow White's, and Beauty's mothers all die inexplicably, leaving their daughters to face their fates alone. As to the cause of death—there were numerous possibilities. Maybe the famine that worried the stepmother had taken the true mother long ago. Maybe death was a disease that had claimed the mother, just as cancer had claimed her own grandmother. Lindsey looked for explanations that matched other stories she knew—both in books and in life.

Whatever the reason, the security provided by the true mother was gone and the stepmother's actions were predictably evil. When we reached the point in the story where Hansel and Gretel follow the stones home, I asked Lindsey what the stepmother would say. Lindsey gave no specific words but screamed gibberish in an angry voice, wagging her index finger and scrunching up her face in a menacing manner. The words were unimportant; it was the tone that carried the message.

Even when the words were spoken with care, Lindsey was not fooled. Her numerous readings of the story made her wary of the spoken lie. When the children are taken into the forest, the stepmother promises, *"Now lie down by the fire, children, and have a good rest. We're going farther into the forest to chop wood. When we've finished, we'll come back and fetch you."* After I had read this passage, Lindsey stopped me.

"No, what they do is tie a stick, a big heavy stick, and make it whack against the trees and it sounds like they're cutting down the tree."

"You're exactly right," I commented. "Right there, like they're there in the vicinity really close by."

"Yeah. And it's whacking and it's whacking and pough!" She made the explosive sound of a tree falling in the forest. "They should make it really an ax flying through the air 'cause then it would chop down . . ."

"But I wonder if it would get stuck in the chop," I countered. "You know, if the ax entered the wood it's usually only the person's strength that pulls the ax back out."

Lindsey changed course. "Yeah. So it's a good thing it's a stick, but they should tie a stick on each tree 'cause then it would really sound like he was chopping down lots of trees."

"Oh, oh, I see," I said. "Instead of the same sort of continuous sound . . . a different kind of sound."

"Yeah," she nodded, pleased with her final configuration. (April 9, 1990, 7;5)

Lindsey's reformulation reflected her need to make the stepmother's plan more effective. The monotonous sound of the same branch hitting the same tree would not have been enough to fool the children. But with refinement, the plan might work. In her attempt to improve the plan, Lindsey worked as an editor might—pointing out fallacies in the logic. When I countered with my own comments, she reconfigured her original plan. Though the method changed, her message remained the same: for the plan to work, more than one tree had to fall.

While Lindsey worried about the trees, I worried about the character of the father. The weakness of the father is well known in fairy tales. He stands idly by or often disappears from the tale—exchanging his children for a little peace of mind. When Hansel and Gretel return home by following the trail of stones, the story tells us that the stepmother was bitter but that *"their father was glad, for it had broken his heart to leave them behind all alone."* I was skeptical.

> "You know," I said, "the stepmother in the story always gets the worst criticism, like she's the meanest character."
>
> "I know!" Lindsey agreed, "Why?"
>
> "But the father . . ." I began.
>
> Lindsey picked up the hesitation in my voice and responded with sarcasm: "He's sooo nice and duh!" She dragged the last word out, for "duh" is the ultimate put-down among her first-grade friends.
>
> "But he doesn't . . . I mean, but he doesn't save the children or . . . I mean, he seems kind of . . ." I struggled to articulate my thoughts.
>
> "Weird!" Lindsey suggested. This word ranks with "duh."
>
> "He makes me mad," I continued. "I mean the stepmother . . . you know that she's being mean. She's outrageously mean. But the father—he should be doing something. I don't know."
>
> In a quiet voice, Lindsey reminded me, "But then the stepmother might kick *him* out." (April 9, 1990, 7;5)

While I struggled for words, wanting the father to break out of his traditional character, Lindsey knew he could not. As Gwen Strauss writes in her poem "Their Father" from *Trail of Stones* (p. 2):

> *Her anger was more*
> *than I had courage for;*
> *her eyes, soft beneath me,*
> *could turn in a frenzy.*

The stepmother's power over the children was minor compared to her ability to manipulate their father. For all he knew, he would be the next one left alone in the forest.

When the stepmother tries to rid herself of the children once more, *"Hansel got up to collect pebbles as before, but the woman had locked the door and he could not get out"* (Grimm Brothers / Browne).

> "Why doesn't he follow the same pebbles?" Lindsey suggested. She then quickly modified her own plan. "Oh, but there isn't so much 'cause they're going to take them *deep* in the forest. *Oh!* Go to the witch's house. Take all the candy apart and drop *those* on the ground."
>
> I commented on the implausibility of this latter plan, "But don't you think the same thing would happen to the candy as happened to the . . ."
>
> "Bread," Lindsey finished my sentence.
>
> I returned to her original idea. "But I thought your idea about following the same pebbles was a good one, except that they are going to go deeper."
>
> "But! Guess what?" Lindsey elaborated on her plan. "Follow the same pebbles but pick up new ones . . ."
>
> "Along the way!" This time *I* completed the thought. (April 9, 1990, 7;5)

The illogical or ineffective aspects of story were open for improvement. Surely Hansel was smart enough to see pebbles in the daylight as well. Couldn't he make use of the original trail, and then add to it along the way? Lindsey's suggestion for Hansel aligned with her own interpretation of story. She picked up the trail offered by the author and illustrator and then extended it to make her own meaning.

As Lindsey learned to reformulate text, she ceased to admire the witch's candy cottage the way she had when she had been a three-year-old. "I wish our house was like that. But then our house would get eaten up by the birds," she commented. Still, she imitated the feeding frenzy of the children and projected that the lead between the windowpanes of sugar was made of licorice, a detail omitted by the author. Her ultimate compliment for the book was, "I wish I could break this book apart and eat it!"

As with the analysis she had made as a six-year-old of the power of the word "lazybones" in the mouth of the witch to trigger an association with the stepmother, Lindsey, over a year later, still looked for clues to prove her point that the witch and the stepmother were one and the same. Anthony Browne's strikingly similar portraits of the two characters supported her case.

> "Do you know what I think? You know how her mother said, 'Get up, lazybones'? I think the witch *is* the mother."
>
> She began to flip back and forth between the two pictures, "Now, look at the mother and look at the witch." Pointing to the mole on the stepmother's face, she exclaimed, "See that black spot?" She then pointed to a matching feature on the witch, "See *that* black spot?" She shuffled back and forth between the pages again. "See the red cheeks and see her frown? See *her* frown?"
>
> "It's the same frown. It's the same mole." I agreed.
>
> "In the same place!" Lindsey compared the stepmother framed by the door of the cottage and the witch framed by the window. (April 9, 1990, 7;5)

Some of the illustrated hints are more subtle.[17] Browne supplies two pictures of the children's house. The house at the beginning of the story is rather gray and shabby, with ugly smudge marks on the door and a black bird perched ominously on its roof. But the home that the children triumphantly return to, with the witch's jewels in hand, is lighter and cleaner. The smudge marks are replaced by a soft shadow. Most important, the stepmother has died. I paid little attention to the difference, but Lindsey noticed it right away.

> "Now look at their house . . . it's all new 'cause they used all the jewels," she exclaimed.
>
> "Do you think that they can make that house new?" I turned back to the illustration at the beginning of the story. "Certainly looks brighter than it did there."
>
> "And that," Lindsey pointed to the door. "Look at the door."
>
> "Oh, yeah. Looks brightly painted." Then, following up on her earlier suggestion, I added, "Maybe they could turn in some of the jewels."
>
> Though I continued to read the tale to completion, Lindsey took the book and turned back to the beginning illustration. "Maybe the house was darker 'cause the mother's really dark and mean."
>
> "Oh, yeah," I agreed. "And now that she's gone the house is lighter . . ."
>
> "And newer," Lindsey continued. "'Cause she was old and ugly."
>
> Extending her interpretation, I asked, "Do you think that people

have that ability to make, you know, a whole atmosphere, where they live, sort of dark and somber?"

"Because of them?" Lindsey asked.

"Because of them," I nodded.

"I don't know," Lindsey mused. "But in story tales they definitely could do that!" (April 9, 1990, 7;5)

The visual features of the house had changed, and Lindsey offered two possible explanations. The first was a logical assumption: jewels were like money and money could be used for renovation. The second was symbolic: the personality of the stepmother cast a "mean and ugly" light over the house, but with her death the house became new again. In Lindsey's eyes, both home and heart were restored.

Both author and illustrator lay down "stones" for the child to gather and use in creating her own trail of story. Lindsey picked up several that I had overlooked, and used them to extend on her thesis of witch/mother while I stopped the story for her comments and countered with my own bits of logic. I also modeled the perplexity and ambiguous emotions often found in interpretations of time-honored literature. Interactive conversations and negotiated interpretations made us partners in analysis, as we both struggled to articulate our ideas.

For Lindsey, story was open: she was free to wander down her own paths and retrace her steps, if necessary, to expand upon an idea. Though Hansel and Gretel eventually find their way back home, the trail of story has no end. Each rereading, each discussion, and each individual event in the child's life can send her further. As children grow, their interpretations expand and incorporate new information and change to meet present needs, as well as cycle back to repeat and reflect on older assumptions. In the recycling of ideas and emotions, interpretation often takes on new forms, as the dramatic play of the younger child transforms into the older child's verbal analysis of characters' intentions and motivations. But unlike theories that try to fix every child's development in response to literature in predictable steps, there is no final destination in which the child's vision will ultimately match that of the "experts." Being literate means being thoughtful, not "right." The child will move across situations and over time, pocketing the stones needed to create her own path through the world.

The Cases of Reading

One night, the girls were in high spirits as I tried to settle them into bed and read them their evening stories. Ashley ran about the room whooping and calling, turning lights on and off while Lindsey laughed and egged her on. I lay on Lindsey's bed watching and issuing admonitions. "Settle down, now. It's time to go to bed." After my third "Don't turn off the light again," Ashley extinguished the light once more.

Sighing against the complete darkness, I got up and left the room, telling the girls that they should each get a book and settle down. I would return to read them their story after five minutes of quiet. I got into my own bed and had just begun reading my own book (*Oldest Living Confederate Widow Tells All*, Gurganus) when Lindsey appeared in my room. "We're quiet now. Are you coming?" she whispered in as low a voice as she could manage (January 30, 1990, 7;2 and 4;1). I told her I would be there in a minute, and after finishing a brief section of the widow's tale, I returned to their room. Both girls were the picture of pretense, studiously examining their books. Ashley was poring over *Caps for Sale* (Slobodkina), while Lindsey was immersed in *Bedtime for Frances* (Hoban).

Lindsey asked me to read from *The Water of Life* (Grimm Brothers / Hyman), which she had seen lying on my bedside dresser. I explained to the girls that I had bought the book for their cousin Danny and that we were going to wrap it and send it to him for his fifth birthday. Lindsey was worried that I was sending Danny her own copy and asked several times if this was another copy. I assured her that it was.

As usual, she recognized the illustrator's work, but she questioned me about the author. "Did she write *Saint George and the Dragon*, too?" she asked. I explained that Margaret Hodges had written that story but that in reality both stories were retellings. I continued by saying that *The Water of Life* was really written by the Brothers Grimm, to which Lindsey replied, "Yeah, they wrote a lot of stuff." I went on to say that the Brothers Grimm had not really made up all the stories in their heads; they had traveled around Germany listening to the stories people told in their homes and in taverns, and then they had written them down. Lindsey listened intently to my explanation while Ashley played with the ribbons on her nightgown.

The story is typically Grimm. One by one, three brothers set out to look for the water of life to save their dying father. The first two are black of heart, but the third is sincere in his attempt. The true nature of the older boys is quickly recognized by a dwarf, who tests each boy by stopping them in their paths and asking a simple question: *"Where are you going so fast?"* The oldest son scoffs at the little man and rudely hurries by. In retaliation, the dwarf curses him, and he becomes stuck in a steep-sided ravine: *"No matter how much he pushed or poked or prodded or yelled, the prince and his horse could move neither forward nor backward. So there they stayed, wedged between the walls of the ravine."* I asked Lindsey what she thought the message of this passage was.

> "You mean the moral?" She corrected my imprecise technical vocabulary. Then she took a guess: "If you don't tell when you should, things won't work out for you." She seemed unsatisfied with her statement, tried to restate it, and then left it alone. She began complaining that Ashley's feet were touching her.
>
> "Stop it, Ash," she hissed. I told her not to be so rude—that if she asked in a nice voice, Ashley would probably stop. Lindsey shot me a disagreeable smirk. I looked at her and said that if she continued to be rude I would curse her and stick her in a ravine for the rest of her life!
>
> "Oh, sure, Mom!" she replied with disdain, but she watched me warily for the next page or two.

The second son is as rude as the first and likewise receives the dwarf's curse:

> *The prince came to a steep-sided ravine, and the same thing happened. The farther he rode, the narrower it became, until finally he was stuck fast and could move neither forward nor backward. This is what happens to those who have too much pride.*

At this point in the story Lindsey grabbed my arm and cried triumphantly, "That's the moral!" And I agreed. (January 30, 1990, 7;2 and 4;1)

There are no morals in case studies, but a summing up—and even a look back at children's literature—are in order.

No Universals of Story

How does literature shape children's cultural performance with stories—in settings ranging from storytelling to dramatic renderings? Is there any way to generalize from the experiences of one child to those of other children? Such questions lead us to a more fundamental question: Who are those children who have a body of literature specially written and printed for them, who are aided in their interpretations by adults during intimate occasions reserved for the reading of such literature?

When we begin searching for answers to this question, we learn that relatively few modern societies have either an established tradition or a widespread definition of children's literature. The retold tale, the spontaneously created oral weaving of parts by several tellers, and the proverb or riddle more often store the wisdom, adventure, and humor of societies than do commercially prepared written texts. Only among northern European and English-speaking societies has children's literature in print come to be an accepted native tradition and a widespread ideal.[1]

As public schooling spread in these societies in the nineteenth century, teachers and the general public came to assume that experience with children's literature, defined as a body of literature either written for children or reclassified as appropriate for children, would come to school with youngsters as naturally and readily as their bookbags and lunchpails. The fireside gathering, the magic of story hour, and the bedtime story: these romanticized moments of connection between adult and child, mediated by a book, slipped into the public belief system in Great Britain, northern Europe, Australia, New Zealand, and North America. Magazines offering parents advice on raising their children and educational journals outlining steps to academic readiness supported these perceptions. Public schools based their recommended methods of teaching reading on expectations of children's prior experiences with literature. Parlor games, read-aloud family sessions, and bedtime reading became occasions of coordinated leisure shared by young and old. Reading and talk about reading climbed to the top of the ladder of idealized family times in which all members participated in "exercising" the mind. The notion of story as a guide for behavior and as a frame for what was logical, moral, or fantastic came to dominate educators' expectations of what children should bring from literature to their more academic performance.

By the end of the nineteenth century, in the English-speaking world and northern Europe, pedagogues assumed that academically successful children would base their in-school experiences on habits of thinking and responding developed through family patterns of reading children's literature. In the twentieth century, as the study of literature and its "critical" reading came to assume a central place in the academic curriculum, few observers of modern society questioned the generalized faith of educators in the ubiquity of children's literature, especially in those genres that came increasingly to be referred to as "classics" (fairy tales, fables, myths) and the writings of authors such as Robert Louis Stevenson, Charles Dickens, Lewis Carroll, and Mark Twain.

By the 1970s it had been recognized that children of all cultures had stories but that these were not the stories known as "classics"; many conformed neither to the schools' expectations of recognizable plot nor to society's endorsement of a moral ending. Children's literature received labels such as "ethnic," "multicultural," and "folk," and school librarians sought out new sources of literature in the homelands of many of the newly arrived immigrants from Mexico, Central America, and Southeast Asia. Such attempts, however, led to the unsettling discovery that many of these nations had no tradition of a literature written for children by specialized authors who could assume that families had leisure hours to spend in reading to and with the young. The stories of many of these nations existed in the form of "oral literature," tales told and retold during hours of labor that brought young and old together, during children's routines of play, as well as during periods of respite around campfires, in villages, in city apartments, or in urban slums where electricity worked irregularly at best.

As librarians, educators, and social historians recognized the need to expand definitions of children's literature, social scientists focused attention on the need to look again at the intricacies of just how adults read with and to children. Teachers often assumed that questions of fact and interpretation followed "naturally" upon the reading of a story to children, and that all children would know that the answers to such questions should come from the previously read text and its illustrations. Closer looks at youngsters' responses to literature revealed that in some cultures, children learned to attend to the expectations of human interactions and the logic of real-world actions as primary; these children found questions about fictionalized plots of stories in books curiously framed in a world of rules peculiar to learning to read in school.

In the 1980s, some parents and social scientists began to question the assumption that all children could enter the world of story as easily as Cinderella stepping into her pumpkin carriage. They began to try to "make strange" their own familiar habits of reading books with young children, in order to perceive the intricate, complex, and interdependent patterns of seeing, saying, and remembering that permeate this activity. They pushed their noses harder against the carriage window and thought carefully about how they could get inside the wonderland of children coming to know literature written primarily for a young audience.

Their bump against the glass jolted them into an awareness that their ways of looking had to diverge from earlier, cursory and culturally biased portrayals of children's experiences with literature. The majority of such accounts had been extended in a free-wheeling manner to suggest that their descriptions and prescriptions represented *all* children, *normal* children, *natural* habits, children from *good families*. In the 1980s, in an era of attention to differences among children, across families, and through cultures, each such account had to be acknowledged as a *particular case study*. Scholars pointed out that even carefully controlled experimental studies of children responding to testers' prompts told less about children's abilities than about the accessibility of their families to university research sites and the familiarity of these children with decontextualized questions about texts. In response to the increasing studies of children from different backgrounds and family settings, scholars acknowledged that children's reading could be influenced by such cultural elements as extent of leisure time, belief in the authority of texts, and assumptions about when and how adults talked with young children.[2]

As more and more educators came to admit, the long-standing assumption that children's literature "should" exist in all families was a value judgment. In the final decades of the twentieth century, children's literature, like certain foods, songs, forms of play, and health provisions, could be acknowledged as being native only to certain societies. Perhaps most important, educators recognized that access to such literature and to adult-child reading sessions was possible only with the literacy skills and family leisure that came with certain levels of economic security. A child's access to children's literature and to the routines of reading and talking that surround it was conditioned in every society—and indeed in every family—by expectations of parental roles and values, by the extent and use of space within the household, and by patterns of choice regarding the spending of family income and the maintenance of the adults' status.[3]

The bulk of writing about children's reading has focused on children *learning to read*—learning to be individual agents in silently decoding texts or reading aloud singly upon command.[4] Yet studies in the 1980s showed that *reading to learn* predominated in those families in which adults and children wove interpretive talk about written texts and printed illustrations into their joint readings. Here adults modeled the extension of meaning from print through their side-sequences of telling stories, queries about illustrations and words, and openings for children to tell their own stories and ask their own questions. Reading books together became a joint cultural performance between adult and child.

Until the 1980s, in the relatively small amount of research on children reading outside the context of school lessons, "reading" referred almost exclusively to making meaning from written texts for the purposes of pleasure. Yet closer looks at children interacting with print outside school settings revealed that their reading texts were prompts: commercial logos from brand-name products, television advertising, and T-shirts stood as guides for action. These studies called attention to the ways in which children became familiar with print in their everyday lives, and how the extent of print in commerce, trade, and religious life enabled them to acquire an early familiarity with the shapes, alignments, and even the meanings of script systems. Studies of children's response to literature after the 1980s also urged educators to look well beyond occasions of interaction around the book itself to the economic, social, and cultural contexts of reading. By the end of the twentieth century, scholars had come increasingly to recognize children's capacity to reconstruct their worlds (if allowed to do so) with words and rules from both life and literature. An environmental approach—describing children and the surroundings that might touch on their response to literature—emerged as highly desirable for understanding how language, literature, and learning were interrelated.

The Place of the Recorder

Redefinitions of and reorientations to the child reader, and the creation of multiple definitions of that reader, have led naturally to serious reconsiderations of the adults who recorded young children's experiences with literature. In every study of individuals or groups of children interacting with children's literature, professional expectations on the part of the adults observing and participating with child readers helped shape children's literary worlds. But especially in those cases in which the observers and recorders were the children's intimates, cultural and personal norms needed delineation as an element of the ecology of reading and readers. Just as child language researchers who have studied their own children's acquisition of spoken language provided the language models, the care-giving interactions, and the loving commitment that created the context for talk, so adults who have read with their children or assisted in their preschool programs have built the print environment they recorded. Thus, adults who have "tuned in" to preschoolers' literary life in order to record such a life have both searched for and experienced the evidence they recorded: choices of books and occasions for reading, selected points of recording data, and filtered perceptions of meaning. They have self-consciously played back or retracked incidents, trying, in most cases, to keep the act and its apprehension as close together as possible, knowing that every rethinking as well as retelling is interpretive.

Moreover, all such parent observers and recorders in northern Europe, Great Britain, Australia, New Zealand, and North America have been shaped by public mythology about children's literature and its effects on children's learning to read to prepare for school. To offer what actually happens rather than what they believed should have occurred has been their challenge. Certain key beliefs surround notions of children's literature, and holding these up for tests against the facts can prove disruptive. The public media, educators and parental advisers, and experts on children's literature have consistently promoted the following ideas:

- Pleasure and the stirring of the imagination are the fundamental offerings of children's literature.
- Stages of moral development, story understanding, metaphor making and comprehension, and genre shaping apply universally to children.
- Children's manipulations of literature center on life-to-literature and literature-to-life comparisons.
- The key to understanding the meaning of literature for children is in the actual process and duration of the decoding of text by either the child or the adult reader.
- Children regard the words of the written text as unchangeable and texts as autonomous in their meanings.

Any recorders of preschool children's responses to literature are therefore part of the full context—or ecology—of children's literature through their direct interactions with children and books, as well as through their reduction and selection of events to be recorded. In their representations, recorders must guard carefully against the influence of widespread truisms on the words, wishes, and wills of those children whose everyday life with books they present.

Something so seemingly "neutral" as a focus on the reading event and on its immediate consequences of pleasurable talk bears the influence of generalized perceptions about the way in which adults and the actual text reading directly influence children's responses. It is true that a good deal of the justification for why young children should read literature and have an early exposure to oral and written stories has been based on arguments that literature enhances the child's creativity or imagination and gives pleasure. It is a truism that books and stories transport us across time and space and let us enter, through imagination, worlds that we can never know through immediate experience. In so doing, books and parental readings can easily be seen as guiding children to stages of moral understanding, competence with language, and facility with literary language.

Thus, any long look by an observing participant—especially a parent—raises questions about the thin and permeable lines between fact and fiction, between subjectivity and objectivity, between science and persuasion. Diary studies by parents of their own children raise particularly difficult questions about bias, selectivity, and forms of persuasive rhetoric. Though in most parts of the world, common wisdom holds parents' knowledge of their own children in high regard, those who esteem science and fact tend to distrust not only parents' recordings of their own children's development, but also studies of any group or situation done by an involved member or participant. Thus, it is only in fiction and indeed in all literature that readers place faith in the knowledge of the insider, that they let the world "in there" onto the page. Social science has until recently insisted that researchers be outsiders and that they be faithful to the world "out there" by using techniques to make their studies reliable and valid.

But in the final two decades of the twentieth century, some social scientists began to substitute *retrievability* for *reliability* and to argue for contextual validity in accounts of readers interacting with texts. They acclaimed the power of the direct words of those being studied and the additional insight to be gained by allowing the subjects of study to reflect often on their own interpretations of their behavior and beliefs. Diary notes, audio and video tapes, and artifacts come in retrievable forms that allow numerous returns to the data over time, not only by the researcher but also by those being studied and by other researchers.

A parent well trained in the theory and methods of a particular discipline brings other perspectives, in addition to those of the personal role. Strong ecological validity comes from studies based on diary records, all artifacts of daily use, and unlimited access to the key subjects of the study for follow-up questions. Longitudinal records extending over years, as well as comparability of activity, response, and language across situations, result when the researcher is a native and continuing member of a group. Access to numerous types of data, ranging from handwritten notes and audio and video recordings to reviews of these data with key subjects, flows easily from sustained membership within a group. Moreover, both longitudinal work and access to multiple sources of data provide a necessary developmental perspective on the behaviors of any individual or group of individuals.

Prior to the 1970s, the dichotomy of subjectivity and objectivity dominated discussions of research methods, particularly on those occasions when social scientists felt compelled to hold their work up for validation by colleagues more oriented to the physical sciences. However, during the 1970s, the writings of both philosophers and literary theorists led social scientists to reflect on the extent to which many time-honored methods reduced and selected data, as well as determined highly limiting ways of reshaping data for presentation. Increasingly, social scientists reflected not only on their processes of studying their subjects but also on their ways of reporting their results. The sharp dichotomies of earlier decades fell away as scholars acknowledged that novelists and scientists alike test and challenge generalizations, use facts to build their cases, work for internal consistency, and structure their rhetoric to persuade. Moreover, especially for those scholars engaged in longitudinal studies of either a particular group or a specific topic, it is pointless to argue that engagement and emotion do not influence how researchers collect, analyze, and report their data. Thus, researchers have been encouraged to look within themselves and at their own roles as research instruments and to report these reflections along with their observations and theoretical conclusions.

These remarks on the state of understanding of how knowledge is created and displayed should not be construed as an apology for the fact that the data of this book are those of a parent studying her own children. Our point here is that Shelby is writing not merely as an autobiographical self but also as a scholar grounded in the literatures of education, anthropology, and children's literature. She supplemented her nature as a parent with her training as a scholar. Thus, there is a blend here of the individual inferences and intentions that emerged naturally through her personal commitment to literature and her role as parent, and of analysis and reflection made possible through the retrievability of her data, her own intellectual growth as a scholar, and accessibility to another scholar from a different field and focus. Similarly, Shirley, in her capacity as social scientist, has been able to view Shelby's observations from a greater distance. She also brought to the study a mass of personal experiences with her own children, as well as knowledge gained through long-term close studies of the children of other classes and cultures in the United States and societies in distant parts of the world.

Across professional fields, individuals tend to reject the idea that what one learns in becoming a professional can be sustained in parallel fashion in one's personal life, along with the daily roles of parent, friend, or member of a particular culture, religion, or racial group. The ordinary view is that the emotional strains of these roles must push aside the skills and underlying theoretical knowledge of one's own training; hence, physicians are expected not to treat members of their own families, family counselors are judged inappropriate advisers for members of their own intimate circle, and so on. Teachers have traditionally been the last to be consulted by education researchers, for their "inside" knowledge has been construed as untrained and undisciplined for research. Their constant considerations of technique and assessment of reasons for outcomes have until recently been rejected as lacking legitimacy.

However, certain circumstances most assuredly override these limitations. For those trained to study children's language, "turning off" technical knowledge drawn from the discipline becomes almost impossible. Individuals can and do bring their professional expertise to bear, when necessary, on what are essentially personal situations. Teacher "training" actively influences teachers as parents, aunts, or even casual advisers to other parents. Shelby's reading of cases of research done in the social sciences, as well as those of children's reading and language development, certainly influenced her perception as parent. Thus, professional knowledge need not and indeed does not operate at the fore in one's personal roles and relationships, but it can legitimately be called on under appropriate circumstances, even when these are in one's own home or in the classroom.

The longitudinal and comprehensive range made possible by almost total access to the lives of Lindsey and Ashley—at home, with friends, and at school—enabled Shelby to move in this study beyond the book-reading episodes themselves (when parent and child were engaged over a book) to the extensions, modifications, and replays by Lindsey and Ashley of their reading experiences. Thus, this study comes as close as possible to being an introspective record of two very young child readers carrying texts, illustrations, and knowledge about authors around in their heads far beyond any direct encounter with the text. Through direct verbal references, metaphorical connections, and sociodramatic play, the girls provided irrefutable evidence of the extensions of literature into their own relationships with their emerging identities, their worlds of friends and family, and their encounters with written and oral texts.

Such a comprehensive record provides important substantiating data for several theories that call our attention to the fact that any text, on the page or in the head, is not a single text. Instead, each text includes within it multiple texts—the words and ideas of other occasions, other persons, and other authors. Shelby's records of Lindsey's and Ashley's speech allow us to hear these multiple voices—their own mingled with

those of the authors they have come to know, as well as their ;
reworkings, retalkings, and rereadings of these texts in ordina
dramatically created events of everyday life. Only with an inter
mersion in the socialization of an individual as a single case over
period of time can we have direct evidence of the source, rete
reshaping, and rejection of particular texts—written and oral.

Off the Page and into the World

Anthropologists who have studied other children of similar
grounds have described preschoolers very much like Lindsey and
ley as "being literate" before they could read.[5] What are we to
of the world of direct experience and the knowledge that is acc:
lated beyond the book-reading event but filtered in part thr.
perceptions shaped and remembered from such occasions? This t
illustrates how, if we look carefully, we will find the extended ex
ences to which children transport their reading of literature. For I
sey and Ashley, their actual performance with book-as-artifact at the
time of reading spread beyond such occasions to their own and their
parents' reminders, comparisons, and commentaries about the contents of books found again in new shapes and sounds in shopping malls,
at the grocery store, on car rides, on television, and in videos. In
addition, both girls reshaped written texts into partial bits of song,
dance, drama, and revoicings in their own tales and critical reflections
on the world. Problem solving by analogy with literature lifted them
in their own flights of reason and emotion, as they used literary scenes,
events, and characters to negotiate, control, and alter everyday situations.

The patterns and periods within which Lindsey and Ashley accom-
plished these flights challenge broadly accepted notions about both the
effects of children's literature and the stages when children will develop
certain capabilities with literary texts. The individual stories of Lindsey
and Ashley tell us the following:

- The fundamental offerings of their reading experiences were not
  just pleasure; they were also connections to problem solving and
  long-running negotiations with adults about the rules and roles of
  everyday life.
- Through multiple readings of cumulative texts, the girls shifted

and recycled their perspectives on how stories and traditional formulas worked, what was right and wrong in text worlds and their own, and how characters expressed their intentions.

- The girls' manipulations of literature centered not only on life-to-literature and literature-to-life transferrals, but also on criticisms that brought within-text reshapings and text-to-text comparisons.
- For Lindsey and Ashley, their experiences of reading children's literature with adults extended far beyond the actual moments of reading to grasping the creative and continuing possibilities of literary language, character, and plot for both their own literary inventions and their relations with friends and family.
- The girls regarded the words of written texts as available and ready resources for their own unique connections to other words, altered meanings, and new settings.

In these and other patterns, clear developmental trends—beyond those associated with physical maturation and increased life experiences—do not make themselves immediately evident. The individual differences in the stories of Lindsey and Ashley stand out far more than any adherence to highly specific developmental patterns.

Between the ages of one and four, Lindsey responded to literature with motion far more than with verbal expression. Especially during her third and fourth years, she used pantomime and costume to play out her reshaped stories with family and friends. At four, she was reworking texts to meet her own moral criteria and preferences for happy endings, but by the age of seven she had accepted the most obvious facts of texts. She then made evident her view that interpretations of characters or intentions were not fixed but open to her needs and imaginary flights. Though she continued to respect the general flow of the story, she did not hesitate to wrinkle its details to fit her current frame of what made sense and felt safe. Between the ages of three and four, Lindsey came to recognize motifs and traditional formulas within genres. Within the next year, in her global representations of storybook characters, she began to shift her attention from their external features to their emotions, motivations, and intentions. During her preschool years, Lindsey held fast to her desire to portray feminine figures who needed outside intervention for rescue; by the age of eight, she had begun to claim the power of male roles. She always preferred dramatic stories of fantasy and happily-ever-after endings to books of information or collections of poetry.

On the other hand, between the ages of one and four, Ashley did not take on flights of dramatic motion but instead preferred quiet and often solitary study of texts. By the age of four, she had become a verbal comic and poet, delighting in language play from texts and often announcing she was *not* a character in a book but *Ashley*. Whereas Lindsey at age four searched for costumes and props, Ashley at the same age experimented in both drawings and her language play with shapes, patterns, and details of texts and illustrations. Preferring from an early age books of fact and poetry, Ashley made few elaborations of fantasy motifs or genre conventions until the age of five. By the age of four, however, she had connected rhyme, wordplay, and particular intonation patterns to the genre of poetry.

Such uses of literary references in the various corners of children's growing up depended on many factors that are easily out of awareness (and out of reach) for the adult recorder of children interacting with books. Shelby and Kenny had to recognize that the individual differences in their personalities, as well as their particular ideals of parenting, pushed and pulled the girls toward fantasizing or fictionalizing the real world. Similarly, their own notions of authority determined the extent to which Lindsey and Ashley tested literary fictions against their own "facts" of the everyday world, or against their assertion of other literary texts as "facts" to compare with different or subsequent book readings. In rescripting written texts and in reshaping the rules that applied within them, Lindsey and Ashley often insisted on naming or renaming customary roles and would announce their shifts into domains where they had made up the rules. They transferred information and solved problems through narratives that were consciously modeled on those of literature. Their memories of chunks of literary language became contrails of discourse in their own talk and drawings.

Their knowledge from stored memory and immediate sensed experience merged also with their own reciprocal exchanges between literature and life—exchanges that went far beyond the control of their parents. Motivated by affect, desire, and intention, they drew on literary texts in their process of testing the everyday experience of learning to be daughter, sibling, friend, individual, and societal member. Literature helped initiate Lindsey and Ashley into mental activities they carried out on their own, well beyond the story-reading or -telling hours. They built hypotheses, tested propositions, compared one object, event, or setting to another, and imagined how changing one factor within a total context would alter a subsequent scene. Within literary texts and in daily operations of achieving some role among family and friends, they linked figure and ground, built categories of associations, and sensed or reasoned out that any effect or consequence usually had multiple and ever-changing causes and several possible settings.

[handwritten margin note: The Narrative mode (Bruner 1986)]

We should remember that two extreme reactions are possible as we read the story of Lindsey and Ashley. The first is a "so what?" response: their story is just what we might expect. Wouldn't all youngsters be literate in just these ways if their parents spent so much time and energy on literature? The opposite response declares: this is a rare story and these people live in a dream world—no family has that kind of time to commit to literature with children these days, so these girls will be the exception when they get to school.

We recognize the plausibility of these responses but must challenge the premises of each. Concerning the first, we would say that previously there has not been such a detailed description of the extent to which reading and talking about books influences the everyday planning, rescripting, and framing of life. If the details here seem obvious or "just what we might expect," their familiarity comes not necessarily through direct experience but through the collective idealistic memory that the English-speaking, mainstream, middle-class public has about family reading. In the United States, especially during the early decades of the nation's history and well into the twentieth century, many families across numerous cultures read books and played games together in their leisure time. To be sure, class membership and geographic region helped determine access to books as well as times and places for either solitary reading or group story telling. But across classes, parlors and front porches centered these activities; talk of books and exchanges of aphorisms seasoned mealtimes. Exercise of the mind depended on conversation and the reading of books. Schools saw these family times as predictable preparation for education and part of the fulfillment of challenge for youngsters' minds. This collective memory of yesteryear became the fictionalized frame many educators transferred to families at the end of the twentieth century. For those who hold that this fiction applies to all families, the story of Lindsey and Ashley may strike a familiar chord.

Those who do not share this collective memory might respond that the story of Lindsey and Ashley sets an unreasonable model for current families, and that the young have no time, preference, or tolerance for such activities in today's world. We would challenge this view by pointing out that for this family, books provided the texts of interpretation and the basis for extension of literate behaviors. For other families, books may not serve such a central role, but other types of texts can serve to some extent as bases from which children extend their premises for testing and challenging real-world roles and rules. Television, movies, video tapes, popular music, and video games provide texts that can be interpreted, talked about, and considered for their internal rules and possible extensions into life.[6]

A major difference between the role of these texts in the lives of youngsters and that of books lies in both the nature of children's literature as mediating tool and the roles of adults interacting with this literature. The stories of Lindsey and Ashley suggest that both interactive and adaptive roles are demanded by books; other texts noted above, particularly those of television and video, generally depend more on passive roles. Thus, it is the guided activity of participation and interaction that adapts itself around books, as well as the openings the language of children's literature offers for interpretation by and from the reader, changing across age, situation, and mood, that differentiates such literature from other interpretive texts available to fill the leisure hours of the young. Hence, the ultimate challenge is that adults must make the choice of whether they will spend time *with* children or let children spend their time *alone* with currently available technology and entertainment. The children of those adults who find ways to talk with and about the texts of television, movies, and video tapes and who exert choices to ensure that a range of possible roles and interpretations is possible from such texts could no doubt demonstrate many, if not most, of the literate behaviors described here for Lindsey and Ashley. But choice is critical; some of these technological texts are—just as are many children's books—devoid of literary language, and they leave no room for interpretation. They invite no concern with abstractions, such as beauty, love, intention, loyalty, faith, and persistence. The literary language of texts must be such that it enters into a dialogue or debate with predecessors, leaves bits of texts for recycling, and offers new perspectives and unexpected twists and shuffling of all the components that matter—character, action, affect, and intent. It is in narratives that children find the holes they can fill through talk with adults and through their own rethinkings and rescriptings. Thus, they can come to know why story-rules work in the world and how story rules in the world.

But what of a comparative perspective? Is this book to be interpreted as saying that all families *should* use children's literature that contains rich literary language to enable their children to become literate? Do we claim that their preparation through literature will ensure the academic or other success of Lindsey and Ashley? The answer to both questions is no. We acknowledge numerous other routes by which children may become literate, and we also recognize that flexibility, creativity, and a critical attitude, as well as an ability to challenge the authority of texts, may themselves create problems in school for the girls. The nuances and subtle everyday features by which Lindsey and Ashley came to be literate stand in sharp contrast to many educational institutions' ways of acknowledging someone as literate (in reading circles, in school series of library reports, or in standardized tests that call only for titles, names and dates of texts, authors, and facts and figures about these). The comparatively stripped-down life of learning to read and write in school, the few opportunities for extended discussion, and the emphasis on facts rather than interpretation bear little resemblance to what the girls knew to be reading-to-learn at home. To be successful in school, they would need to adapt their abilities to the tasks of schooling and limit their understandings to finding the prescribed answers for the relatively simple stories of basal readers and other textbooks in classrooms. They would need to keep separate what "literacy" means for schooling and what "being literate" means for life.

Opportunities to talk about and act out stories do not guarantee that children will become smooth decoders. Reading is a complex activity that requires familiarity with the patterns within and between words, and those patterns quite often need to be amplified by an adult. Just as talk about multiple stories allows children to increase their understanding of character motivation and diverse story genres, talk about the patterns of language enables children to decode familiar words, as well as unlock new configurations. While it would be easy to be enchanted with children's imaginative performances and thoughtful comments, it is only through careful observation and questioning that the full scope of a child's reading—both the larger thematic issues, as well as the specific skills to unlock language—is revealed.

For despite the experience Lindsey had with text, she had difficulty with decoding. At the end of her year in first grade, she was still unsure of herself and feeling frustrated because the words on the page did not reveal themselves in the same way that images and themes did. Shelby and Lindsey spent the summer between first and second grades focusing on decoding, talking about the patterns of language rather than the patterns of people's behavior. A focus on the rules governing decoding fit within the larger rule systems of interpreting and expanding literature. Lindsey knew that letters convey sounds which translate into words of action and emotion—the seemingly constricted black letters on a white page transport the reader into others' lives, times, spaces, and thoughts. She also recognized that reading brought new ideas and information and that it could be called upon to challenge, synthesize, and complement other knowledge. In addition, she understood that reading and talk about books held a central place in the institutional community of her family and friends. The challenge, then, of learning how to unlock the code was not dependent on understanding the purposes of the code. These purposes she understood.

Having concentrated on the patterns in the code, Lindsey read more independently and comfortably in second grade. Still, reading by herself was not a chosen activity. For Lindsey, reading was a social act. And though she rarely refused to be read to, she often balked at the suggestion that she read alone. Without a reading partner, how could a discussion take place? During her silent reading, she often stopped to say, "Hey, Mom, listen to this!" drawing her mother in and eliminating the isolation of interpretation.

Ashley, on the other hand, developed an interest in the code quite early. She wanted to know "what letters said" and would write strings of letters on paper asking, "What does 'XLMDETQ' spell?" She often insisted on reading her favorite stories to us, interpreting the illustrations and reformulating the story as we had read it to her previously. Prior to kindergarten, she could read simple road signs and could write the names of all family members, as well as the name of her best friend, Nate. Ashley viewed reading as an independent activity, and often studied and wrote texts on her own, interpreting our "help" as interference in a process she well understood.

For a comparative perspective, it is necessary to ask also about what this book says for single-parent families, cultures incorporating oral story-telling habits, and extended families that must cram three generations into a one-bedroom apartment. We hope that the story of Lindsey and Ashley would suggest a message far beyond the role that children's literature can play in youngsters' preschool lives. The deeper intent here is to suggest that if we could gain a similarly detailed description of the lives of children from a pueblo family in northern Mexico or a Tlingit family in Alaska or an inner-city family, we would be forced to acknowledge the power of all symbols that lend themselves to interpretation by children. To study such symbols, whether they be books, oral tales, the music of radio stations, artistic patterns carved in wood, or rituals performed before hunting, we must go beyond the moment of encounter to try to trace the reshaping of these moments and the ways in which they are used in the narrative so as to help solve the problems of roles and rules in life.

Moreover, though Lindsey and Ashley made the task of studying their responses relatively easy by their habit of talking aloud about their thoughts, children of other cultures or of extended families living in cramped quarters may not use talk to reframe and reshape their encounters with culture's symbols. Thus, the challenge is greater in those cultures in which knowledge is not habitually displayed primarily through talk. Similarly, in single-parent families, children are more likely to spend time alone or with peers than to spend it with adults, and tracking interpretive talk among peers becomes extremely difficult for adult researchers. The story of Lindsey and Ashley is one that should make us more clear-eyed about the extent to which their habits of talk and verbal introspection made their literate connections relatively easy to document, in contrast to the differently developed and displayed habits of children of other family circumstances and other cultures.

Moreover, the story of Lindsey and Ashley should enable us to hear clearly how oral language echoes and overlaps with written words. Researchers and educators must be more open to acknowledging that, for children, talk about texts plays a large role, along with other ways of knowing that are not demonstrated only through words. Schools insist that children demonstrate what they know through the written— and only occasionally the oral—word; schools admit wide-ranging interpretations and reshapings of texts as problem-solving devices only as extra credit in the early years and as advanced learning for older students. Yet in the twenty-first century, other institutions—businesses, bureaucracies, and religious and community organizations—will depend on individuals who can interpret texts, both oral and written, and, in addition, use their powers of observation, invention, and retention to function effectively.

The British writer George Eliot closed her novel *Middlemarch* with a description of what happened to the characters beyond the pages of her book. She knew well that literature has a way of slipping into life for readers who believe the literary characters they have come to know persist beyond the author's pen and the covers of the book. As Eliot reminded her readers, "The fragment of a life, however typical, is not the sample of an even web."

Just as readers do not remain the same each time they return to a book, neither do those individuals or situations described in case studies, ethnographies, or biographies of living individuals remain as they have been described. Any authoring of another's life must limit the space and time in which characters move, and the stance of any author necessarily frames the fragments of life the reader will see. Moreover, no life or "web" is "typical": each is unique, despite efforts by the social sciences to categorize and label such lives as "cases" of generalized phenomena.

We make no claim that Lindsey, Ashley, and their family are "typical" or in any sense a model; we do claim that they represent a case of what "being literate" means in *one* young family of relatively limited economic means, little leisure, much fondness for literature, and considerable commitment to teaching. We also claim that they reflect for the English-speaking world and northern Europe much of the general public's collective memory and ideals of children's literature.

What Shelby and Kenny modeled, through their choices to spend money buying books and to spend time reading literature themselves and with their children, played itself out in different ways in the individual personalities of Lindsey and Ashley. In turn, the girls influenced each other—Lindsey with her passion for drama, and Ashley with her quiet play with words. The bundlings of nuances, subtle moves, quick references during a meal, ways of selecting movies, coaxing, and rewarding are what add up to the literate socialization of the two girls. They had opportunities to step into and out of texts as they read them and as they carried them into their daily problem solving. Moreover, they saw both parents negotiate over what was in books, genuinely puzzle and wonder about the contents of children's literature, and use their own scarce leisure time reading books they were willing to summarize for their children. A large share of their socialization into being literate came through the authority that books gave them—to control their interpretations, to carry extended powers of rescripting beyond the texts, and to challenge both directly and indirectly the rules, roles, and dialogues of their everyday concerns and interactions with adults. But their parents *let* books give them this authority. As young children, Lindsey and Ashley had opportunities to become authoritative about texts; moreover, they became continuous and continuing carriers of these texts as they included them in their own dialogues (both internal and external) about the wonders and ways of the everyday world.

This story of Lindsey and Ashley demonstrates the innumerable ways in which books and other written texts lay beneath much of the everyday life of their family, and the ways in which texts may play similar roles in other families who hold strong values about "being literate." The narrative frames for problem solving that come from books transfer into the basic frames for planning toward goals and slipping intentions into actions. Through the story of Lindsey and Ashley, we see and hear the full and immediate access both children had to varieties of spoken and written texts, to audiences for their dramatic renderings of stories, and to critics that challenged their analogies and questioned their creative propositions about the world.

The three strands which form the braid of literature—creativity, connections, and criticism—are not meant to imply standardized ways of interpreting, linking, and critiquing a set group of texts. Instead, the strands intertwine in unique and personal ways in the words and worlds of the girls' literary experiences. Each strand has its individual characteristics. Each, in turn, dominates and hides elements of the other two. And their relationships, the continual crossings of the strands, change over text and time, weaving between life and literature. For Lindsey and Ashley, the braid symbolized the beauty of the fairy princess and her link to the handsome prince. The braid also reveals to us the surface and hidden dimensions of the girls' dramatic interpretations, insights, and interactions, and their links to literate lives.

Prologue

1. Though adults have long watched childhood, language, and learning with keen interest and occasional amusement and exasperation, the twentieth century marked a turn toward careful documented scrutiny of young children's language development and interactions with books. With regard to language development, three studies are of particular note: Leopold's extensive study (1939, 1949) of his bilingual daughter Hildegard, from her eighth week to her seventh year; Weir's study (1962) of the presleep soliloquies of her two-and-a-half-year-old son, Anthony; and Halliday's study (1975) of his son Nigel's language from the age of nine months. The earliest long-term study of literacy is that of White (1954), who records her daughter Carol's interactions with literature from her second birthday to a month before she entered school. Butler (1975) then set out to explore her severely handicapped granddaughter Cushla's special friendship with books and their characters. The joint parental study carried out by the Cragos (1983) of their daughter Anna records her reading interactions between the ages of three and five, as well as her book-related play and many conversations of which books were a part. Baghban (1984) documents the reading and writing of daughter Giti from birth to three; Haussler (1985) similarly reports the development of her daughter's "self-made" readiness for reading. In the abundance of studies of daughters and their preschool readings, Bissex's (1980) story of her young son's entry into reading and writing is an exception. All of the above studies focus on the reading of actual children's books in the home with intimate participant-observers over relatively long periods of time; Cochran-Smith (1984) outlines the relative merits of these studies over those carried out with children under experimental or testing conditions in laboratories by nonintimates.

2. By the end of the twentieth century, the focus on earlier concerns about "good" books or interpretations by adult readers had shifted to numerous theories that celebrated the "play of the text" and the power of literary language to stimulate many readings. In the 1980s particular stress fell on how readers make sense of texts and how literary language serves "not as representation or communication but as a series of forms which comply with and resist the production of meaning" (Culler, 1975, p. 259). The power of literary language to engage many faculties of perception, as well as knowledge of individuals, social groups, spirituality, and history, ensures "the profuse inventiveness of the text's language . . . and of its constructed world . . . , our enlistment by the text as players in one of the most elaborate and various games that human culture has devised" (Alter, 1989, p. 228). The exceptional creativity of children with language, as well as their eternal willingness to enter into play, endows them with qualities fundamental for taking advantage of the open-endedness of literature. Metaphor and irony—and the potential reversibility inherent in these—are primary manifestations of children's capacity to perceive, visualize, wonder, and communicate about events, objects, people, and themes as other than they might first appear (Winner, 1988). Numerous philosophers and scholars studying creativity have noted the analogy between childhood wonder and adult creativity, as well as the intensive role of the arts and humanities in the early lives of highly creative scientists (Root-Bernstein, 1989).

3. The ultimate paradox of the language of literature has been described as "at once centripetal and centrifugal"—pulling toward an imaginative center, while never enabling us to specify precisely what that center is or what it means (Alter, 1989, pp. 236–237). Literature constantly presents the reader with the possibilities of difference—one reading as different from the next, one segment of the text as resisting another. The list of possibilities of differing goes on and on. Though linguists and humanists have repeatedly tried to pinpoint the qualities of literary language, the early work on poetic language by members of the Prague School of Linguistics in the 1920s and 1930s still stands as central (Garvin, 1964; Mukarovsky, 1977; Jakobson, 1960, 1985). V. Propp (1968) pioneered work that revealed the intuitive knowledge readers display each time they read, recount, or create a plot structure; thus readers carry literary forms around in their heads without being aware that they do so.

4. Following Spellman (1990), we use notes "to announce the company we're in, even if that's not actually the company we keep." In these notes, we provide the names and dates of cited research, and at times a brief summary of the research, though often the notes serve as guideposts for readers' further exploration. In the case of children's literature, we provide

the names and dates in the main body of the text, with complete information in our "Bibliography of Books Read to the Children." This bibliography extends beyond the children's literature texts cited in our book to provide a more well-rounded, though by no means complete, list of books with which Lindsey and Ashley were familiar. Direct quotations from children's literature are in italics, and acknowledgments for these quotations appear in the endmatter of the book.

5. Though long-term, careful documentation of the imaginary flights, critical reasoning, and highly active comparative frames of young children in cultures without written children's literature is woefully absent in social science literature, folkloric studies and ethnographies offer some useful evidence. Studies of the games, riddles, teasing, and dramatic rituals of children in these studies illustrate numerous types and occasions of language play, multiple ways of making sense of texts, and dramatic renderings of adult roles and rules (Schwartzman, 1978).

6. One of the best-loved sources of children's language play and ability to reshape their social world is the account by Opie and Opie (1969) of children's games in the playgrounds of England, Scotland, and Wales. Galda and Pellegrini (1985), Goodwin (1990), and Heath (1983) illustrate repeatedly the extent to which children's play, stories, and jokes offer perceptive critical commentary on adult life and the extent to which children use these to test the astuteness of authority figures. Children take note of whether or not adults pick up on figurative language, recognize sources of metaphor and irony, and acknowledge their critical commentary with good humor.

7. Numerous studies since the 1970s have described the storybook reading of mainstream (middle-class, school and public media–oriented) parents (many of whom were either linguists or psychologists strongly interested in education) with their children. Among the earliest was that by Ninio and Bruner (1976), who outlined patterns of extended reading which focused on labeling and increased expectations for accuracy as the child progressed in age. Snow (1983) also followed the interactions of one child-mother dyad, suggesting that story reading centered on semantic contingency, scaffolding, and accountability procedures. Although each of these categories has its own characteristics, each is also related to the "coaching" nature of mother-child interaction: listening to children's responses, expanding on these responses, and holding children accountable for increasingly difficult tasks. The term "storybook reading," however, should not be taken to encompass fully the early literate experiences of children in complex modern industrial societies; as Heath (1982), Taylor and Dorsey-Gaines (1988), and Teale and Sulzby (1986) point out, print in a wide variety of reading material permeates the day-to-day

activities of families across classes and cultures. For extensive explorations of the ever-present nature of books and other forms of print in mainstream families, see Baghban (1984), Bissex (1980), Butler (1975), Crago and Crago (1983), Taylor (1983), White (1954), and Woodward and Serebrin (1989).

8. Huck, Hepler, and Hickman (1987) suggest that the lines between adult literature and children's literature are blurred: "The only limitations, then, that seem binding on literature for children are those that appropriately reflect the emotions and experiences of children today. Children's books are books that have the child's eye at the center" (p. 6). A helpful summary of several attempts to define children's literature can be found in Hunt (1991, ch. 3). But it is important to note that children's printed literature as a concept is not universal, and its development in recent centuries in industrialized nations has been closely intertwined with commercial publishing and compulsory schooling. See the section "No Universals of Story" in our epilogue.

9. The anthropologist Clifford Geertz (1986) has written: "Like murals and carnivals, stories matter. So—and this is the thing for anthropologists to remember, as well as their readers—do stories about stories" (p. 377). Our own story about the stories of Lindsey and Ashley deserves some explanation. Shelby's fieldnotes were written in a narrative style, and the study itself is about narratives, about how one family moves the narratives of multiple texts in and out of their talk. To make analytical points, Shelby took notes on the children's remarks on or enactments of story, making verbatim recordings of the speech as close to the communication as possible and paraphrasing speech if the exact wording could not be retrieved. She elaborated on these handwritten notes on a daily basis, adding elements of context, matching chunks of written text, and striving for an initial interpretation of possibilities for why the match was made. She constructed a narrative for each entry in her journal, giving each a title and a date, designating the family's conversations and comments with quotation marks, and placing the text in the vertical paragraph format normally found in books. Like other narratives, each entry had characters, setting, plot, and theme. The characters were predominantly the children and Shelby, although many entries included her husband, Kenny, neighborhood children, relatives, and others. The settings were diverse—from the children's bed, where they read stories each night, to the kitchen, playground, bathtub, and classroom. The plot lines were dissimilar in individual entries but uniform in patterns of action; they were chronological (first giving information that foreshadowed the event to come), usually reaching a climax at the point at which written text entered the children's actions or spoken words, and there was a resolution in which the features

of the written texts bore on the children's speech or action. This "denoue-ment" often stood for the theme in her narratives, but several stories that seemed to share features were chunked under broad headings (for exam-ple, "book-handling knowledge," "seeing connections between stories and life is the result of visual image"). Microethnographer Raymond McDermott (1990) has suggested that "to be rigorous, the researcher must describe empirically some complex phenomena in our world in a way that is consistent with both their internal organization and their conse-quences in our shared experiences; this demands an intimate, and hard to define, fit between what is done with the people in gathering the data, the procedures for operating on the data, and the conclusions reached about the people being studied (including, by necessity, conclusions about us as researchers)." Yet such narratives from researchers can be both enlighten-ing and blinding—expanding, as happens in this book, the vision of the importance of story in the girls' household, and constricting the ability of readers to see other possibilities beyond those of Shelby's narratives. It is worthwhile to remember, then, that in this, as in any story about stories, Shelby opens up the matushka or the Russian "little mother" nested doll of story, reveals stories inside stories inside stories; but she also closes down other features that may not seem a part of the pattern of story. This style emanates from the multiple narratives she reads and lives, and it would therefore have been less "rigorous" to write in a style inconsistent with the lives that generated the accounts here.

1. Living in a World of Words

1. Though children—and all speakers—have always respoken the texts of others, this phenomenon drew intensified interest through the rediscovery by Western scholars in the 1980s of the writings of Mikhail Bakhtin, who reminds us: "Internally persuasive discourse . . . tightly interwoven with 'one's own word' [is] gradually and slowly wrought out of others' words that have been acknowledged and assimilated, and the boundaries be-tween the two are at first scarcely perceptible." All internally persuasive words then become creative and productive because they link, organize, and awaken "new and independent words" (1981, p. 345). Wertsch (1991) explores further the Bakhtinian question "Who is doing the talk-ing?"

2. Anthropologists and linguists have increasingly emphasized the "ritual of theatre" and sociodramatic play as metacommentaries on the "rules un-derlying the structures of familiar sociocultural life or experienced social reality" (Turner, 1982, p. 104). Usually these are dramas that children act out to replay society, but in the case of acting out a scene or adaptation

of children's literature spontaneously, children effectively hold up to daily reality not just one mirror—that of play—but two mirrors; they see and enact the play within the literary tale that is itself a play on social experience. The symbolic transformation of objects, people, voices, movements, and relationships is characterized by a metacommunicative message which emphasizes that, in play, actions are not what they seem. Bateson (1955), for example, suggests that in a play fight, "the playful nip denotes the bite, but it does not denote what would be denoted by the bite" (p. 121). Lindsey, in explaining to her father her reenactment of Billy as rocking horse, must tell *the story of the story* she reenacts to subvert strictures on her activities. By replaying the story of the work of literature that her father had approved, she ensures acceptance, for she has transformed her own escape from disobedience into obedience. The cognitive complexity and degrees of social sensitivity necessary for such sociodramas receive only slight attention in the scant work on children's spontaneous sociodramas. Yet Smilansky (1968), in her pioneering training study, recognized the interweaving of role portrayal, situation substitution, and object substitution with the development of cognitive, social, and verbal skills. More recently Kelly-Byrne (1989), in her case study of the play of one child, and Garvey (1990), in her summary of research on play, have explored the complexity of play and its positive influence on children's development. Garvey, in particular, stresses the relationship between literary play and the acquisition of reading and writing skills (1990, ch. 10).

3. We can understand the "equipment" that texts provide for manipulation through the writings of the philosopher-poet Kenneth Burke (1966, 1968). His early notions of "dramatism" view the study of language and thought as situated modes of action, motivated in origin and thus dramatic (and dialectic) in form and function. From him, we learn that every text becomes a strategy for encompassing a situation dramatically as well as referentially; thus, motives and functions, or the goal directions of language use, give meaning far beyond that of the pure naming or referencing role of words. Moreover, the language in verbal performance depends upon kinds of symbolic competence that include movement, action, and emotion and expect the interplay of a dialectic approach to text.

4. The problem-solving powers of narratives in which children explain and interpret are amply illustrated in the evening crib monologues of a two-year-old girl named Emily, who used narratives to take up the puzzles or contradictions of her day (Nelson, 1989). Emily's thinking aloud in these narratives enabled her to achieve cognitive goals of logical inference and to qualify her knowledge states by specific linguistic choices such as *but, because, so,* and *probably* or *maybe*. Like Lindsey, Emily shifted propositions around, combined them, and resequenced them in "pragmatically rich,

story-like frames" (Feldman, 1989, p. 101). For a convincing argument on how stories and theories (the latter often set forth as steps to solutions of problems) intermingle, see Coles (1989, ch. 1). Psycholinguists have explored the relative priority of perceptual features (size, shape, texture, and so on) versus functional roles, animacy, and the like in the child's acquisition of vocabulary, but the variety and complexity of categorial organization have made it difficult to construct total theories of semantic development; for a convenient summary of theoretical approaches, see Clark (1983).

5. Within the extensive work on children's perception and production of the genre of "stories," their acquisition of the subtleties of style and particular markers that distinguish one kind of story from another has received surprisingly little attention from researchers. Yet the few studies available invariably indicate that even very young children achieve awareness of fine distinctions of types of stories much earlier than might be expected and without explicit instruction. For a highly useful summary of children's learning of narrative, see Herrnstein Smith (1978, pp. 124–132). The papers collected in Nelson's *Narratives from the Crib* (1989) tease apart many of the complexities of children's stories, such as dialogue, real-life accounts, hypothetical proposals, reports of mental states, and the role of the listener.

6. Metaphor offers learners the optical, attitudinal, and verbal means to expand that which is within the current instant. The vague, rapidly moving, and frequently indescribable features of the immediate world can often best be captured through metaphor; in addition to their compactness and their immediate encompassing strengths, metaphors are memorable and provide lightweight baggage with which the mind (and verbal expression) can move across highly dissimilar situations and scenes to capture their essence. Chukovsky (1963), Winner (1982, ch. 11), and Winner (1988) provide numerous examples of the interplays between sound and sense that very young children produce and recognize.

7. The term "interpretive community" refers to the contexts of practice for reading that substantially preconstrain perception—ways of organizing experience that bring individuals to share in distinctions and categories of understanding and relevance (Fish, 1980). Any member of a community-constituted interpreting group (such as a family, reading club, or class in English literature) is "never individual in the sense of unique or private, but is always the product of the categories of understanding that are his by virtue of his membership in a community of interpretation. It follows, then, that what that experience in turn produces is not open or free, but determinate, constrained by the possibilities that are built into a conventional system of intelligibility" (Fish, 1989, p. 83). Research in the late

1980s, especially after the appearance of several works on "reader-response criticism" (for example, Tompkins, 1980; Mailloux, 1982; Freund, 1987), turned to the careful delineation of different types of interpretive communities and their underlying attitudes, frames, and approaches to reading choices, habits, and expectations; see especially the collected papers in Davidson (1989) and the case study by Radway (1984). Though not cast within this theoretical frame or research methodology, earlier case studies of the context for the practice of reading by children in their families provide substantive data on ways these children came to understand their membership in reading families; see, for example, Bissex (1980) and Crago and Crago (1983). These studies were carried out by intimate family members; later, ethnographic studies by long-term participant observers expand the contexts of practice to include as much as possible of the environment of written *and* oral language development of young children in their communities; see, for example, Heath (1983) and Schieffelin and Cochran-Smith (1984). Several scholars of social cognition urge psychologists interested in cognitive development to extend their interest to studies of the social environment that shapes the acquisition and valuation of knowledge and skills perpetuated in particular institutional communities; see, for example, Goodnow (1990a, 1990b) and Wertsch and Youniss (1987).

8. This passage aligns with the pattern of story reading outlined by Ninio and Bruner (1976), in which the mother made repeated use of four key utterance types with her child. These are the "ATTENTION VOCATIVE *Look!*, the QUERY *What's that?*, the LABEL *It's an X*, and the FEEDBACK UTTERANCE *Yes*" (p. 6).

9. "Intertextuality" is a term which signifies relationships among written texts. De Beaugrande (1980) suggests that a reader's understanding of one text is dependent on knowledge of other texts. Rosen (1985) further explains that "stories are as they are only because others exist" (p. 15). The word "story" does not define a single narrative confined within the limitations of one combination of setting, character, and plot. Rather, it is the intermingling of texts, where relationships exist among characters, similarities abound among settings, and plots that carry associated themes occur. A story is not one text but many. For a view of intertextuality in children's literature, see Meek's *How Texts Teach What Readers Learn* (1988). The notion of intertextuality does not exclude the text (or the narrative) of the reader. The story in print interacts with the story in the mind. A crucial element of this intertextual learning is the "multiplicity of connections" (Short, 1986, p. 62) that occurs in reading. New connections are formed with each reading, which in turn transforms new expe-

riences. This presents a kaleidoscopic view of intertextual reading with small shimmering bits of experience and text combining and recombining.

10. Throughout Kelly-Byrne's (1989) study of a child's play life, she reiterates the power of play (and its dependence on trust, intimacy, and secrecy) by which children can bring adults to their imaginative worlds, points of view, and possibilities of transformation. See also Sutton-Smith and Kelly-Byrne (1984, pts. 3 and 5). The issue of power here and in Lindsey's assumption of the role of lion-tamer (as queen) deserves comparison with discussions of what effect reading tales of heroines can have on young female readers. Certain types of heroines enclose or constrict possibilities, while others promote a sense of possibility, a raised consciousness that can liberate a girl from "feeling (and therefore perhaps from being) a victim or a dependent or a drudge, someone of no account" (Brownstein, 1982, p. xix). The paradox of the fiction of the heroine is thus that of "pride and prison" (p. 295) that can carry no final judgments regarding absolute effects. Maturation, individual differences in personality and family circumstances, and community norms for age- and gender-appropriate behavior will determine the ultimate transformative potential of the literary heroine on her readers.

11. Theorists of children's play stress three general themes: "(1) play as investigation, (2) experimentation and flexibility in play, and (3) facilitating the transition from concrete to abstract thought through play" (Pepler, 1982, p. 68). These three themes are seen in a developmental light, often as stages through which the child passes. But several important ideas are left out of such a configuration. First and foremost is affect. As Vygotsky explains (1976, p. 540), "Play is essentially wish fulfillment, not, however, isolated wishes but generalized affects" that are created in an imaginary situation which follows certain rules. In play the rule becomes a source of pleasure: "play gives a child a new form of desires, i.e., teaches him to desire by relating his desires to a fictitious 'I'—to his role in the game and its rules. Therefore, a child's greatest achievements are possible in play—achievements which tomorrow will become his average level of real action and morality" (p. 549). An overriding "rule" is that in play, meaning takes precedence and its social nature guides its internal directions. As Garvey explains, "Social play is defined here as a state of engagement in which the successive, non-literal behaviours of one partner are contingent on the non-literal behaviors of the other partner. Viewed from the standpoint of either partner, this means leaving interstices in one's behaviours for the other's acts and modifying one's successive behaviours as a result of the other's acts" (1976, p. 570). The varying roles of parents in children's play have been explored in the work of Fein (1979), who

suggests that the play of the mothers she studied fell into three categories: (a) *unrelated* play in which the mother played alongside her child, (b) *imitative* play in which the mother basically copied the actions of her child, and (c) *elaborative* play in which the mother introduced subtle changes in the child's play.

12. Individual differences in oral language learning have been well documented, but the range of such differences in learning written language far exceeds that of oral language-learning variations. Relative strength of visual over auditory memory and preference for system building over imitation as a learning style, as well as matters of motivation and interactional style, bear strong influence on the development of individual differences in both oral and written language usage; see, for example, essays in Fillmore, Kempler, and Wang (1979). For a discussion of differences in children's preferences for language play (with sound, vocabulary, and intonation), see Ferguson and Macken (1983).

13. For an insightful discussion of this particular tale, see Meek's *How Texts Teach What Readers Learn* (1988).

14. Children's book critics (see editions of *The Horn Book Magazine, School Library Journal,* and *The Booklist* among others), as well as those who write comprehensive children's literature textbooks (such as Cullinan, 1989; Huck, Hepler, and Hickman, 1987; Sims, 1982; and Sutherland and Arbuthnot, 1986), all express strong opinions about what constitutes a well-written book. Lukens (1982, p. 23) suggests that classics in children's literature are established because of the "significance of theme, the credibility of character, the continuing reality of the conflict, or the engaging quality of style," while Lurie (1990) has advocated the subversive quality of great children's literature. The clarion call of children's literature experts has been repeated in the educational literature of "whole language" teachers and researchers (for example, Goodman, Bird, and Goodman, 1990), who press for the use of trade books over basal readers.

2. The Sight, Sounds, and Sense of Story

1. Rosenblatt (1938) was the first to emphasize that the reader is an active participant in the reading process, rather than merely a passive recipient. She developed the *transactional* approach to reading, suggesting that when reader and text come together, the "poem" is the result. The reader brings past experience and present personality to the text, which acts as a guide; a new experience emerges to become a "part of the ongoing stream of [the reader's] life experience" (1978, p. 12). Iser (1974) and others, such as those whose essays appear in Tompkins (1980), argue that the transaction of reader and text actually brings the literary work into exis-

tence. Britton (1970) suggests that we distinguish *spectator* from *participant:* the participant is actively engaged, reading to gain information and to accomplish something in the real world; the spectator is "on holiday from the world's affairs, someone contemplating experiences, enjoying them, vividly reconstructing them perhaps—but experiences *in which he is not taking part*" (p. 104, emphasis in the original). Rosenblatt (1978) places the reading event in a continuum from *efferent* reading to *aesthetic* reading. An efferent reader focuses on "the residue *after* the reading—the information to be acquired" (p. 23), whereas the aesthetic reader centers on "what happens *during* the actual reading event" (p. 24). To emphasize where reading goes with the individual reader, some reading theorists see "the world in the head [as] dynamic, constantly changing" (Smith, 1983, p. 122). Such reading creates opportunities to experience as well as to create worlds: "Stories do not *represent* experiences for children; they *are* experiences as immediate and as compelling as actual events" (Smith, 1984, p. 152). The relationships between text and reader can thus be described as those of potentially ever-changing narratives: those of story and those of reader. Bruner (1986) suggests that "narrative deals with the vicissitudes of human intentions" (p. 16). Here he is speaking of story narrative, but the link to a reader's life narrative is clear, for he also suggests that "we construct our lives autobiographically" (1987). Using narrative, we not only tell about ourselves; we live out our lives. Barbara Hardy (1977) explains that "narrative, like lyric or dance, is not to be regarded as an aesthetic invention used by artists to control, manipulate, and order experience, but as a primary act of mind transferred to art from life" (p. 12). She believes that fictional narrative shares the qualities of the "inner and outer storytelling" (p. 13) that occur constantly in our daily lives. We weave a tale, cutting away sections and embroidering others, and the resulting creation is again subject to further alterations. In essence, text is alive, changing with the passage of time.

2. Clay (1972, 1979a, 1979b) developed her *Concepts about Print Test* (*Sand* and *Stones*) to test children's facility with reading behaviors—which included how to hold a book, directionality of both words and pictures, the function of punctuation marks, and understanding of letter and word units. Goodman (1986) reviewed five studies on young children's literacy and concluded that the ability to handle books cut across socioeconomic, linguistic, and racial groups. While children sometime between the ages of three and five came to understand that print carries the message of the book, younger children thought pictures held the message. Though the older children showed an understanding of book-related terms such as "story," "page," and "read," they denied being able to read and perceived the process as a difficult one. The "essential meaningful situations"

(Smith, 1983, p. 9) of parent reading with child also demonstrate "what a story is, how authors put stories together, how pictures and print work together to form a surface text, and how you package the whole thing. Additionally children have demonstrated to them how pages in a book work, how to turn pages as you read, the order in which you read, and the relationship between page turning and movement through the story" (Harste, Woodward, and Burke, 1984, p. 184).

3. The cross-cultural power of book as narrative prop is illustrated in Heath, Branscombe, and Thomas (1986) and in Heath and Thomas (1984), accounts of a young mother not accustomed to reading to her child who finds that as she begins to read with her two-year-old, he starts to tell stories—both factual and fictional. He seeks audiences and collects characters, plots, and dialogues from television, life, books, and his imagination. For other accounts of the strong linkages between oral and written stories, see the cases in Schieffelin and Gilmore (1986).

4. Butler (1975) describes her granddaughter Cushla's involvement in Sendak's *Where the Wild Things Are:* "The monsters are like nothing else encountered in literature; Sendak's three, whole, unlabelled spreads of 'wild rumpus' excite and delight in equal proportions. Cushla was totally captivated" (p. 82). Perhaps Sendak himself has the answer for why children find his pictures so compelling: "[He] was once blamed by an editor for drawing truncated, ugly children in his books, with oversize heads and short legs and arms. As he replied himself, 'I know the proportions of a child's body. But I am trying to draw the way children *feel*—or rather, the way I imagine they feel'" (Hentoff, cited in Tucker, 1981, p. 49). See Lobel (1981) and Nodelman (1988) for analyses of the elements of a "good picture book." Artistic styles, while variable, have similarities that children learn to recognize through the numerous stories of an individual illustrator. Green (1982) found that the five-year-old children she studied were able to identify the illustrative style of particular artists, as well as to "appreciate and discriminate among the literary styles available in books intended for young children" (p. 159).

5. Huck, Hepler, and Hickman (1987) suggest: "Picture-book artists also provide clues to the future action of a story. A close look at the first and second pages of *Where the Wild Things Are* shows the mischievous Max dressed in his wild things suit and stringing up a home-made tent. A stuffed toy looking vaguely like a wild thing hangs near by. Later the tent and wild things appear in Max's dream trip to the far off land of the wild things. His drawing of a wild thing on page two shows his preoccupation with creating these creatures which later inhabit his dreams" (p. 199). Tucker (1981) explains that as children grow older they "begin to understand the rudimentary laws of cause and effect more clearly, and so are

better able to describe what is actually happening in illustrations, whereas before they may simply have been happy to recognise and enumerate the main objects in their pictures" (p. 46).

6. Söderbergh (1988) suggests that children's literary drawings are often "triggered" by emotional factors as they draw scenes of "killing, mortal danger, captivity (followed by liberation), mother-child-separation followed by reunion, loss of irreplaceable property, and everyday drama in the life of a child" (p. 36). This was true for Lindsey's and Ashley's enactments and their drawings, but their portrayals on paper were more often triggered by aesthetic factors marked by an increasing length of luxurious hair and the colorful detailing on the ball gowns of princesses. Hubbard (1989) stresses the interdependence of children's drawings with their words as they learn to deal with space, time, movement, and color. This interdependence was a key feature of Dyson's (1989) study of children's writing. She suggests that as children draw, talk, write and try new forms, they "begin to sense new functional possibilities in their activity, ends that were previously fulfilled through other means" (p. 256). Elaborated talk clears the way for more detailed drawing and writing, which cycles back into more extended talk. The problem-solving nature of children's drawing is thoroughly explored in Goodnow (1977) and their judgments of drawings in Goodnow, Wilkins, and Dawes (1986), while a view of children's art in developmental stages can be found in Lindstrom (1970).

7. The empowering or disabling aspect—especially for female readers—of such tales of heroines in fantasy and romantic fiction has drawn considerable attention from scholars in feminism, children's literature, and psychoanalysis. Such tales often mark older women as evil and frightening and young women as passive creatures waiting for the rescue of marriage; courage, adventure, and achievement rarely come to girls or women. For further discussion of this issue, see the introduction to Phelps (1978), a collection of folk and fairy tales in which the protagonists are heroines that take up active roles and make decisions to shape their own lives. But the issue of the role of women in romantic or fantasy tales does not rest simply on the matter of a favorable or unfavorable portrayal. Brownstein's (1982) characterization of the primary effects of fantasy and romantic fiction applies to both children and adult female readers: "The beautiful person the novel heroine imagines and stands for and seeks for herself is a version of the romantic view of woman as a desired object; as the image of the integral self, she is the inverted image of half of a couple" (p. 295). Inversion—between innocence and experience—is a common theme of classic works of children's fantasy fiction. The literary fantasy typically brings the hero and heroine back to reality at the story's end; thus, there

is a frame of fictional reality—as, for example, in Baum's *The Wizard of Oz*. Bruno Bettelheim (1975) and D. W. Winnicott (1971), child psychotherapists, saw literary fantasy as essentially therapeutic, enabling children to discover that fantasy was not harmful, so long as one did not remain caught in it permanently. Dreams and fantasy help children adjust to the illusion-disillusion cycle of the maturing life, as well as enable them to balance between the unknown and the known. Gilead (1991) maintains that the return-to-reality closures many fantasies offer may, in fact, be too cozy, idealized, and simple, and may turn on themselves to reveal ironies and discords. The separate fictional realms of the frame and central narrative may suggest to children that the frame reality is more escapist than the preceding fantasy, or, ironically, reveal the deep fictionality of both literary and extraliterary versions of reality. It is likely that while children of both sexes sort out these various roles and realities, they move through periods of fixation on particular characters or roles, ignoring or minimalizing other features of the tales in their own dreams and reenactments; thus, the character or feature that may appear heroic, adventurous, or passive on one reading may assume an alternate identity on another reading.

8. Child development researchers have discussed the relationship between language development and Piaget's (1962) explanation of symbolic play (the understanding that one thing can stand for something else, such as Lindsey's use of her yellow blanket to represent Goldilocks' hair); see especially McCune (1984) for strong claims for symbolic play as a prerequisite to language.

9. Theorists (for example, Pepler, 1982) continue to speculate on play and the role of props. Some see the three themes of investigation, exploration, and experimentation in a developmental light: in investigation, the child explores a block, noting its size, shape, or color; investigation leads to experimentation, in which the child studies the objects in terms of practice and relationships to be manipulated, banged together, perched one on top of the other. Finally, after an understanding of concrete properties and practice, the child begins to see an object in the abstract, in terms of its potential; the block becomes a cup of tea, a racing car, a castle. Segal and Adcock (1981) disagree and suggest: "We cannot be sure whether a child has decided first that he needs a certain prop and then found an appropriate object, or has found the object first and then decided that it would make a good prop" (p. 44). What is crucial is the matter of intention that enables the child to see the object's properties as potential. The Soviet psychologist Vygotsky (1978) argued: "The degree of similarity between a plaything and the object it denotes is unimportant. What is most important is the utilization of the plaything and the possibility of executing a representational gesture with it. This is the key to the entire symbolic

function of children's play. A pile of clothes or piece of wood becomes a baby in a game because the same gestures that depict holding a baby in one's hands or feeding a baby can apply to them. The child's self-motion, his own gestures, are what assign the function of sign to the object and give it meaning" (p. 108). Shotwell, Wolf, and Gardner (1979) have explored two basic styles of play and using props: those of "patterners" and those of "dramatists." Patterners are absorbed by the properties and practice of an object, whereas dramatists are absorbed by the social implications of an object. Wolf and Grollman (1982) extended the characteristics of the two styles of play, suggesting that the patterner is noted for her "*object-dependent transformational play* in which the child creates an imaginary world by aptly transforming the objects and arrangements she actually finds around her" (p. 48). The dramatist, on the other hand, is noted for her "*object-independent fantasy play* in which the child creates an imaginary world by inventing events, roles and props 'out of thin air'" (p. 48).

10. The Cragos (1983) found similar questions linked to the same author. Their daughter, Anna, questioned Beatrix Potter's voice in *The Tale of Tom Kitten* as Potter bemoaned that fact that one of her characters had told a lie. "Who said that?" Anna demanded. The Cragos (1983) believed that the confusion was created by the use of the first-person narrative voice, because the author had put "into the mouth of a book character the mode of address that properly (as far as Anna was concerned) belongs to oneself" (p. 254–255). Green (1982) notes that Potter "almost always interrupts her narrative at the end and makes her presence felt" (p. 158), which may account for the similarities in Lindsey's and Anna's reactions, even though the stories were different. The acknowledgment of a text's *author* provides the first step toward children's recognition of the voice of *fictional narrator* in literary texts—a more complex concept signaled by numerous linguistic features. Shift of tense or person, a move away from direct dialogue to explication or interior thought, or insertion of description provide just some of the linguistic signals of narrative voice. The saliency and extent of such shifts depend on the narrator's status in the tale. For example, the narrator may tell a story from which he or she is absent except as author-evaluator or commentator (the role Beatrix Potter often chose), or the narrator may be the hero as well as explicator, and may, in addition, set the tale in a realistic frame in which the sources (or authors) of the story are made prominent (this occurs, for example, in many African and Native American folk tales). Genette (1980, esp. ch. 5) examines the variations on voice that authors can achieve as narrators; Bakhtin (1990, esp. pp. 150–182) considers the various ways in which the author as narrator and as "other" hero-character enables the reader's narration of

his or her own life, engendering a biographical unity of which the reader can say there is "an even minimally intelligible and coherent picture of my life and its world" (p. 154). Authors commonly recall realizing in their childhood the promise of "reading" their own lives someday—another form of escape or exertion of power over adults: "That close relatives don't understand the real meaning of one's life, fail to recognize statements and moments as premonitory, symbolic, definitive, consequential, is very nearly assurance that someday someone will. The gap between the way one appears and the way one is seems to a literary child analogous to the gap between the shelf it comes from and the world inside the book. That gap draws the eyes irresistibly: it is as if the meaning of life is just about to show itself right there" (Brownstein, 1982, p. 142).

11. When Lindsey was four years of age, her preschool teacher remarked that her understanding of the author's role was unique: "I'll oftentimes, if we're reading something by Keats or Lionni or Sendak, ask [the children] if they can think of other things that the author's written, and [Lindsey] can list them. In the end it's such a piece of who Lindsey is" (June 6, 1987, 4;7). From an early age, for Lindsey, the *agent* or *originator* held a strong fascination, and once she grasped the concept of *author,* she latched onto it with relish. The poetry of authors' names and the details of their lives filled her head as much as did their characters and plot lines.

12. Catherine Garvey (1990) asserts that the "use of newly acquired resources for playful exploitation is most striking in children's play with language" (p. 59). From the initial babbling of babies to toddlers' language in the crib (Weir, 1962) to preschoolers' love of nonsensical rhyme, children play with language. Kirschenblatt-Gimblett (1979) suggests that the process of speech play is sometimes more important than the product. She also believes that the "process is not streamlined, but rather is voluntarily elaborated and complicated in various patterned and culture-specific ways" (p. 223). Thus, the process of the creation of language can be an end in itself. Peters (1983) illustrates how "units" or chunks of language may precede segmented sounds or words in first-language acquisition. In addition, children use linguistic chunks acquired as wholes to fuse into new larger units; these expressions are "neither copied directly from nor even directly reduced from adult usage, giving evidence that some sort of construction process may have gone on before the expression became frozen" (p. 82). For second-language learners, Wong-Fillmore (1979) shows the extent to which language play with stretches of speech or formulas can accelerate the social integration of new learners of English. Such language manipulation can also be for pure pleasure, such as the playlike, adventure-filled quality of nonsense verse. Livingston (1981) explains: "Nonsense is a literary genre whose purpose it is to rebel against

not only reason but the physical laws of nature. It rejects established tenets, institutions, pokes fun at rational behavior, and touts destruction. It champions aberrations" (p. 123). Although these chaotic elements would be rejected in the everyday world, they are safely distanced in the world of the imagination, and offer brief respite—or, as Livingston suggests, "complete escape"—from day-to-day demands.

13. Chukovsky (1963) explains that young children's repetitions in poetry lend a songlike rhythm to their renditions and are also used to express strong emotion. He further suggests: "Under the influence of beautiful word sequences, shaped by a pliable musical rhythm and richly melodic rhymes, the child playfully, without the least effort, strengthens his vocabulary and his sense of the structure of his native language" (p. 87).

14. Haussler (1985) noted a similar voice in her daughter Anna's reading and suggests, "By changing voice tone and phrasing as she 'reads,' Anna also demonstrates that she knows that print can be turned into speech" (p. 79). As Harste, Woodward, and Burke (1984) explain in their discussion of demonstration, "Equally important are demonstrations about how one reads, how one corrects in reading, and how the speaking voice changes during reading" (p. 184). Baghban (1984) noted Giti's growing concept of story voice: "From HOW PEOPLE SOUND WHEN THEY READ at 14 months, she determined HOW BOOKS TALK IN A SPECIAL WAY at 30 months" (pp. 40–41).

15. Bettelheim (1975), well-known for his analysis of fairy tales, disregards the bulk of children's literature—books which are often "so shallow in substance that little of significance can be gained from them" (p. 4). He concentrates instead on the fairy tale's invitation to explore human behavior and to carry out the psychosocial work of fantasy. Lurie (1990) suggests that many children's books "told me what grown-ups had decided I ought to know or believe about the world" (p. ix). But there are other books that "recommended—even celebrated—daydreaming, disobedience, answering back, running away from home, and concealing one's private thoughts and feelings from unsympathetic grown-ups" (p. x). Calling this literature "subversive," Lurie chooses it as her subject because it "will endure long after more conventional tales have been forgotten" (p. xi). Knoepflmacher (1983) sees works of fantasy as hovering between innocence and experience, enabling children to resist adult values while engaging disturbing emotional situations with the sharpened perspectives of momentary escape.

16. At issue far beyond the "bad" manners exhibited in Wonderland is the entire dream journey of Alice and the question of whether or not it quiets the restlessness that Alice feels at the beginning of the story. Upon her awakening, has Alice been transformed into accepting a conventional view

of the world or is she now a more intelligent and sensitive observer of life? Within the story itself is the central question of children's fantasy for children: How do the rules evidenced in the fantasy escapade carry over (as liberating, conventionalizing, paralleling) to the frame of reality of the child? See Coveney (1967), Knoepflmacher (1986), Timmerman (1983), and Madden (1986) for discussions of this issue.

17. Maurice Sendak has been under fire from parents and librarians since the publication of his stunning but scary *Where the Wild Things Are,* which turned him "into a sort of 'Peck's bad boy' of children's books" (Lanes, 1980, p. 104). In his Caldecott acceptance speech for the story, Sendak defended his vision: "Certainly we want to protect our children from new and painful experiences that are beyond their emotional comprehension and that intensify anxiety; and to a point we can prevent premature exposure to such experiences. That is obvious. But what is just as obvious—and what is too often overlooked—is the fact that from their earliest years children live on familiar terms with disrupting emotions, that fear and anxiety are an intrinsic part of their everyday lives, that they continually cope with frustration as best they can. And it is through fantasy that children achieve catharsis. It is the best means they have for taming Wild Things. It is my involvement with this inescapable fact of childhood—the awful vulnerability of children and their struggle to make themselves King of all Wild Things—that gives my work whatever truth and passion it may have" (1988, p. 151).

18. Prosodic modifications in parental speech to preverbal infants serve several functions: eliciting attention, communicating affect, facilitating language comprehension, and modulating arousal. See Fernald (1984) and Sachs (1977).

19. Linguists use the term "register" to refer to the special varieties of language that are appropriate for different occasions of use. Children learn these registers very early; for a discussion of their ability to take on the register appropriate for such adult roles as nurse, doctor, teacher, or parent, see Andersen (1989). Registers may differ in subject matter, medium, and style of discourse; for further discussion of this linguistic term, see Hudson (1980, sect. 2.4). Just as teachers, sports announcers, and mothers talking to babies in mainstream middle-class societies use distinctive registers, so the literary language of children's literature (especially that written for children under twelve years of age) carries certain features of vocabulary, syntax, and discourse that set it apart from other uses. Alliterative words, as well as phrases such as "all day long," "right then and there," along with highly unusual proper names and frequently repeated chunks of language, characterize the register of children's literature. Brief sentences beginning with rapid-fire repetitions of the same

pronoun also signal the register of children's literature. For example, the opening of Judith Viorst's story *The Tenth Good Thing about Barney* places the child in the story's woeful tale with multiple repeats of the pronoun "I":

> *My cat Barney died last Friday.*
> *I was very sad.*
> *I cried, and I didn't watch television.*
> *I cried, and I didn't eat my chicken or even*
> *the chocolate pudding.*
> *I went to bed, and I cried.* (p. 3)

20. Herrnstein Smith (1978) suggests that "Tell it again" is a universal among children. They relish the familiar and predictable nature of stories, which only emerges in the *telling* of tales. She separates this from the *reportage* of natural discourse, where redundancy is often rejected. Still, children are often "openly eager for the special pleasures of 'redundancy' in fiction" (p. 128).

21. Vivian Paley (1986) describes three-year-old Molly as a child who "is quicker than most to transfer the process [of integrating bits and pieces] into her stories . . . because, more than most children, she sees life as a unified whole. To her, fantasy characters and real people all communicate in the same language" (p. 33). Dorothy Butler (1975), who studied her granddaughter's literary life, felt that a child's ability to take story language and apply it to other contexts "added to her speech repertoire, and therefore, her cognitive equipment" (p. 94).

22. The primary organizing features of artistic or literary language that enable this creativity have been identified by Soviet literary structuralists and linguists of the Prague School. Such features include repetition, rhythm and meter, rhyme, metaphor, vocabulary with "emotional charge," stage dialogue, and parallelism. All of these characteristics draw listeners' attention, heighten memory, and invite elaboration; see, for example, Mukarovsky (1977) and Lotman (1976, 1977).

23. Donaldson (1978) cites a study claiming that more "privileged" children pay closer attention to the wording of a question. Yet she still concludes that children "rarely ask about the meanings of the words, even when these must clearly be unfamiliar" (p. 91). This was not the case with Lindsey, nor with other children whose parents devoted time to story, for an integral part of Lindsey's questioning was the fact that we encouraged her to ask. Butler (1975) suggests that this ability of the child to stop the story is a part of the creation of a "home environment which provides optimum opportunity for the development of language which will simultaneously express and promote the child's thinking" (p. 94).

24. E. B. White gave Charlotte an extensive vocabulary, but balanced her

erudite ways with Wilbur's childlike demands for definitions. Beatrix Potter was legendary for her use of demanding and often esoteric words, some of which she coined herself. Nicholas Tucker defends her word choice: "'Dignity and repose' is not a phrase one would normally find in an infant's vocabulary, but Beatrix Potter knew what she was about. So long as the general context is clear, the odd expressive phrase, however unfamiliar, can always enliven an otherwise fairly basic vocabulary, which in any unrelieved form can soon become monotonous. This also applies to her famous use of 'soporific' in *The Tale of the Flopsy Bunnies* [1909], with its meaning immediately made clear in the next sentence: '*I* have never felt sleepy after eating lettuce, but then *I* am not a rabbit.' As she once wrote to her publishers, who were sometimes alarmed by her adventurous vocabulary, 'Children like a fine word occasionally,' and so of course does a true author" (Linder, cited in Tucker, 1981, p. 58).

25. Those who study children's language agree that "the child actually learns two sets of linguistic convention, that which governs natural and that which governs fictive discourse: the distinctive features, distinctive occasions, and distinctive consequences of each" (Herrnstein Smith, 1978, p. 131). Theorists of genre suggest that within fictive discourse, genres provide strongly positive support for both memory and problem solving. Genres offer "a habitation of mediated definiteness; a proportioned mental space; a literary matrix by which to order . . . experience" (Fowler, 1982, p. 31). The power of genre is most often revealed in young children by both their "placing" of stories and their "telling back": "Something in the actual text 'triggers' an interpretation of genre in the reader, an interpretation that then dominates the reader's own creation" (Bruner, 1986, p. 6). Study of two-year-old Emily's narrative genres in her crib monologues demonstrates the extent to which these productions exceeded in cognitive and linguistic complexity her daily dialogic language with others: "It is the telling of stories, to oneself in this case, that makes possible the reflective activities of analysis and later of invention. It also suggests a common origin in story forms for two activities that are not usually seen as related in development: problem solving and fantasy" (Feldman, 1989, p. 118).

3. Moving to Possible Worlds

1. Applebee (1978), for example, believes that it is only at the end of text that the pattern of response is revealed. He explains that when we consider the poetic technique "an experience becomes that of a *spectator:* we look on, testing our hypotheses about structure and meaning, but we do not

rush in to interrupt—to do so would obscure the relationships and spoil the effect of the whole" (p. 16).

2. The title of this chapter and many of the ideas here bear the strong influence of Bruner's (1986) approaches to literature, which bring together psychologists' and humanists' views of text, context, imagination, and the mind. Bruner follows the Soviet psychologist Vygotsky (1978) and anthropologist Victor Turner (1982) in emphasizing stories' possibilities in both dramatic motion and verbalization: stories "provide . . . a map of possible roles and of possible worlds in which action, thought, and self-definition are permissible (or desirable)" (Bruner, 1986, p. 66). Vygotsky (1978) reconstructed an earlier study by Stern (cited in Vygotsky, 1978) and asked toddlers to describe pictures in pantomime. Vygotsky found that "the two-year-old child, who according to Stern's schema is still at the separate 'object' stage of development, perceived the dynamic features of the picture and reproduced them with ease through pantomime. What Stern regarded as a characteristic of the child's perceptual skills proved to be a product of the limitations of her *language development* or, in other words, a feature of her *verbalized perception*" (p. 32). Thus, complete reliance on verbalization can cause a skewed perception of the reader's response, for meaning is not completely dependent on speech (Siegel, 1984). Instead, meaning is discovered in movement, sights, and sounds and can be created through dance, drama, art, music, and *play*. Indeed, those who study children's play (Pellegrini and Galda, 1982; Saltz and Johnson, 1974) and children's elaborated language (Pelligrini, 1985) suggest that story comprehension is improved as children re-create a story through fantasy play. Hickman (1983) explains: "Those who work with young children know that language tells only part of the story of what they are feeling and thinking. Not only do young children demonstrate intention and meaning before fluency, but they also characteristically use modes of expression other than language, revealing themselves through gesture and movement, for instance, or in their painting or other art work. The reliance on verbal measures and critical statements which seems generally appropriate for studying the response of young adults is less satisfactory when the subjects are children, since it ignores this important nonverbal aspect of their communication" (p. 344).

3. The Cragos (1983) found similar role choices in their preschool daughter, Anna. She chose female roles over male roles, and "good mothers" over "bad." In fairy tales, the good mother is represented by the many royal heroines, and bad mothers by witches and stepmothers. The Cragos believed that Anna's preoccupation with an assortment of fairy tale prin-

cesses represented "the 'good mother,' an idealized female to be admired and emulated" (p. 233). Bruno Bettelheim (1975) explains: "So the typical fairy-tale splitting of the mother into a good (usually dead) mother and an evil stepmother serves the child well. It is not only a means of preserving an internal all-good mother when the real mother is not all-good, but it also permits anger at this bad 'stepmother' without endangering the goodwill of the true mother" (p. 69).

4. The Cragos (1983) found that Anna "chose the heroine/victim role and assigned the aggressor/antagonist role to a parent—sometimes with elaborate safeguards to distance that character from herself" (p. 106).

5. Bettelheim (1975) explains that "before the 'happy' life can begin, the evil and destructive aspects of our personality must be brought under our control" (p. 214). Scholars of feminism and children's literature have noted that such duality is often reflected in a paired-bird or paired animal-human metaphor in children's literature; for example, the dove and the eagle most often point out the contrast between the feminine, mystical, and peaceful and the aggressive, attacking, and domineering (Moers, 1976). In many fairy tales, children's safety and eventual rescue depend on transformations of the aggressive and avenging into the feminine and caring; such occasions are often either weddings or reunions. In Lindsey's case on this occasion, she grew too uncomfortable with the replacement of her mother by the menacing wolf and did not want to wait for the predictable rescue.

6. Dorothy White (1954) found a similar interest in weddings in her daughter, Carol, whose favorite story contained a grand wedding for an ant. She imitated the scene in dress, creating an ensemble of hair ribbons and her mother's evening gown. The Cragos (1983) also found that their daughter, Anna, would rarely enact a story in its entirety, but instead would repeatedly dramatize a favorite scene. Saltz and Brodie (1982) believe that in "pretend play children often take the roles of others; such changes in perspective could serve as a basis for their understanding the emotions and reactions of others" (p. 98). Such shifts among roles complement the major transformations that come with rituals such as weddings. Through a wedding, the unloved (Cinderella, Snow White, and so on) find love and acceptance, as well as exchange their helplessness and poverty for power and riches, but the wedding also marks the drastic change of the formerly ugly and fearsome male creature (Beast, Frog Prince) into a compassionate and kind hero. Among adult women who have read romantic novels or romances over the past two centuries, similar convictions about the transformative power of the ideal romance have constituted much of the appeal of this genre (Brownstein, 1982; Radway, 1984).

7. In the fourth essay of *The Dialogic Imagination* ("Discourse in the

Novel"), Bakhtin (1981) stresses that multiple voices of discourse are a social phenomenon exemplified in the novel. He defines the novel as "a diversity of social speech types (sometimes even diversity of languages) and a diversity of individual voices, artistically organized" (p. 262). The term he uses for this diversity is "heteroglossia," and its use in the novel allows for a dialogue among languages. Bakhtin explains that as the centripetal forces of unification work to standardize language, the centrifugal forces of heteroglossia push language out of any prescribed mold. Language of the novel, like language of the carnival, spills out into a "lively play" among languages. In this process, Bakhtin suggests that words are only half one's own. When authors use words from the mouths of others in time and space, they do not empty out past intentions. Rather, they welcome words "that are already populated with the social intentions of others . . . to serve . . . new intentions, to serve a second master" (p. 300). To extend Bakhtin's idea, perhaps this is, in turn, what happens to the child. The child becomes the third master, using part of the intention of the author and others but creating her own shape as well.

8. Voloshinov (1973) defines reported speech as "speech within speech, utterance within utterance, and at the same time also *speech about speech, utterance about utterance*" (p. 115). He suggests that it "is regarded by the speaker as an utterance belonging to *someone else,* an utterance that was originally totally independent, complete in its construction, and lying outside the given context" (p. 116). Tannen (1989), however, emphasizes the constructed nature of the use of other's talk, suggesting that "the construction of the dialogue represents an active, creative, transforming move which expresses the relationship not between the quoted party and the topic of talk but rather the quoting party and the audience to whom the quotation is delivered" (p. 109). Lindsey and Ashley did not usually regard literary speech as borrowed talk—it was their own. Still, when the chunks of language were larger or prototypical of certain characters, they would give the author credit. In their constructed dialogue, often without attribution to the literary source, the girls' "real" feelings were identified with those of the character who uttered the original words. When the chunks of language were larger and only slightly altered, their speech often included a citation.

9. *Text* becomes in this sense *activity*—and thus capable of transformation between subjective form or image and objective results or products. The Soviet psychologist A. Leont'ev (1981) argues for a sociocultural approach to cognition by asking social scientists and psychologists to consider the unit of analysis as an individual engaged in goal-directed activity—usually with the mediation of objects and language in a process of interaction: "The human individual's activity is a system in the system of social rela-

tions. It does not exist without these relations" (p. 47). Thus, activities are systems of coordination among individuals, in the service of goals carried out through motivations. For Lindsey and Ashley, the language, images, and illustrations of literary texts became objects for transport into their daily activities with their friends and family. Literary language, as distinct from their own words, carried more "objective" weight, since the authority of the text, its imminent retrievability, and its potential for expansion always lurked in the background for negotiating power.

10. Such uses of literary texts to escape consequences occur often in mainstream school-oriented families where children are allowed and often encouraged to make up stories, even when the tale borders on the fantastic. As Heath (1982) explains, "Any initiation of a literacy event by a preschooler makes an interruption, an untruth, a diverting of attention from the matter at hand (whether it be an uneaten plate of food, a messy room, or an avoidance of going to bed) acceptable. Adults jump at openings their children give them for pursuing talk about books and reading" (p. 53).

11. In a sense, the child becomes an actor, imagining her life from within and imaging it in playacting as an aesthetic experience for an audience—a type of coexperiencing of words, feelings, and situations (Bakhtin, 1990, p. 78).

12. Children's focus on formal features of routines and genres prior to, or with occasional persistence over, comprehensible content has been widely reported by child-language researchers. For example, folklorists studying acquisition of riddles and "knock-knock" jokes point out that children comprehend the formal structures of riddle and joke routines and use these, before they understand what content demands there may be, to make "sense" in such routines. For example, children under the age of five often know how to ask the solicitational question that begins a joke: "What color is blood?" But they may then give the arbitrary answer "It's black and blue," without understanding why their joke has failed. Similarly, they learn early the "Knock-knock—who's there?" routine through these first two lines, but then fail to be able to supply the appropriate critical third line upon which the resolution of the next two depends (Bauman, 1977; Sutton-Smith, 1976).

13. Ashley's verbal art here carried features that in general mark children's language play as distinct from that of adults. Her utterances are relatively short, with stylistic devices structured over short spans; the irregularities in her rhyme scheme and stanza structure conform to various sets of rules (some of sense and some of sound); and she carefully observes phonological structure with an end-rhyme pattern of *aa, b, cc, b*. This work, unlike

other pieces of verbal art composed almost entirely of sounds put together for their similarity of phonological structures, unites small segments of formerly independent lines for an expanded creation that fulfills phonological, syntactic, and semantic rules. For extended discussions of children's verbal art as a reflection of their understanding of the various rule systems of language (sound, syntax, and meaning), see Sanches and Kirschenblatt-Gimblett (1976, esp. pp. 86–106) and Iwamura (1980).

14. Most theories of socialization have characterized children as passive recipients of adults' teachings, puzzling those parents who recognized their children as active participants in their own socialization processes. By the end of the twentieth century, theory caught up with common experience as numerous researchers of learning documented ways in which children themselves chose salient features of their environment to remember, compare, expand, or deny. Many concepts characterize the interactive nature of child and adult learning together. Among the earliest was Wundt's (1916) idea of "mental products" that could not be explained in terms of an individual consciousness but had to presuppose reciprocal actions. Many years later, others, such as the British psychiatrist Winnicott (1986), developed similar ideas. For Winnicott, the key notion was that of "transitional phenomena"—ideas that the child uses while trying to separate objective perceptions from their subjective contexts (especially those of the family). During this phase, the child is helped by someone who adapts sensitively in the use of objects such as toys until the child can use fantasy and play to separate his or her own manipulation of the object from that of the immediate adult interaction and carry the symbol away for future use (see esp. pp. 130–137). More well-known in the last decades of the twentieth century has been Vygotsky's "zone of proximal development"— that difference between a child's actual development "as determined by independent problem solving" and the higher level of potential development "through problem solving under adult guidance or in collaboration with more capable peers" (1978, p. 86). Subsequent elaborations of this idea have maintained that culture and cognition create each other (Cole, 1985) and have stressed the importance of tacit and distal social interaction beyond that of explicit face-to-face behaviors (Rogoff, 1990). This latter extension suggests the need to bridge from the adults' roles to focus on the child as independent silent creative thinker and to shift from a strong focus on verbal images to visual images—on what Winnicott terms "apperception as opposed to perception" (1986, p. 41). For example, Shepard (1988) suggests that highly creative thinkers may benefit from an early environment without the constraints of conventional, verbalized, and guided explorations of objects or events; in fact, the power of *visual*

imagination may be inhibited by the heavy verbal directions of others. Feldman (1988) echoes similar views regarding transformative *insights*, in which the mind is enabled to "make new things" spontaneously (p. 287).

15. Numerous psychologists point out the problem-solving power of "what-if" play, much of which often precedes the actual pretend of sociodramatic engagements. In planning for or imagining the upcoming sociodramatic play, the child explores in analytic and constructive ways the counterfactual conditions about to be enacted: a living room will be transformed into a forest, a wagon into a funeral bier or a prince's chariot, and friends into dwarfs, Snow White, and a witch (Sutton-Smith and Kelly-Byrne, 1984). Anthropologists underscore the cognitive complexity of such imaginary explorations that precede and accompany play—especially sociodramatic episodes; during these occasions, children maintain two narratives simultaneously in their heads, with the relevant roles, language, and props of each. In addition, their play often masks other dimensions—they experiment with cruelty, intimacy, power, or danger (Bateson, 1972, 1982; Turner, 1982).

16. The most comprehensive discussions of the acquisition of conditionals by children are those of Reilly (1986) and Bowerman (1986). For an examination of the use of conditionals by children in the game of baseball, see Heath (1991).

17. Bruno Bettelheim (1975) explains: "As with all great art, the fairy tale's deepest meaning will be different for each person, and different for the same person at various moments in his life. The child will extract different meaning from the same fairy tale, depending on his interests and needs of the moment. When given the chance, he will return to the same tale when he is ready to enlarge on old meanings, or replace them with new ones" (p. 12). This is a lesson that can be applied to a broad range of children's literature, including traditional fairy tales and many modern tales. Children do not look upon a story as having a separate existence; its meaning is an integral part of their own story. Their search for meaning in the world of written language would be enervated without the vision to see enchantment in the ordinary, to weave their context and other texts into the tale, and to express their understanding in nonverbal ways.

4. Wings of Meaning

1. The most comprehensive and readable account of the efforts by psychologists and child development specialists to move "inside the head," while facing increasing pressures within their own field as well as from other social sciences to consider meaning and culture, is given in Bruner (1990). See also Goodnow (1990a, 1990b).

2. One of the most fruitful areas for considering the "lag time" between actual reading of a literary text and its use for problem solving or rescripting in another context has consisted of studies of children's drawings (Goodnow, 1977). Söderbergh (1988) indicates the extent to which texts "echo" each other across time and media, in the mind of the five-year-old in her study. Paley's stories of her kindergarten class amply illustrate the ways in which bits and pieces of text and illustration work themselves into everyday problem solving time and time again. The motto of the children as readers seemed to be, "An idea could be examined on two levels: the obvious fact seen by the adult and the possibilities seen by the child" (1981, p. 203).

3. The image of Galatea is an effective metaphor for traditional studies of response to literature—studies that often effectively trapped the heart of a young reader's interaction with story within the confines of a cold, hard shape. The expert response was set on a pedestal and, in comparison, the young child's response was too often labeled literal, simple, and naive. While the image of a perfectly calculated response may have beauty, it is essentially passive, unyielding in its expertly defined form. More recently, understandings in response to literature have moved from an expert/novice dichotomy (Purves and Beach, 1972) to the poem as a creation of worlds (Rosenblatt, 1978; Bruner, 1984; Smith, 1984; Teale, 1984). Rather than listening for the child's concept of story to align itself with expert understanding, recent studies release the construction of story to the child (or to any reader—see Tompkins, 1980) to allow for the individual meaning to come in and thus bring the poem to life in a multiplicity of meanings and connections.

4. The Cragos (1983) found that their daughter, Anna, had "no night fears, and her few nightmares had no relationship to her books" (p. 232), but this was not true for Lindsey and Ashley.

5. The Cragos (1983) found consistent links between the feelings of the reader and the feelings of the story characters. They wrote: "It is widely accepted that young children can become intensely involved in stories, that they can openly demonstrate a range of emotional responses to events and characters, and that they readily align themselves with a fictional protagonist to the point of sharing many of his/her feelings" (p. 215).

6. Kohlberg (1981) posits several levels of moral understanding and describes a developmental sequence, from subjective self-centered judgments through reference to authority figures to rational objective and universal standards. Recent scholars have criticized the extent to which Kohlberg's elicitations of data were heavily biased toward children of Westernized elites and too dependent on children's ability to verbalize their understandings; see Shweder, Mahapatra, and Miller (1990) and Coles (1986)

for discussions of moral development in cross-cultural perspective. The case of Lindsey and Ashley suggests that requests for their verbal explications of moral reasoning would not adequately capture either their moral reflection and analysis or their enactments of moral decisions triggered by literature.

7. Those who bring together the study of social development with that of cognitive development make a fundamental assumption in their work—namely, that cognitive growth emerges not only out of social dialogue and conflict but also out of cultural practices and social interactions. But in acquiring knowledge, we also acquire values about knowledge that are closely linked with intentionality—"the very core of the self" (D'Andrade, 1990, p. 105), and a phenomenon that is much less talked about in mainstream socialization of children than *thought, feeling, emotion,* or *ideas.* Yet the intentionality of individuals continually meets the intentionality of the world, and the two "continuously make each other up, perturbing and disturbing each other, interpenetrating each other's identity, reciprocally conditioning each other's existence" (Shweder, 1990, p. 27).

8. In the mid-1950s, "the intentional fallacy"—the alleged wish on the part of some critics to use the author's intention as a standard for judging the success of a work of literary art—drew considerable attention in literary criticism. Opponents of the use of such a standard argued strongly that to focus on the psychological causes of literary art or to apply terms such as "sincerity," "authenticity," or "integrity" in judgments of aesthetic achievement did not constitute appropriate critical inquiry (Wimsatt and Beardsley, 1954). Uses of children's literature in churches and schools have often leaned toward moralistic or didactic readings, justified through claims of authorial intention and emphasis on biography and history; see Zinsser (1986) and Meek, Warlow, and Barton (1977, sect. 3). Examples of children's reading outside "the intentional fallacy" or other strained directives to interpretation appear in Meek (1988), as well as in parental studies of children's reading, such as Crago and Crago (1983). Cochran-Smith (1984) and Schieffelin and Gilmore (1986, pt. 2) provide studies of such reading of literature in preschools and primary schools.

9. As Rosen (1985) explains, "Any story presupposes the existence of other stories. For both reader and listener threads of connection exist, threads of many different kinds—shapes, devices, signals, echoes, explicit references and, more generally, a sense of how a story belongs with others as a verbal act" (p. 33). Yet these kinds of connections are often given less credence in the early years of school than they are in later years. Rowe and Harste (1985) assert that "young children, prior to instruction, have very proficient strategies . . . After only 20 days of phonics instruction, all too many of these very successful language users were willing to turn in their

strategies for the ones taught in school. As learners, if what we know is not valued, that knowing will atrophy" (p. 134). All learners need both structure and challenge, which can come through a variety of materials, prompts to comprehension, and calls for critical reactions (Chall, Jacobs, and Baldwin, 1990).

10. Applebee (1978) believes that to a young child, stories are immutable. They become caught up in the language of story and allow few changes. Parents who substitute words or entire passages quickly find themselves challenged by the child who will brook no deviation from the text. Rather than interpreting this as a child's sense of immutable story, we could also view it as an opportunity for the child to make firm claims for the knowledge she has gained.

11. Baghban (1984) suggests that "the use of predictable books promotes successful literacy by matching knowledge of the world through oral language to written" (p. 40).

12. In her study of six mainstream families, Denny Taylor (1983) found that literacy allowed children to "build new social connections" (p. 26). Erickson (1984) and others have used the term "cultural capital" (p. 538).

13. Margaret Meek (1988) explains that those "who know how to recognize bits and pieces of other texts in what they read find it is like the discovery of old friends in new places . . . They become 'insiders' in the network" (p. 22).

14. Vygotsky (1978) suggests: "Looking at the matter from the opposite perspective, could one suppose that a child's behavior is always guided by meaning, that a preschooler's behavior is so arid that he never behaves spontaneously simply because he thinks he should behave otherwise? This strict subordination to rules is quite impossible in life, but in play it does become possible: thus, play creates a zone of proximal development of the child. In play a child always behaves beyond his average age, above his daily behavior; in play it is as though he were a head taller than himself. As in the focus of a magnifying glass, play contains all developmental tendencies in a condensed form and is itself a major source of development" (p. 102). By calling on story language, each girl was able to dramatize her zone of proximal development—to stretch her language beyond the boundaries of everyday life, introduce shifts in tone and scene, and express strong positive emotion in an otherwise emotionally negative situation.

15. Janet Hickman (1984) believes that children spontaneously share response to literature. She found that the children she studied "frequently gave each other cues for acting like a reader, in effect teaching one another reader behaviors and strategies for responding" (p. 281).

16. Since authors write more than one book or series, they must have to

struggle for devices of the nonordinary. But some of the disconnections possible in children's literature give them a certain flexibility. Stories begin and move and come to an end within the covers of a single book, but these ends are not always tied to a specific book. Authors may write more than one book about the same or similar characters; they may pick up the same themes in other books, and they may also break their longer books into sections, which seem to have temporary ends but do not finalize the events in the characters' lives. Thus, Laura Ingalls and her family (Wilder, 1932, 1935) move from house to house and from book to book, while Ramona (Cleary, 1968, 1981) moves from scrape to scrape and year to year. Illustrators, too, have volition, but their wills are tied to their stylistic preference and to the written text. And authors and illustrators are not exclusive pairs. Garth Williams, for example, was paired with Laura Ingalls Wilder for her "Little House" books, with E. B. White for *Charlotte's Web*, and with George Selden for *The Cricket in Times Square*.

17. In many ways, Lindsey's interpretation matches Bruno Bettelheim's: "After they have become familiar with 'Hansel and Gretel,' most children comprehend, at least unconsciously, that what happens in the parental home and at the witch's house are but separate aspects of what in reality is one total experience. Initially, the witch is a perfectly gratifying mother figure . . . Only on the following morning comes a rude awakening from such dreams of infantile bliss . . . This is how the child feels when devastated by the ambivalent feelings, frustrations, and anxieties of the oedipal stage of development, as well as his previous disappointment and rage at failures on his mother's part to gratify his needs and desires as fully as he expected. Severely upset that Mother no longer serves him unquestioningly but makes demands on him and devotes herself ever more to her own interests—something which the child had not permitted to come to his awareness before—he imagines that Mother, as she nursed him and created a world of oral bliss, did so only to fool him—like the witch of the story" (1975, p. 163). Experts in children's literature (Huck, Hepler, and Hickman, 1987) tell us that illustrators purposefully make these comparisons to nudge the child into a realization that may be hard to understand: "Jeffers' witch [see Grimm Brothers, 1980] is wrapped in a shawl identical to the stepmother's, hinting that the two may be the same person. Anthony Browne, in his startling contemporary version [see Grimm Brothers, 1981], makes the same connection by the placement of a mole on each woman's cheek" (p. 275).

Epilogue

1. Prior to the 1800s, books specifically designed for children's amusement did not exist. Along with the adults in their community, children listened

to tales of the highborn in medieval castles and of the common people in cottages. The first books for the young were often instructional in nature, containing religious themes and didactic morals. The publication of the first folk and fairy tales (such as those by Charles Perrault, or *The Thousand and One Nights*) were intended for adults, though they were soon expropriated by children. The idea of specific books for children perhaps originated with John Locke's admonition that children's education could be improved by "play and recreation." His words strongly influenced the emergence and continued popularity of "engaging books" for children beginning early in the eighteenth century (Pickering, 1981). John Newbery, who followed Locke's advice, is usually credited with being the first to publish books for children's amusement. The predominance of northern Europe, and especially England, in the production of children's literature has continued, in spite of great advances in some other countries. One outstanding shift came in Russia, where in prerevolutionary times there was very little written just for children. Under the Soviets, children's literature became quite copious and varied—novels, poetry, popularized science, and biography; this expansion of children's literature, encouraged by a regime that regarded the child as a potential Soviet citizen, also took place in other countries in the Communist bloc. For thorough summaries of the history of children's literature, see Cullinan (1989, ch. 12), Huck, Hepler, and Hickman (1987, ch. 3), Sutherland and Arbuthnot (1986, ch. 4), Darton (1958), and Opie and Opie (1974).

2. Many of these scholars recognized the need to flesh out the language story into a literacy lesson (Harste, Woodward, and Burke, 1984). Cochran-Smith (1984) called for a "broad consideration of context," with emphasis on the "cultural and social notions of literacy" (p. 16). Fundamental examinations of the meanings of literacy included the researchers' explorations of their own assumptions about literacy, as well as their close look at the demands placed on the family life of children and adults under different cultural and socioeconomic circumstances. Thus, scholars came to include in their studies of children's reading such environmentally and culturally shaped behaviors as uses of space and time, so that they could offer naturalistic accounts of children in the full round of their daily activities. Such research featuring children of subordinated populations led some educators to recognize the extent to which oral and written language structures and uses intertwined with each other, as well as with children's sense of what was immediately practical. See, for example, Heath (1983, esp. chs. 5, 6, and 7), Schieffelin and Ochs (1986), Schieffelin and Gilmore (1986), and Taylor and Dorsey-Gaines (1988).

3. Anthropological studies of play, as well as collections of children's games and folklore (as distinct from those created by adults for children), proliferated after the late 1960s, underscoring the wide range of linguistic,

cognitive, and social contributions of these forms (Opie and Opie, 1969; Schwartzman, 1978; see also the newsletter of the Association for the Study of Play, which became the journal *Play and Culture* in 1988). These studies also encouraged researchers in disciplines beyond anthropology to take additional factors into account—for example, the writings of Gregory Bateson (1955) on play, and the linkages children made between their play and their observations and critiques of adults' economic and social habits.

4. Such studies usually focus on the child literally in the act of reading—decoding and encoding written texts—and not on the child as "reading" one written text into others or into events and situations of everyday life. Stages of the child's reading development as defined by reading experts such as Jeanne Chall move from "pseudo" or "pretend" reading through decoding, fluency, and reading to learn new information, gain multiple viewpoints, and construct and reconstruct written information for one's own purposes (Chall, 1983). When children can enter children's literature in the social act of reading, with adults acting as decoders, they are freed very early to enter texts for all the purposes of the later stages they achieve for themselves in their private reading, once they master decoding.

5. Scollon and Scollon (1981), in a comparative study of literacy behaviors across cultures, pointed out the extensive ways in which children from literate homes displayed, long before they could read, their sense of how to use language in literate ways. In addition, such children exhibited remarkable facility in "storying" themselves by telling tales in which they made themselves and their actions analogous to those of characters they had heard about in children's literature.

6. A work parallel in function to social scientists' studies of the effects of written texts on individuals and their cultures is that of Silko (1981). Though well outside the genre of ethnography, case study, or autobiography, this work tells the story of the effects of oral storytelling on Silko and members of her Native American community. She discusses the multiple interpretations of stories, occasions of their telling and retelling, differences in telling and interpretation across ages and genders, and stories' interdependence with pragmatics, human relations, and spirituality.

REFERENCES

Alter, R. (1989). *The pleasures of reading in an ideological age*. New York: Simon and Schuster.

Andersen, E. S. (1989). *Speaking with style: The sociolinguistic skills of children*. London: Routledge, Chapman, and Hall.

Applebee, A. N. (1978). *The child's concept of story*. Chicago: University of Chicago Press.

Baghban, M. (1984). *Our daughter learns to read and write*. Newark: International Reading Association.

Bakhtin, M. M. (1981). *The dialogic imagination*. Austin: University of Texas Press.

——— (1990). *Art and answerability: Early philosophical essays*. M. Holquist and V. Liapunov, eds. Austin: University of Texas Press.

Bateson, G. (1955). A theory of play and fantasy. *Psychiatric Research Reports*, 2, 39–51.

——— (1972). *Steps to an ecology of mind*. New York: Ballantine.

——— (1982). Difference, double description, and the interactive designation of self. In F. Allan Hanson, ed., *Studies in symbolism and cultural communication* (pp. 3–8). Lawrence, Kans.: University of Kansas Publications in Anthropology.

Bauman, R. (1977). Linguistics, anthropology, and verbal art: Toward a unified perspective, with a special discussion of children's folklore. In M. Saville-Troike, ed., *Georgetown University Round Table on Languages and Linguistics 1977* (pp. 13–36). Washington, D.C.: Georgetown University Press.

Bettelheim, B. (1975). *The uses of enchantment: The meaning and importance of fairy tales*. New York: Alfred A. Knopf.

Bissex, G. (1980). *Gnys at wrk: A child learns to write and read*. Cambridge, Mass.: Harvard University Press.

Bowerman, M. (1986). First steps in acquiring conditionals. In E. C. Traugott, A. Ter Meulen, J. S. Reilly, and C. A. Ferguson, eds., *On conditionals* (pp. 285–309). Cambridge: Cambridge University Press.

Britton, J. (1970). *Language and learning.* Harmondsworth: Penguin.

Brownstein, R. M. (1982). *Becoming a heroine: Reading about women in novels.* New York: Viking Press.

Bruner, J. (1984). Language, mind, and reading. In H. Goelman, A. Oberg, and F. Smith, eds., *Awakening to literacy* (pp. 193–200). London: Heinemann Educational Books.

—— (1986). *Actual minds, possible worlds.* Cambridge, Mass.: Harvard University Press.

—— (1987). *Narrative and the structure of experience.* Paper presented at a Psychology Department colloquium, Stanford University. May.

—— (1990). *Acts of meaning.* Cambridge, Mass.: Harvard University Press.

Burke, K. (1966). *Language as symbolic action: Essays on life, literature, and method.* Berkeley: University of California Press.

—— (1968). Dramatism. *International encyclopedia of the social sciences, 7:* 445–452. New York: Macmillan.

Butler, D. (1975). *Cushla and her books.* Boston: Horn Book.

Chall, J. S. (1983). *Stages of reading development.* New York: McGraw-Hill.

——, V. A. Jacobs, and L. E. Baldwin. (1990). *The reading crisis: When poor children fall behind.* Cambridge, Mass.: Harvard University Press.

Chukovsky, K. (1963). *From two to five.* M. Morton, trans. Berkeley: University of California Press.

Clark, E. V. (1983). Meaning and concepts. In P. H. Mussen, ed., *Handbook of child psychology,* 4th ed., vol 3: *Cognitive development,* J. H. Flavell and E. M. Markman, eds., pp. 787–840. New York: Wiley.

Clay, M. (1972). *Sand: Concepts about print test.* Auckland, New Zealand: Heinemann.

—— (1979a). *Stones: Concepts about print test.* Auckland, New Zealand: Heinemann.

—— (1979b). *The early detection of reading difficulties.* Hong Kong: Heinemann.

Cochran-Smith, M. (1984). *The making of a reader.* Norwood, N.J.: Ablex.

Cole, M. (1985). The zone of proximal development: Where culture and cognition create each other. In J. Wertsch, ed., *Culture, communication and cognition: Vygotskian perspectives* (pp. 146–161). Cambridge: Cambridge University Press.

Coles, R. (1986). *The moral life of children.* Boston: Houghton Mifflin.

—— (1989). *The call of stories: Teaching and the moral imagination.* Boston: Houghton Mifflin.

Coveney, P. (1967). *The image of childhood: The individual and society—A study of the theme in English literature.* Baltimore: Penguin.

Crago, H., and M. Crago. (1983). *Prelude to literacy: A preschool child's encounter with picture and story.* Carbondale: Southern Illinois University Press.

Culler, J. (1975). *Structuralist poetics.* Ithaca, N.Y.: Cornell University Press.

Cullinan, B. (1989). *Literature and the child.* San Diego: Harcourt Brace Jovanovich.

D'Andrade, R. (1990). Some propositions about the relations between culture and human cognition. In J. W. Stigler, R. A. Shweder, and G. Herdt, eds., *Cultural psychology: Essays on comparative human development* (pp. 65–129). Cambridge: Cambridge University Press.

Darton, F. J. H. (1958). *Children's books in England.* 2nd ed. Cambridge: Cambridge University Press.

Davidson, C. N., ed. (1989). *Reading in America: Literature and social history.* Baltimore: Johns Hopkins University Press.

de Beaugrande, R. (1980). *Text, discourse, and process.* Norwood, N.J.: Ablex.

Donaldson, M. (1978). *Children's minds.* New York: Norton.

Dyson, A. H. (1989). *Multiple worlds of child writers: Friends learning to write.* New York: Teachers College Press.

Erickson, F. (1984). School literacy, reasoning, and civility: An anthropologist's perspective. *Review of Educational Research, 54:* 525–546.

Fein, G. (1979). Play with actions and objects. In Brian Sutton-Smith, ed., *Play and learning* (pp. 69–82). New York: Gardner Press.

Feldman, C. F. (1989). Monologue as problem-solving narrative. In K. Nelson, ed., *Narratives from the crib* (pp. 98–122). Cambridge, Mass.: Harvard University Press.

Feldman, D. H. (1988). Creativity: Dreams, insights, and transformations. In R. J. Sternberg, ed., *The nature of creativity* (pp. 271–297). Cambridge: Cambridge University Press.

Ferguson, C. A., and M. A. Macken. (1983). The role of play in phonological development. In K. E. Nelson, ed., *Children's language,* vol. 4 (pp. 231–254). Hillsdale, N.J.: Erlbaum.

Fernald, A. (1984). The perceptual and affective salience of mother's speech to infants. In L. Feagans, C. Garvey, and R. Golinkoff, eds., *The origins and growth of communication* (pp. 5–29). Norwood, N.J.: Ablex.

Fillmore, C. J., D. Kempler, and W. S. Wang. (1979). *Individual differences in language ability and language behavior.* New York: Academic Press.

Fish, S. (1980). *Is there a text in this class? The authority of interpretive communities.* Cambridge, Mass.: Harvard University Press.

——— (1989). *Doing what comes naturally: Change, rhetoric, and the practice of theory in literary and legal studies.* Durham, N.C.: Duke University Press.

Fowler, A. (1982). *Kinds of literature: An introduction to the theory of genres and modes.* Cambridge, Mass.: Harvard University Press.

Freund, E. (1987). *The return of the reader: Reader-response criticism.* London: Methuen.

Galda, L., and A. D. Pellegrini, eds. (1985). *Play, language, and stories.* Norwood, N.J.: Ablex.

Garvey, C. (1976). Some properties of social play. In Jerome S. Bruner, Alison Jolly, and Kathy Sylva, eds., *Play: Its role in development and evolution* (pp. 570–583). New York: Penguin.

—— (1990). *Play.* Cambridge, Mass.: Harvard University Press.

Garvin, P. L. (1964). *A Prague School reader on esthetics, literary structure, and style.* Washington, D.C.: Georgetown University Press.

Geertz, C. (1986). Making experience, authoring selves. In V. W. Turner and E. M. Bruner, eds., *The anthropology of experience* (pp. 373–380). Urbana: University of Illinois Press.

Genette, G. (1980). *Narrative discourse: An essay in method.* J. E. Lewin, trans. Ithaca, N.Y.: Cornell University Press.

Gilead, S. (1991). Magic abjured: Closure in children's fantasy fiction. *Publications of the Modern Language Association of America,* 106, no. 2: 227–293.

Goodman, K. S., L. Bird, and Y. M. Goodman. (1990). *The whole language catalog.* Santa Rosa, Calif.: American School Publishers.

Goodman, Y. M. (1986). Children coming to know literacy. In E. Sulzby and W. H. Teale, eds., *Emergent literacy: Writing and reading* (pp. 1–14). Norwood, N.J.: Ablex.

Goodnow, J. J. (1977). *Children drawing.* Cambridge, Mass.: Harvard University Press.

—— (1990a). The socialization of cognition: What's involved? In J. W. Stigler, R. A. Shweder, and G. Herdt, eds., *Cultural psychology: Essays on comparative human development* (pp. 259–286). Cambridge: Cambridge University Press.

—— (1990b). Using sociology to extend psychological accounts of cognitive development. *Human Development, 33:* 81–107.

——, P. Wilkins, and L. Dawes. (1986). Acquiring cultural forms: Cognitive aspects of socialization illustrated by children's drawings and judgments of drawing. *International Journal of Behavioral Development,* 9: 485–505.

Goodwin, M. H. (1990). *He-said-she-said: Talk as social organization among black children.* Bloomington: Indiana University Press.

Graetz, M. (1979). Loving with stories. *Orana,* 15: 56–65.

Green, G. (1982). Competence for implicit text analysis: Literary style discrimination in five-year-olds. In D. Tannen, ed., *Analyzing discourse: Text and talk* (pp. 142–163). Washington, D.C.: Georgetown University Press.

Gurganus, Allan. (1989). *Oldest living Confederate widow tells all.* New York: Alfred A. Knopf.

Halliday, M. A. K. (1975). *Learning how to mean: Explorations in the development of language.* London: Edward Arnold.

Hardy, B. (1977). Narrative as a primary act of mind. In M. Meek, A. Warlow, and G. Barton, eds., *The cool web: The pattern of children's reading* (pp. 12–23). New York: Atheneum.

Harste, J., V. Woodward, and C. Burke. (1984). *Language stories and literacy lessons.* Portsmouth, N.H.: Heinemann.

Haussler, M. (1985). A young child's developing concepts of print. In A. Jaggar and M. T. Smith-Burke, eds., *Observing the language learner* (pp. 73–81). Newark: International Reading Association.

Heath, S. B. (1982). What no bedtime story means: Narrative skills at home and school. *Language in Society,* 11: 49–76.

———— (1983). *Ways with words: Language, life, and work in communities and classrooms.* Cambridge: Cambridge University Press.

———— (1991). "It's about winning!" The language of knowledge in baseball. In L. Resnick, J. Levine, and S. Behrend, eds., *Perspectives on socially shared cognition* (pp. 101–124). Washington, D.C.: American Psychological Association.

————, A. Branscombe, and C. Thomas. (1986). The book as narrative prop. In B. B. Schieffelin and P. Gilmore, eds., *The acquisition of literacy: Ethnographic perspectives* (pp. 16–34). Norwood, N.J.: Ablex.

Heath, S. B., and C. Thomas. (1984). The achievement of preschool literacy for mother and child. In H. Goelman, A. Oberg, and F. Smith, eds., *Awakening to literacy* (pp. 51–72). London: Heinemann Educational Books.

Herrnstein Smith, B. (1978). Children at the gates of the marketplace. In B. Herrnstein Smith, *On the margins of discourse: The relation of literature to language* (pp. 124–132). Chicago: University of Chicago Press.

Hickman, J. (1983). A new perspective on response to literature in an elementary school setting. *Research in the Teaching of English,* 15: 343–354.

———— (1984). Research currents: Researching children's response to literature. *Language Arts,* 61: 278–284.

Hubbard, R. (1989). *Authors of pictures—draughtsmen of words.* Portsmouth, N.H.: Heinemann.

Huck, C., S. Hepler, and J. Hickman. (1987). *Children's literature in the elementary school.* New York: Holt, Rinehart and Winston.

Hudson, R. A. (1980). *Sociolinguistics.* Cambridge: Cambridge University Press.

Hunt, P. (1991). *Criticism, theory, and children's literature*. Oxford: Basil Blackwell.

Hyman, T. S. (1985). Caldecott medal acceptance speech. *The Horn Book*. July–August.

Irving, John. (1989). *A prayer for Owen Meany*. New York: William Morrow.

Iser, W. (1974). *The implied reader*. Baltimore: Johns Hopkins University Press.

Iwamura, S. G. (1980). *The verbal games of pre-school children*. London: Croom Helm.

Jakobson, R. (1960). Linguistics and poetics. In T. Sebeok, ed., *Style in language* (pp. 350–377). Cambridge, Mass.: MIT Press.

——— (1985). *Verbal art, verbal sign, verbal time*. Minneapolis: University of Minnesota Press.

Kelly-Byrne, D. (1989). *A child's play life: An ethnographic study*. New York: Teachers College Press.

Kirschenblatt-Gimblett, B. (1979). Speech play and verbal art. In B. Sutton-Smith, ed., *Play and learning* (pp. 219–238). New York: Gardner Press.

Knoepflmacher, U. C. (1983). The balancing of child and adult: An approach to Victorian fantasies for children. *Nineteenth-Century Fiction*, 37: 497–530.

——— (1986). Avenging Alice: Christina Rossetti and Lewis Carroll. *Nineteenth-Century Literature*, 41: 299–328.

Kohlberg, L. (1981). *The philosophy of moral development: Moral stages and the idea of justice*. Vol. 1 of *Essays on moral development*. San Francisco: Harper and Row.

Lanes, S. G. (1980). *The art of Maurice Sendak*. New York: Abradale Press and Harry N. Abrams.

Leont'ev, A. N. (1981). The problem of activity in psychology. In J. V. Wertsch, ed., *The concept of activity in Soviet psychology* (pp. 37–71). Armonk, N.Y.: Sharpe.

Leopold, W. (1939). *Speech development of a bilingual child—A linguist's record, I: Vocabulary growth in the first two years*. Evanston: Northwestern University Press.

——— (1949). *Speech development of a bilingual child—A linguist's record, IV: Diary from age two*. Evanston: Northwestern University Press.

Lindstrom, M. (1970). *Children's art*. Berkeley: University of California Press.

Livingston, M. C. (1981). Nonsense verse: The complete escape. In B. Hearne and M. Kaye, eds., *Celebrating children's books* (pp. 122–139). New York: Lothrop, Lee and Shepard.

Lobel, A. (1981). A good picture book should . . . In B. Hearne and M. Kaye, eds., *Celebrating children's books* (pp. 73–80). New York: Lothrop, Lee and Shepard.

Lotman, J. (1976). *Analysis of the poetic text*. D. B. Johnson, trans. Ann Arbor, Mich.: Ardis.

―――― (1977). *The structure of the artistic text*. R. Vroon, trans. Ann Arbor, Mich: University of Michigan Press.

Lukens, R. J. (1982). *A critical handbook of children's literature*. Glenview, Ill.: Scott, Foresman.

Lurie, A. (1990). *Don't tell the grown-ups: Subversive children's literature*. Boston, Mass.: Little, Brown.

Madden, W. A. (1986). Framing the *Alices. Publications of the Modern Language Association of America*, 101: 362–373.

Mailloux, S. (1982). *Interpretive conventions: The reader in the study of American fiction*. Ithaca, N.Y.: Cornell University Press.

McCune, L. (1984). Play-language relationships: Implications for the theory of symbolic development. In A. W. Gottfried and C. C. Brown, eds., *Play interactions* (pp. 67–79). Lexington, Mass.: D. C. Heath.

McDermott, R. (1990). Qualitative research methods (course syllabus). Stanford University. Winter–Spring.

Meek, M. (1988). *How texts teach what readers learn*. Exeter, England: The Thimble Press.

―――― , A. Warlow, and G. Barton, eds. (1977). *The cool web: The pattern of children's reading*. New York: Atheneum.

Moers, E. (1976). *Literary women: The great writers*. New York: Oxford University Press.

Morrison, Toni. (1987). *Beloved*. New York: Alfred A. Knopf.

Mukarovsky, J. (1977). *The word and verbal art*. J. Burbank and P. Steiner, trans. New Haven: Yale University Press.

Nelson, K., ed. (1989). *Narratives from the crib*. Cambridge, Mass.: Harvard University Press.

Ninio, A., and J. Bruner. (1976). The achievement and antecedents of labelling. *Journal of Child Language*, 5: 1–15.

Nodelman, P. (1988). *Words about pictures*. Athens, Ga.: University of Georgia Press.

Opie, I., and P. Opie. (1969). *Children's games in street and playground*. Oxford: Oxford University Press.

―――― (1974). *The classic fairy tale*. London: Oxford University Press.

Paley, V. (1981). *Wally's stories*. Cambridge, Mass: Harvard University Press.

―――― (1986). *Molly is three: Growing up in school*. Chicago: University of Chicago Press.

Pellegrini, A. D. (1985). Relations between preschool children's symbolic play and literate behavior. In L. Galda and A. D. Pellegrini, eds., *Play, language, and stories: The development of children's literate behavior* (pp. 79–97). Norwood, N.J.: Ablex.

Pellegrini, A. D., and L. Galda. (1982). The effects of thematic-fantasy play training on the development of children's story comprehension. *American Educational Research Journal*, 19: 443–452.

Pepler, D. J. (1982). Play and divergent thinking. In D. J. Pepler and K. H. Rubin, eds., *The play of children: Current theory and research* (pp. 64–78). Basel: S. Karger.

Peters, A. M. (1983). *The units of language acquisition*. Cambridge: Cambridge University Press.

Phelps, E. J. (1978). *Tatterhood and other tales*. Old Westbury, N.Y.: Feminist Press.

Piaget, J. (1962). *Play, dreams and imitation in childhood*. New York: Norton.

Pickering, S. F. (1981). *John Locke and children's books in eighteenth-century England*. Knoxville: University of Tennessee Press.

Propp, V. (1968). *Morphology of the folktale*. L. Scott, trans. Austin: University of Texas Press. Orig. pub. 1958.

Purves, A., and R. Beach. (1972). *Literature and the reader: Research in response to literature, reading interests, and the teaching of literature*. Urbana, Ill.: National Council of Teachers of English.

Radway, J. A. (1984). *Reading the romance: Women, patriarchy, and popular literature*. Chapel Hill: University of North Carolina Press.

Reilly, J. S. (1986). The acquisition of temporals and conditionals. In E. C. Traugott, A. Ter Meulen, J. S. Reilly, and C. A. Ferguson, eds., *On conditionals* (pp. 309–332). Cambridge: Cambridge University Press.

Rogoff, B. (1990). *Apprenticeship in thinking: Cognitive development in social context*. New York: Oxford University Press.

Root-Bernstein, R. S. (1989). *Discovering*. Cambridge, Mass.: Harvard University Press.

Rosen, H. (1985). *Stories and meanings*. Winnipeg: National Association for the Teaching of English.

Rosenblatt, L. (1938). *Literature as exploration*. New York: D. Appleton-Century.

——— (1978). *The reader, the text, the poem: The transactional theory of the literary work*. Carbondale: Southern Illinois University Press.

Rowe, D., and J. Harste. (1985). Reading and writing in a system of knowing: Curricular implications. In M. Sampson, ed., *The pursuit of literacy: Early reading and writing*. Dubuque, Iowa: Kendall/Hunt.

Sachs, J. (1977). The adaptive significance of linguistic input to prelinguistic infants. In C. E. Snow and C. A. Ferguson, eds., *Talking to children: Language input and acquisition* (pp. 51–61). Cambridge: Cambridge University Press.

Saltz, E., and J. Brodie. (1982). Pretend-play training in childhood: A review and critique. In D. J. Pepler and K. H. Rubin, eds., *The play of children: Current theory and research* (pp. 97–113). Basel: S. Karger.

Saltz, E., and J. Johnson. (1974). Training disadvantaged preschoolers on various fantasy activities: Effects on cognitive functioning and impulse control. *Child Development,* 66: 623–630.

Sanches, M., and B. Kirschenblatt-Gimblett. (1976). Children's traditional speech play and child language. In B. Kirschenblatt-Gimblett, ed., *Speech play* (pp. 65–110). Philadelphia: University of Pennsylvania Press.

Schieffelin, B. B., and M. Cochran-Smith. (1984). Learning to read culturally: Literacy before schooling. In H. Goelman, A. Oberg, and F. Smith, eds., *Awakening to literacy* (pp. 3–23). London: Heinemann.

Schieffelin, B. B. and Gilmore, P., eds. (1986). *The acquisition of literacy: Ethnographic perspectives.* Norwood: N.J.: Ablex.

Schieffelin, B. B., and E. Ochs. (1986). Language socialization across cultures. Cambridge: Cambridge University Press.

Schwartzman, H. B. (1978). *Transformations: The anthropology of children's play.* New York: Plenum Press.

Scollon, R., and S. Scollon. (1981). *Narrative, literacy, and face in interethnic communication.* Norwood, N.J.: Ablex.

Segal, D., and M. Adcock. (1981). *Just pretending.* Englewood Cliffs, N.J.: Prentice-Hall.

Sendak, M. (1988). *Caldecott & Co.: Notes on books and pictures.* New York: Farrar, Straus and Giroux.

Shepard, R. (1988). The imagination of the scientist. In K. Egan and D. Nadaner, eds., *Imagination and education* (pp. 153–185). New York: Teachers College Press.

Short, C. (1986). Literacy as a collaborative experience. Dissertation, Indiana University, Bloomington.

Shotwell, J., D. Wolf, and H. Gardner. (1979). Exploring early symbolization: Styles of achievement. In B. Sutton-Smith, ed., *Play and learning* (pp. 127–156). New York: Gardner Press.

Shweder, R. A. (1990). Cultural psychology: What is it? In J. W. Stigler, R. A. Shweder, and G. Herdt, eds., *Cultural psychology: Essays on comparative human development* (pp. 130–204). Cambridge: Cambridge University Press.

———, M. Mahapatra, and J. G. Miller. (1990). Cultural and moral development. In J. W. Stigler, R. A. Shweder, and G. Herdt, eds., *Cultural psychology: Essays on comparative human development* (pp. 130–204). Cambridge: Cambridge University Press.

Siegel, M. (1984). Reading as signification. Dissertation, Indiana University, Bloomington.

Silko, L. M. (1981). *Storyteller.* New York: Little, Brown.

Sims, R. (1982). *Shadow and substance: Afro-American experience in contemporary children's fiction.* Urbana, Ill.: National Council of Teachers of English.

Smilansky, S. (1968). *The effects of sociodramatic play on disadvantaged preschool children.* New York: Wiley.

Smith, F. (1983). *Essays into literacy.* London: Heinemann Educational Books.

——— (1984). The creative achievement of literacy. In H. Goelman, A. Oberg, and F. Smith, eds., *Awakening to literacy* (pp. 143–153). London: Heinemann Educational Books.

Snow, C. E. (1983). Literacy and language: Relationships during the preschool years. *Harvard Educational Review,* 53: 165–189.

Söderbergh, R. (1988). A five-and-a-half-year-old reader's book-illustrating drawings: Transformation into the pictorial mode and a window towards an inner world of language. In *Early reading and writing,* Paper no. 3, pp. 33–56. Lund, Sweden: Child Language Research Institute.

Spellman, E. V. (1990). Sisterhood is intimidating. *New York Times Book Review,* May 27, p. 8.

Sutherland, Z., and M. H. Arbuthnot. (1986). *Children and books.* Glenview, Ill.: Scott, Foresman.

Sutton-Smith, B. (1976). A developmental structural account of riddles. In B. Kirschenblatt-Gimblett, ed., *Speech play* (pp. 111–120). Philadelphia: University of Pennsylvania Press.

——— and D. Kelly-Byrne. (1984). The masks of play. In B. Sutton-Smith and D. Kelly-Byrne, eds., *The masks of play* (pp. 184–197). New York: Leisure Press.

Tannen, D. (1989). *Talking voices: Repetition, dialogue, and imagery in conversational discourse.* Cambridge: Cambridge University Press.

Taylor, D. (1983). *Family literacy.* Exeter, N.H.: Heinemann Educational Books.

——— and C. Dorsey-Gaines. (1988). *Growing up literate: Learning from inner-city families.* Portsmouth, N.H.: Heinemann.

Teale, W. (1984). Reading to young children: Its significance for literacy development. In H. Goelman, A. Oberg, and F. Smith, eds., *Awakening to literacy* (pp. 110–121). London: Heinemann Educational Books.

——— and E. Sulzby. (1986). *Emergent literacy: Writing and reading.* Norwood, N.J.: Ablex.

Timmerman, J. H. (1983). *Other worlds: The fantasy genre.* Bowling Green, Ohio: Bowling Green University Popular Press.

Tompkins, J. P., ed. (1980). *Reader-response criticism: From formalism to post-structuralism.* Baltimore: Johns Hopkins University Press.

Tucker, N. (1981). *The child and the book.* Cambridge: Cambridge University Press.

Turner, V. (1982). *From ritual to theatre: The human seriousness of play*. New York: PAJ Publications.

Voloshinov, V. N. (1973). *Marxism and the philosophy of language*. New York: Seminar Press.

Vygotsky, L. S. (1976). Play and its role in the mental development of the child. In Jerome S. Bruner, Alison Jolly, and Kathy Sylva, eds., *Play: Its role in development and evolution* (pp. 537–554). New York: Penguin.

—— (1978). *Mind in society*. Cambridge, Mass.: Harvard University Press.

Warlow, A. (1977). What the reader has to do. In M. Meek, A. Warlow, and G. Barton, eds., *The cool web: The pattern of children's reading* (pp. 91–96). New York: Atheneum.

Weir, R. (1962). *Language in the crib*. The Hague: Mouton.

Wertsch, J. (1991). *Voices of the mind: A sociocultural approach to mediated action*. Cambridge, Mass.: Harvard University Press.

—— and J. Youniss. (1987). Contextualizing the investigator: The case of developmental psychology. *Human Development*, 30: 18–31.

White, D. (1954). *Books before five*. Portsmouth, N.H.: Heinemann Educational Books.

Wimsatt, W. K., Jr., and M. C. Beardsley. (1954). *The verbal icon: Studies in the meaning of poetry*. Louisville: University Press of Kentucky.

Winner, E. (1982). *Invented worlds: The psychology of the arts*. Cambridge, Mass.: Harvard University Press.

—— (1988). *The point of words: Children's understanding of metaphor and irony*. Cambridge, Mass.: Harvard University Press.

Winnicott, D. W. (1971). *Playing and reality*. Harmondsworth: Penguin.

—— (1986). *Home is where we start from*. New York: Norton.

Wolf, D., and S. H. Grollman. (1982). Combinatorial competency in symbolic play and language. In D. J. Pepler and K. H. Rubin, eds., *The play of children: Current theory and research* (pp. 46–63). Basel: S. Karger.

Wong-Fillmore, L. (1979). Individual differences in second language acquisition. In C. J. Fillmore, D. Kempler, and W. S. Wang, eds., *Individual differences in language ability and language behavior* (pp. 203–228). New York: Academic Press.

Woodward, V. A., and W. G. Serebrin. (1989). Reading between the signs: The social semiotics of collaborative storyreading. *Linguistics and education*, 1: 393–414.

Wundt, W. (1916). *Elements of folk psychology*. London: Allen and Unwin.

Zinsser, C. (1986). For the Bible tells me so: Teaching children in a fundamentalist church. In B. B. Schieffelin and P. Gilmore, eds., *The acquisition of literacy: Ethnographic perspectives* (pp. 55–74). Norwood, N.J.: Ablex.

BIBLIOGRAPHY OF BOOKS READ TO THE CHILDREN

Aardema, Verna. (1975). *Why mosquitoes buzz in people's ears.* Ilustrated by Leo and Diane Dillon. New York: Dial.

—— (1977). *Who's in rabbit's house?* Illustrated by Leo and Diane Dillon New York: Dial.

—— (1984). *Oh, Kojo! How could you!* Illustrated by Marc Brown. New York: Dial.

Aesop. (1964). *Aesop: Five centuries of illustrated fables.* Selected by John J. McKendry. New York: Metropolitan Museum of Art.

—— (1976). *Tales from Aesop.* New York: Random House.

Ahlberg, Janet, and Allan Ahlberg. (1986). *The jolly postman, or other people's letters.* Boston: Little, Brown.

Aliki. (1969). *My visit to the dinosaurs.* New York: Harper and Row.

Allard, Harry. (1977). *Miss Nelson is missing!* Illustrated by James Marshall. Boston: Houghton Mifflin.

—— (1982). *Miss Nelson is back.* Illustrated by James Marshall. Boston: Houghton Mifflin.

Andersen, Hans Christian. (1978). *The princess and the pea.* Illustrated by Paul Galdone. New York: Seabury.

—— (1979a). *Thumbelina.* Retold by Amy Ehrlich and illustrated by Susan Jeffers. New York: Dial.

—— (1979b). *The ugly duckling.* Retold and illustrated by Lorinda Bryan Cauley. San Diego: Harcourt Brace Jovanovich.

—— (1984). *The little mermaid.* Adapted by Anthea Bell and illustrated by Chihiro Iwasaki. Natick, Mass.: Picture Book Studio.

—— (1985). *The nightingale.* Translated by Anthea Bell and illustrated by Lisbeth Zwerger. Natick, Mass.: Picture Book Studio.

Bach, Alice, and J. Cheryl Exum. (1989). *Moses' ark: Stories from the Bible.* Illustrated by Leo Dillon and Diane Dillon. New York: Delacorte Press.

Barrie, J. M. (1911). *Peter Pan.* New York: Tundra Books.

Base, Graeme. (1987). *Animalia*. New York: Harry N. Abrams.

———— (1989). *The eleventh hour: A curious mystery*. New York: Harry N. Abrams.

Bate, Lucy. (1975). *Little Rabbit's loose tooth*. Illustrated by Diane De Groat. New York: Scholastic.

Battaglia, Aurelius. (1973). *Mother Goose*. New York: Random House.

Baum, L. Frank. (1900). *The wizard of Oz*. Illustrated by W. W. Denslow. Chicago: Reilly and Lee.

Baylor, Byrd. (1972). *When clay sings*. Illustrated by Tom Bahti. New York: Macmillan.

Bemelmans, Ludwig. (1939). *Madeline*. New York: Simon and Schuster.

———— (1953). *Madeline's rescue*. New York: Viking.

———— (1985). *Madeline's Christmas*. New York: Viking.

Berger, Melvin. (1985). *Germs make me sick!* Illustrated by Marylin Hafner. New York: Harper and Row.

Bishop, Claire Huchet. (1938). *The five Chinese brothers*. Illustrated by Kurt Wiese. New York: Coward-McCann.

Brett, Jan. (1987). *Goldilocks and the three bears*. Retold and illustrated by Jan Brett. New York: Dodd, Mead.

Brown, Marcia. (1947). *Stone soup*. New York: Scribner's.

Brown, Margaret Wise. (1942). *The runaway bunny*. Illustrated by Clement Hurd. New York: Harper and Row.

———— (1947). *Goodnight moon*. Illustrated by Clement Hurd. New York: Harper and Row.

———— (1954). *The little fir tree*. Illustrated by Barbara Cooney. New York: Harper and Row.

Browne, Anthony. (1983). *Gorilla*. New York: Alfred A. Knopf.

Bunting, Eve. (1989). *The Wednesday surprise*. Illustrated by Donald Carrick. New York: Clarion Books.

Burnett, Frances Hodgson. (1905). *A little princess*. Illustrated by Graham Rust. Boston: David R. Godine.

———— (1910). *The secret garden*. Illustrated by Michael Hague. New York: Henry Holt.

Burton, Virginia Lee. (1942). *The little house*. Boston: Houghton Mifflin.

Carle, Eric. (1969). *The very hungry caterpillar*. New York: Philomel Books.

Carroll, Lewis [Charles L. Dodgson]. (1978). *Alice's adventures in Wonderland*. Illustrated by Arthur Rackham. New York: Weathervane Books.

———— (1979). *The nursery "Alice."* Illustrated by Sir John Tenniel. New York: Mayflower Books.

———— (1985). *Jabberwocky*. Illustrated by Kate Buckley. Niles, Ill.: Albert Whitman.

Cauley, Lorinda Bryan. (1983). *Jack and the beanstalk*. New York: Putnam's.

Cendrars, Blaise. (1982). *Shadow*. Translated and illustrated by Marcia Brown. New York: Scribner's.

Chaucer, Geoffrey. (1988). *Canterbury tales*. Selected, translated, and adapted by Barbara Cohen and illustrated by Trina Schart Hyman. New York: Lothrop, Lee and Shepard.

Childcraft folk and fairy tales. (1949). Vol. 3. Chicago: Field Enterprises.

Childcraft poems of early childhood. (1949). Vol. 1. Chicago: Field Enterprises.

Cleary, Beverly. (1968). *Ramona the pest*. Illustrated by Louis Darling. New York: Dell.

———— (1981). *Ramona Quimby, age 8*. Illustrated by Alan Tiegreen. New York: Dell.

Cole, Joanna. (1989). *The magic school bus inside the human body*. Illustrated by Bruce Degen. New York: Scholastic.

Dahl, Roald. (1961). *James and the giant peach*. Illustrated by Nancy Ekholm Burkert. New York: Alfred A. Knopf.

———— (1982). *The Twits*. Illustrated by Quentin Blake. New York: Bantam Books.

D'Aulaire, Ingri, and Edgar P. D'Aulaire. (1957). *Abraham Lincoln*. Garden City, N.Y.: Doubleday.

———— (1962). *Book of Greek myths*. Garden City, N.Y.: Doubleday.

De Brunhoff, Jean. (1933). *The story of Babar, the little elephant*. Translated from the French by Merle S. Haas. New York: Random House.

———— (1938). *Babar and his children*. Translated from the French by Merle S. Haas. New York: Random House.

———— (1940). *Babar and Father Christmas*. Translated from the French by Merle S. Haas. New York: Random House.

De Brunhoff, Laurent. (1973). *Meet Babar and his family*. New York: Random House.

de Paola, Tomie. (1975). *Strega Nona*. Englewood Cliffs, N.J.: Prentice-Hall.

———— (1978). *The clown of God*. San Diego: Harcourt Brace Jovanovich.

———— (1984a). *Mother Goose story streamers*. New York: Putnam's.

———— (1984b). *The first Christmas*. New York: Putnam's.

———— (1987). *The miracles of Jesus*. Retold from the Bible and illustrated by Tomie de Paola. New York: Holiday House.

de Regniers, Beatrice Schenk. (1972). *Red Riding Hood*. Illustrated by Edward Gorey. New York: Atheneum.

———— (1988). *Sing a song of popcorn: Every child's book of poems*. Selected by Beatrice Schenk de Regniers, Eva Moore, Mary Michaels White, and Jan Carr and illustrated by nine Caldecott Medal artists. New York: Scholastic.

Ets, Marie Hall, and Aurora Labastida. (1987). *Nine days to Christmas: A story of Mexico*. Illustrated by Marie Hall Ets. New York: Viking.

Flack, Marjorie. (1933). *The story about Ping*. Illustrated by Kurt Wiese. New York: Viking.

Fleischman, Paul. (1988). *Joyful noise: Poems for two voices*. Illustrated by Eric Beddows. New York: Harper and Row.

Fonteyn, Margot. (1989). *Swan lake*. Illustrated by Trina Schart Hyman. San Diego: Harcourt Brace Jovanovich.

Fox, Mem. (1985). *Wilfrid Gordon McDonald Partridge*. Illustrated by Julie Vivas. New York: Kane/Miller.

Gág, Wanda. (1928). *Millions of cats*. New York: Coward-McCann.

Galdone, Paul. (1968). *Henny Penny*. New York: Scholastic.

———— (1970). *The three little pigs*. New York: Scholastic.

Garelick, May. (1970). *Where does the butterfly go when it rains?* Illustrated by Leonard Weisgard. New York: Scholastic.

Goble, Paul. (1978). *The girl who loved wild horses*. New York: Bradbury Press.

Goldin, Augusta. (1965). *Ducks don't get wet*. Illustrated by Leonard Kessler. New York: Harper and Row.

Grimm Brothers. (1972). *Snow White*. Translated by Randall Jarrell and illustrated by Nancy Ekholm Burkert. New York: Farrar, Straus and Giroux.

———— (1973a). *"The juniper tree" and other tales from Grimm*. Translated by Lore Segal and Randall Jarrell, and illustrated by Maurice Sendak. New York: Farrar, Straus and Giroux.

———— (1973b). *Grimm's fairy tales: Twenty stories*. Illustrated by Arthur Rackham. New York: Viking.

———— (1974). *Snow White*. Freely translated from the German by Paul Heins and illustrated by Trina Schart Hyman. Boston: Little, Brown.

———— (1977a). *The sleeping beauty*. Retold and illustrated by Trina Schart Hyman. Boston: Little, Brown.

———— (1977b). *Grimms' tales for young and old*. Translated by Ralph Manheim. Garden City, N.Y.: Anchor/Doubleday.

———— (1980). *Hansel and Gretel*. Illustrated by Susan Jeffers. New York: Dial.

———— (1981). *Hansel and Gretel*. Illustrated by Anthony Browne. New York: Alfred A. Knopf.

———— (1982). *Rapunzel*. Retold by Barbara Rogasky and illustrated by Trina Schart Hyman. New York: Holiday House.

———— (1983). *Little Red Riding Hood*. Retold and illustrated by Trina Schart Hyman. New York: Holiday House.

———— (1984). *Hansel and Gretel*. Retold by Rika Lesser and illustrated by Paul O. Zelinsky. New York: Dodd, Mead.

———— (1986a). *Rapunzel*. Illustrated by Michael Hague. Mankato, Minn.: Creative Education.

———— (1986b). *Rumpelstiltskin*. Retold and illustrated by Paul O. Zelinsky. New York: Dutton.

────── (1986c). *The water of life.* Retold by Barbara Rogasky and illustrated by Trina Schart Hyman. New York: Holiday House.

────── (1988). *Hansel and Gretel.* Translated by Elizabeth D. Crawford and illustrated by Lisbeth Zwerger. Saxonville, Mass.: Picture Book Studio.

Grimm, Wilhelm. (1988). *Dear Mili.* Translated by Ralph Manheim and illustrated by Maurice Sendak. New York: Farrar, Straus and Giroux.

Hamilton, Edith. (1940). *Mythology.* New York: New American Library.

Hale, Sara Josepha. (1984). *Mary had a little lamb.* Illustrated by Tomie de Paola. New York: Holiday House.

Haley, Gail. (1970). *A story a story.* New York: Atheneum.

Hall, Donald. (1979). *Ox-cart man.* Illustrated by Barbara Cooney. New York: Viking.

Hamilton, Virginia. (1985). *The people could fly: American Black folktales.* Illustrated by Leo Dillon and Diane Dillon. New York: Alfred A. Knopf.

────── (1988). *In the beginning: Creation stories from around the world.* Illustrated by Barry Moser. San Diego: Harcourt Brace Jovanovich.

Harris, Joel Chandler. (1986). *Jump! The adventures of Brer Rabbit.* Adapted by Van Dyke Parks and Malcolm Jones, and illustrated by Barry Moser. San Diego: Harcourt Brace Jovanovich.

Henry, Marguerite. (1947). *Misty of Chincoteague.* Illustrated by Wesley Dennis. New York: Rand McNally.

────── (1948). *King of the wind.* Illustrated by Wesley Dennis. New York: Rand McNally.

Henry, O. [William Sidney Porter]. (1982). *The gift of the Magi.* Illustrated by Lisbeth Zwerger. Saxonville, Mass.: Picture Book Studio.

Heyward, Du Bose. (1939). *The country bunny and the little gold shoes.* Illustrated by Marjorie Flack. Boston: Houghton Mifflin.

Hoban, Russell. (1960). *Bedtime for Frances.* Illustrated by Garth Williams. New York: Harper and Row.

────── (1964). *A baby sister for Frances.* Illustrated by Lillian Hoban. New York: Harper and Row.

Hoban, Tana. (1985). *Is it larger? Is it smaller?* New York: Greenwillow Books.

Hodges, Margaret. (1984). *Saint George and the dragon.* Illustrated by Trina Schart Hyman. Boston: Little, Brown.

Hoffmann, E. T. A. (1984). *Nutcracker.* Translated by Ralph Manheim and illustrated by Maurice Sendak. London: Bodley Head.

Hutchins, Pat. (1968). *Rosie's walk.* New York: Macmillan.

────── (1985). *The very worst monster.* New York: Greenwillow Books.

Hutton, Warwick. (1985). *Beauty and the beast.* New York: Atheneum.

Isadora, Rachel. (1979). *Ben's trumpet.* New York: Greenwillow Books.

Joyce, William. (1988). *Dinosaur Bob and his adventures with the family Lazardo.* New York: Scholastic.

Keats, Ezra Jack. (1962). *The snowy day*. New York: Viking.

—— (1964). *Whistle for Willie*. New York: Viking.

—— (1967). *Peter's chair*. Harper and Row.

Kellogg, Steven. (1979). *Pinkerton, behave!* New York: Dial.

—— (1984). *Paul Bunyan*. New York: William Morrow.

Kennedy, Jimmy. (1983). *The teddy bears' picnic*. Illustrated by Alexandra Day. La Jolla, Calif.: Green Tiger Press.

Kimmel, Eric. (1989). *Hershel and the Hanukkah goblins*. Illustrated by Trina Schart Hyman. New York: Holiday House.

Kipling, Rudyard. (1987). *Just so stories*. Illustrated by Safaya Salter. New York: Henry Holt.

Kotzwinkle, William. (1982). *E.T. the extra-terrestrial storybook*. Based on a screenplay by Melissa Mathison, with photographs from Steven Spielberg's film. New York: Putnam's.

Kraus, Robert. (1970). *Whose mouse are you?* Illustrated by José Aruego. New York: Macmillan.

—— (1971). *Leo the late bloomer*. Illustrated by José Aruego. New York: Crowell.

Krauss, Ruth. (1945). *The carrot seed*. Illustrated by Crockett Johnson. New York: Scholastic.

Kunhardt, Dorothy. (1962). *Pat the bunny*. New York: Golden.

Lamorisse, Albert. (1957). *The red balloon*. London: Unwin Paperbacks.

Langstaff, John. (1967). *Over in the meadow*. Illustrated by Feodor Rojankovsky. San Diego: Harcourt Brace Jovanovich.

Leaf, Munro. (1936). *The story of Ferdinand*. Illustrated by Robert Lawson. New York: Viking Penguin.

Lee, Harper. (1960). *To kill a mockingbird*. New York: Warner Books.

Lionni, Leo. (1959). *little blue and little yellow*. New York: Astor-Honor.

—— (1985). *Frederick's fables: A Leo Lionni treasury of favorite stories*. New York: Pantheon.

Lobel, Arnold. (1971). *Frog and Toad together*. New York: Scholastic.

—— (1979). *Days with Frog and Toad*. New York: Harper and Row.

—— (1980). *Fables*. New York: Harper and Row.

—— (1982). *Ming Lo moves the mountain*. New York: Scholastic.

—— (1986). *The Random House book of Mother Goose*. Selected and illustrated by Arnold Lobel. New York: Random House.

Mathis, Sharon Bell. (1986). *The hundred penny box*. Illustrated by Leo Dillon and Diane Dillon. New York: Viking Penguin.

Mayer, Marianna. (1978). *Beauty and the beast*. Retold by Marianna Mayer and illustrated by Mercer Mayer. New York: Four Winds Press.

Mayer, Mercer. (1973). *What do you do with a kangaroo?* New York: Scholastic.

—— (1980). *East of the sun and west of the moon*. New York: Macmillan.

McClintock, Barbara. (1979). *The little red hen.* New York: Random House.

McCloskey, Robert. (1941). *Make way for ducklings.* New York: Viking.

———— (1948). *Blueberries for Sal.* New York: Viking.

McDermott, Gerald. (1974). *Arrow to the sun: A Pueblo Indian tale.* Harmondsworth: Penguin.

McGovern, Ann. (1967). *Too much noise.* Illustrated by Simms Taback. Boston: Houghton Mifflin.

McKissack, Patricia C. (1988). *Mirandy and Brother Wind.* Illustrated by Jerry Pinkney. New York: Alfred A. Knopf.

McMurtry, Larry. (1985). *Lonesome Dove.* New York: Pocket Books.

McNaught, Harry. (1977). *Animal babies.* New York: Random House.

McSpadden, J. Walker. (1989). *Robin Hood.* Illustrated by Greg Hildebrandt. Morris Plains, N.J.: Unicorn.

Miles, Miska. (1971). *Annie and the old one.* Illustrated by Peter Parnall. Boston: Little, Brown.

Milhous, Katherine. (1950). *The egg tree.* New York: Scribner's.

Milne, A. A. (1928). *The house at Pooh Corner.* Illustrated by Ernest H. Shepard. New York: Dell.

Minarik, Else Holmelund. (1968). *A kiss for Little Bear.* Illustrated by Maurice Sendak. New York: Harper and Row.

Montgomery, L. M. (1908). *Anne of Green Gables.* Illustrated by Jody Lee. New York: Grosset and Dunlap.

Moore, Clement. (1976). *The night before Christmas.* Illustrated by Arthur Rackham. New York: Crown.

Morimoto, Junko. (1988). *The inch boy.* New York: Viking Penguin.

Mosel, Arlene. (1968). *Tikki Tikki Tembo.* Illustrated by Blair Lent. New York: Scholastic.

———— (1972). *The funny little woman.* Illustrated by Blair Lent. New York: Dutton.

Munsch, Robert. (1980) *The paper bag princess.* Illustrated by Michael Martchenko. Toronto: Annick Press.

———— (1986). *Love you forever.* Illustrated by Sheila McGraw. Ontario: Firefly Books.

Musgrove, Margaret. (1976). *Ashanti to Zulu: African traditions.* Illustrated by Leo Dillon and Diane Dillon. New York: Dial.

Paterson, Diane. (1976). *Smile for Aunty.* New York: Dial.

Patterson, Francine. (1987). *Koko's story.* Photographs by Ronald H. Cohn. New York: Scholastic.

Perrault, Charles. (1954). *Cinderella.* Translated and illustrated by Marcia Brown. New York: Scribner's.

Piper, Watty. (1930). *The little engine that could.* New York: Platt and Munk.

Polacco, Patricia. (1988a). *The keeping quilt.* New York: Simon and Schuster.

———— (1988b). *Rechenka's eggs*. New York: Philomel Books.

Potter, Beatrix. (1902). *The tale of Peter Rabbit*. London: Frederick Warne.

———— (1903). *The tailor of Gloucester*. London: Frederick Warne.

———— (1904). *The tale of Benjamin Bunny*. London: Frederick Warne.

———— (1906). *The tale of Mr. Jeremy Fisher*. London: Frederick Warne.

———— (1907). *The tale of Tom Kitten*. London: Frederick Warne.

———— (1908). *The tale of Jemima Puddle-Duck*. London: Frederick Warne.

———— (1909). *The tale of the Flopsy Bunnies*. London: Frederick Warne.

Prelutsky, Jack. (1970). *The terrible tiger*. Illustrated by Arnold Lobel. New York: Macmillan.

———— (1984). *The new kid on the block*. Illustrated by James Stevenson. New York: Greenwillow Books.

———— (1989). *Poems of A. Nonny Mouse*. Selected by Jack Prelutsky and illustrated by Henrik Drescher. New York: Alfred A. Knopf.

Prokofiev, Sergei. (1980). *Peter and the wolf*. Illustrated by Erna Voigt. Boston: David R. Godine.

Provensen, Alice, and Martin Provensen. (1977). *Old Mother Hubbard*. New York: Random House.

Pyle, Howard. (1986). *King Stork*. Illustrated by Trina Schart Hyman. Boston: Little, Brown.

Ransome, Arthur. (1968). *The fool of the world and the flying ship*. A Russian tale retold by Arthur Ransome and illustrated by Uri Shulevitz. New York: Farrar, Straus and Giroux.

Rey, H. A. (1941). *Curious George*. Boston: Houghton Mifflin.

———— (1952). *Curious George rides a bike*. Boston: Houghton Mifflin.

Romanova, Natalia. (1985). *Once there was a tree*. Illustrated by Gennady Spirin. New York: Dial.

San Souci, Robert D. (1989). *The talking eggs: A folktale from the American South*. Illustrated by Jerry Pinkney. New York: Dial.

Scarry, R. (1963). *Richard Scarry's best word book ever*. New York: Golden Press.

Selden, George. (1960). *The cricket in Times Square*. Illustrated by Garth Williams. New York: Farrar, Straus and Giroux.

Sendak, Maurice. (1962a). *One was Johnny*. New York: Harper and Row.

———— (1962b). *Chicken soup with rice*. New York: Harper and Row.

———— (1962c). *Pierre*. New York: Harper and Row.

———— (1962d). *Alligators all around*. New York: Harper and Row.

———— (1963). *Where the wild things are*. New York: Harper and Row.

———— (1970). *In the night kitchen*. New York: Harper and Row.

———— (1981). *Outside over there*. New York: Harper and Row.

Seuss, Dr. [Theodor Seuss Geisel]. (1938). *The 500 hats of Bartholomew Cubbins*. New York: Vanguard.

———— (1957). *How the Grinch stole Christmas*. New York: Random House.

Sharmat, Marjorie Weinman. (1975). *Nate the Great and the lost list*. Illustrated by Marc Simont. New York: Dell.

———— (1985). *Nate the Great and the fishy prize*. Illustrated by Marc Simont. New York: Dell.

Silverstein, Shel. (1964). *The giving tree*. New York: Harper and Row.

———— (1981). *A light in the attic*. New York: Harper and Row.

Slobodkina, Esphyr. (1940). *Caps for sale: A tale of a peddler, some monkeys and their monkey business*. New York: Harper and Row.

Spier, Peter. (1977). *Noah's ark*. New York: Doubleday.

———— (1980). *People*. New York: Doubleday.

———— (1983). *Christmas!* New York: Doubleday.

———— (1985). *The book of Jonah*. New York: Doubleday.

Star wars. (1979). Burbank, Calif.: Lucasfilm.

Steig, William. (1969). *Sylvester and the magic pebble*. New York: Simon and Schuster.

———— (1971). *Amos and Boris*. New York: Farrar, Straus and Giroux.

———— (1976). *The amazing bone*. New York: Farrar, Straus and Giroux.

———— (1977). *Caleb and Kate*. New York: Farrar, Straus and Giroux.

———— (1978). *Tifky Doofky*. New York: Farrar, Straus and Giroux.

———— (1982). *Dr. De Soto*. New York: Scholastic.

———— (1985). *Solomon the rusty nail*. New York: Farrar, Straus and Giroux.

———— (1986). *Brave Irene*. New York: Farrar, Straus and Giroux.

Steptoe, John. (1987). *Mufaro's beautiful daughters: An African tale*. New York: Lothrop, Lee and Shepard.

Strauss, Gwen. (1990). *Trail of stones*. Illustrated by Anthony Browne. New York: Alfred A. Knopf.

Tarcov, Edith H. (1974). *The frog prince*. Retold by Edith H. Tarcov and illustrated by James Marshall. New York: Scholastic.

Taylor, Mildred D. (1976). *Roll of thunder, hear my cry*. New York: Dial.

Ungerer, Tomi. (1971). *The beast of Monsieur Racine*. New York: Harper and Row .

Van Allsburg, Chris. (1981). *Jumanji*. Boston: Houghton Mifflin.

———— (1984). *The mysteries of Harris Burdick*. Boston: Houghton Mifflin.

———— (1985). *The polar express*. Boston: Houghton Mifflin.

———— (1986). *The stranger*. Boston: Houghton Mifflin.

Viorst, Judith. (1969). *I'll fix Anthony*. Illustrated by Arnold Lobel. New York: Harper and Row.

———— (1971). *The tenth good thing about Barney*. Illustrated by Erik Blegvad. New York: Macmillan.

———— (1972). *Alexander and the terrible, horrible, no good, very bad day*. Illustrated by Ray Cruz. New York: Atheneum.

———— (1974). *Rosie and Michael.* Illustrated by Lorna Tomei. New York: Atheneum.

Waber, Bernard. (1972). *Ira sleeps over.* Boston: Houghton Mifflin.

Watson, Richard Jesse. (1989). *Tom Thumb.* Retold and illustrated by Richard Jesse Watson. San Diego: Harcourt Brace Jovanovich.

Wells, Rosemary. (1973). *Noisy Nora.* New York: Dial.

———— (1981). *Timothy goes to school.* New York: Dial.

White, E. B. (1952). *Charlotte's web.* Illustrated by Garth Williams. New York: Harper and Row.

Wilder, Laura Ingalls. (1932). *Little house in the big woods.* Illustrated by Garth Williams. New York: Harper and Row.

———— (1935). *Little house on the prairie.* Illustrated by Garth Williams. New York: Harper and Row.

Willard, Nancy. (1981). *A visit to William Blake's inn: Poems for innocent and experienced travelers.* Illustrated by Alice Provensen and Martin Provensen. New York: Harcourt Brace Jovanovich.

Williams, Jay. (1976). *Everyone knows what a dragon looks like.* Illustrated by Mercer Mayer. New York: Four Winds Press.

Williams, Margery. (1983). *Velveteen rabbit.* Illustrated by Allen Atkinson. New York: Alfred A. Knopf.

Wood, Audrey. (1985). *King Bidgood's in the bathtub.* Illustrated by Don Wood. San Diego: Harcourt Brace Jovanovich.

———— (1987). *Heckedy Peg.* Illustrated by Don Wood. San Diego: Harcourt Brace Jovanovich.

———— (1988). *Elbert's bad word.* Illustrated by Audrey and Don Wood. San Diego: Harcourt Brace Jovanovich.

Yashima, Taro. (1983). *Crow boy.* New York: Viking.

Yolen, Jane. (1987). *Owl moon.* Illustrated by John Schoenherr. New York: Philomel Books.

———— (1988). *The emperor and the kite.* Illustrated by Ed Young. New York: Philomel Books.

———— (1989). *Dove Isabeau.* Illustrated by Dennis Nolan. San Diego: Harcourt Brace Jovanovich.

Yorinks, Arthur. (1986). *Hey, Al.* Illustrated by Richard Egielski. New York: Farrar, Straus and Giroux.

Young, Ed. (1989). *Lon Po Po: A red-riding hood story from China.* New York: Philomel Books.

Zemach, Harve. (1969). *The judge.* Illustrated by Margot Zemach. New York: Farrar, Straus and Giroux.

Zemach, Margot. (1976). *Hush, little baby.* New York: Dutton.

———— (1988). *The three little pigs: An old story.* New York: Farrar, Straus and Giroux.

Zolotow, Charlotte. (1962). *Mr. Rabbit and the lovely present*. Illustrated by Maurice Sendak. New York: Harper and Row.

———— (1972). *William's doll*. Illustrated by William Pène Du Bois. New York: Harper and Row.

———— (1983). *But not Billy*. Illustrated by Kay Chorao. New York: Harper and Row.

INDEX